English Language Teaching @ World Wide Web

English Language Teaching @ World Wide Web

Dr. Ashok K. Saini
Deptt. of English
State Council of Educational Research & Training
Uttarakhand, India.

AUTHORSPRESS
Publishers of Scholarly Books

Worldwide Circulation through Authorspress Global Network
First Published 2011
by
Authorspress
E-35/103, Jawahar Park
Laxmi Nagar, Delhi-110 092
e-mail: authorspress@yahoo.com

English Language Teaching @ World Wide Web
ISBN 978-81-7273-570-8

Printed in India at Tarun Offset, Delhi.

Foreword

English language teaching and learning is taking quick turns worldwide in general and India in particular. Indeed, the stance of English language is enriched and strengthened greatly due to the application of World Wide Web and extreme advancement of Information & Communication Technologies (ICT) these days. The uses of World Wide Web and ICT in language learning are having encouraging consequences on learners' motivation too. Thus their use contributes to language teaching and learning greatly. An enhanced understanding of motivational aspects of the use of ICT makes it more effective and increase potential for ICT to be more widely used in language teaching and learning around the world. Now children are more enthralled toward computers and Information & Communication Technologies. Technology enabled campus—a green campus—is also being preferred by students to get admission these days, where every effort is made to preserve the environment, lower the energy consumption and harness the power of green computing and green communication.

This book is one of the modest attempts to make employment of World Wide Web and Information & Communication Technologies more effective, more natural, more fun-filled and more enjoyable in the process of English Language Teaching. The world-widely submitted research papers may be divided into various categories, like theoretical, exploratory, applied, evaluative, and research-oriented. To make it more elaborative, Dr. Ashok K. Saini theorizes the different issues of language and technology. They are two most significant centers of attention of educational transformation in Indian today. A fundamental interpretative study is in use to identify with how and why teachers accomplish the information and communications technology into their language teaching and to ascertain the issues and barriers that teachers encountered when trying to incorporate modern technology into their teaching practice. The study implies that unvarying professional enhancement involving technology integration, specifically for language teachers, should be thoroughly designed.

The Internet is a driving force for much development and innovation in both developed and developing countries. To be able to do so, a cadre of professionals has to be educated with sound ICT backgrounds and independent of specific computer platforms or software environments. Technological developments lead to changes in work and changes in the organization at work, and required competencies are therefore swiftly changing. These days video teleconferencing is also introduced in the classrooms, subsequently students are being benefited from this facility to a great extent. Internet has become the greatest means of expression where people learn, share, and collaborate in ways not possible years before. On the other hand, a great deal of the success comes from preparing students to interact and learn in this online environment. Consequently, wide-ranging efforts are considered necessary to integrate technologies in English Language Teaching in the present day.

On the other hand, the book additionally has some common center of attention also. To illustrate it further, the research papers, in general, indicate a very bright future of the application of World Wide Web and Information & Communication Technologies in English Language Teaching. Besides, several of these research papers, by using established theories, meticulously provide a clear position & proposition of the application of World Wide Web and ICT. Taking all these facts into consideration, the book may be treated as a milestone in the area of the application of World Wide Web and

Information & Communication Technologies in English Language Teaching. Besides, educational planners and policy makers in future may also consider the book as an important point of reference.

Sep. 2010.

R. P. Singh
Deputy Director,
State Council of Educational Research & Training,
Uttarakhand

Acknowledgement

My acknowledgement at first goes to the Almighty before whom I bow my head with great devotion. This volume concerning *English Language Teaching @ World Wide Web* would have not been translated into reality without the kind co-operation and guidance of my teachers, friends, and well wishers. I place on record my regards to Dr. Dharam Singh Saini, Minister of Education (Govt. of Uttar Pradesh, India); Prof. Pashupati Jha (IIT, Roorkee), M.R. Verma, Prof. & Head, Deptt. of English, Gurukul Kangari University, Haridwar; Prof. Binod Mishra (IIT, Roorkee); Prof. Saryug Yadav (RIE, Ajmer); Shri Ram Awadh Prashad (Joint Director, SCERT Uttarakhand); Shri Jokhan Prasad Yadav (Joint Director, SCERT Uttarakhand); Dr. Amrendra Sharma, Prof. of Linguistics (Dhofar University, Salalah, Sultanate of Oman); Dr. Nasrah M. Ismail, Prof. of English, English Language Center (Taif University, Saudi Arabia) for their academic guidance, sane suggestions and applauding my efforts from time to time. Special thanks are due to Shri R.P. Singh, Deputy Director S.C.E.R.T. Uttarakhand for specific suggestions in addition to writing a concise foreword of this volume. Every effort has been made to trace or contact all copy right holders. We apologise for some omissions, and will greatfully acknowledge them as soon as they can be traced. The publisher/editor will be pleased to make good any omissions or rectify any mistakes brought to their attention at the earliest opportunity.

I also attest my admiration and cordiality to all my family members and kinsmen who have encouraged me in my adventurous project. I register my heartfelt gratitude to all the contributors for their scholarly contributions. Besides contributing their articles, they have been quite instrumental in reminding me of bringing the anthology well in time. I appreciate their continuous reminders, which have spurred me in my venture. Finally, I express my deep sense of gratitude to Authorspress for undertaking the publication of this book.

Dr. Ashok K. Saini

Introduction

Education never takes place in a vacuum but is deeply embedded in a socio-cultural milieu. Thus learning is a matter not only of cognitive development but also of shared social practices. The cognitive and the social development go hand in hand in classroom learning. The moral and cultural values give opportunity for sympathetic mutual collaboration among different countries, nations and borders. Once the configuration of global cultural values is amended or accepted in English Language Teaching (ELT) curriculum, monotony and complexity can be avoided. The impact of advanced information and communication technology and multimedia in classroom has revolutionized the whole teaching pattern. Not only does ELT serve as the infrastructure for vocational institute and performing effective role in enabling students with the knowledge of the global aspects and phenomena at all levels (individual, group and community) but also for the integration of language and culture. Internet and World Wide Web have great potentials and are the greatest boon of technical era in teaching English.

For centuries technology has been used by language teachers. "Comenius created his picture and word lessons in the seventeenth century for the teaching of Latin. We know that the forerunner of the slide projector was used as early as the eighteenth century, and even a bona-fide language course using phonograph records, text, and pictures was in use in Paris in the early 1099s" (Price, Karen, 1987: 155-159). When used appropriately, different Information and Communication

Technologies (ICTs) help to expand access to education, strengthen the relevance of education to the increasingly digital workplace, and raise educational quality, among others, helping make teaching and learning into an engaging, active process connected with real life.

Nevertheless, the twenty-first century has already welcomed such ICT tools that may cover up the maximum of the time, space, and activities in the classroom, i.e., excellent whiteboards and associated softwares. Although the major recommendations are:

a) Both the teachers and the taught in ELT classes should have access to ICT tools,

b) The English teachers should update themselves to the latest innovations taking place in methods, materials and also practice in English teaching areas, and

d) The ICT tools must bring to them innovations catering to the needs and requirement of the classroom.

Talking about cinema, it can be easily said that it provides an environment which is required for learning a language. It can be made clear with the help of the example, that the person who watches a foreign movie in English language, would be more familiar with its culture and will learn the language more easily than a person who gets knowledge from other sources (or lecture). Undoubtedly the person would go deep into the movie, would feel as if he himself were living among all the characters of the movie and would identify himself with others. Their way of speaking, culture, background and mind will give the learner a better understanding of the society whose language he is trying to attain, and it results in the increase of level of comprehension on the part of the learner. Cinema and media have been entered into the life of even the common man: literate and non-literate for long. These can be proved beneficial sources in imparting language training to the learners in India. Novels, magazines, comics, movies and newspapers are considered on the same pedestal in language training with that of Internet, computer, radio, television and music. Each source, here, is equally important to reach the destination of learners: to acquire English language.

Consequently, the challenge for higher educational institutions, particularly teacher education, has been to create a new generation of teachers capable of employing a variety of technology tools into all phases of academic, administrative, research, and extension functions. A teacher being a pivot in the process of teaching learning, knowledge of ICT and skills to use ICT in teaching learning has gained immense importance for contemporary teacher. A teacher is expected to know successful integration of ICT into his/her subject area to make learning meaningful. This knowledge development during pre-service training has gained much importance with the notion that exposure to ICT during this time is helpful in increasing student teachers' willingness to integrate technology for classroom teaching. ICT integration in institutions is being perceived as a necessity and is growing exponentially. The pervasive use of technology in all spheres of life, the knowledge economy and the paradigm shift together generate demands on the institutions to adopt ways that help inculcate twenty-first century skills amongst students.

Finally it can be concluded that technological devices like computers, videotapes and audiotapes can be used in various ways to facilitate language learning. They can be used not only in developing basic language skills but also in vocabulary development and verbal language development as well. But we have to keep one important fact in mind that computers are not a substitute for effective teaching. Computers are a tool; they are simply one type of supplement to the regular curriculum in teaching English language students as they develop language skills. Basically the key role is to be played by the teachers. The teachers who use technology as a part of their language-learning environment should ensure that they are familiar with the technological options available and their suitability to particular learning goals. This is a necessary but somehow a difficult balance to achieve. On the one hand it requires teachers to be aware of new technological developments while, on the other hand, keep a focus on learning goals and the technologies related to them.

This anthology begins with an opening research paper by ***Dr. Ashok K. Saini.*** Language and technology are two most significant centres of attention of educational transformation in India today. English language teachers have to cape with the challenges of technological and pedagogical swing taking place in the teaching profession. A fundamental interpretative study is in use to identify with how and why teachers accomplish the information and communications technology into their language teaching, and to ascertain the issues and barriers that teachers encounter when trying to incorporate modern technology into their teaching practice. The study implies that unvarying professional enhancement involving technology integration, specifically for language teachers, should be thoroughly designed. Latest guidelines concerning vision and goals of accomplishment should be made apparent to teachers.

Dr. Anju Bala Agrawal in her very incisive article explores the use of ICT in language learning which has encouraging consequences on motivation, and its use can contribute to language teaching and learning. An enhanced understanding of motivational aspects of use of ICT can make it more effective and increase potential for ICT to be more widely used in language teaching and learning around the world. Now children are more attracted towards computers. Teachers design an individualized programme for developing the language and literacy processes, and improving the understandings and abilities while they work on computer publication and drawing applications, then gradually towards text work to increase reading and writing competencies of students. She further says, a teacher should be ingenious in introducing the language to the students, specially in means of communication which is the foremost rationale of learning a language. Hence, the teachers should explore using technology without just sticking to the course books.

Ashu Tomar explains that a technology-enabled campus is also a green campus, where every effort is made to preserve the environment, lower the energy consumption and harness the power of green computing and green communication.

Typically, such a campus will be designed in a way that minimizes the carbon footprint. It will use smart approaches to cut energy usage and make life easier and better. Another crucial element of a connected campus is a set of affordable, robust, collaborative systems and tools. One such example is the synchronous learning technology, which provides real time, anywhere, anytime education to students, bringing them face-to-face with professors and industry leaders from across the world. This two-way, bi-directional, interactive learning technology is proving to be critical in instances where the learners and faculty are separated by vast geographic distances. In a world where shortage of competent and experienced faculty is being considered a huge challenge to education, synchronous technology has appeared as a panacea. She further says, by using it, reputed global universities can make available their faculty to other institutions where this expertise is lacking.

Dr. Ashok Singh Rao in his research paper concludes that ICT has also enabled learning through multiple intelligences as it has introduced learning through simulation games; this enables active learning through all senses. ICT tools can be used to find, explore, analyze, exchange and present information responsibly and without discrimination. It can be employed to give users quick access to ideas and experiences from a wide range of people, communities and cultures. It permeates the business environment, it underpins the success of modern corporations, and it provides governments with an efficient infrastructure. At the same time, it adds value to the processes of learning, and in the organization and management of learning institutions. The Internet is a driving force for much development and innovation in both developed and developing countries. Countries must be able to benefit from technological developments. To be able to do so, a cadre of professionals has to be educated with sound ICT backgrounds, independent of specific computer platforms or software environments. Technological developments lead to changes in work and changes in the organization of work, and required competencies are therefore changing.

Dr. K. Sandhya and Afsha Jamal in their joint venture emphasize that technology has provided plenty of opportunities for both teachers and students. They are privileged to have Internet access, a few computers and appropriate guidance. These days video-teleconferencing is introduced in the classrooms, subsequently students are being benefited from this facility to a great extent. Synchronized collaboration applies between desktop computers hooked to a projection system so that many people in the same location can participate. All the desktops are connected through the Internet. An instructor sits at a desktop workstation and communicates with a "classroom" of students, each of whom has a workstation in front of him and a connection to the Internet. Another feature of it is that the students no longer have to be in the same room; they can interact with other students and teachers in different locations.

Thus, practical English is being taught through technology in almost all the technical colleges. Undoubtedly, technology has revolutionized society in many places around the globe, including how language instruction is taught and delivered. In particular, the Internet has become a means of expression where people can learn, share, and collaborate in ways not possible years before. On the other hand, a great deal of the success comes from preparing students to interact and learn in this online environment. Hence, an extensive effort is needed to integrate technology in teaching. A refocused approach to teaching will boost the learners a long way to making technology and the Internet a more rewarding partner in the teaching and learning process.

Kavita Chauhan states that the potential of each technology varies according to how it is used. She has identified at least five levels of technology used in educational presentation, demonstration, drill and practice, interaction and collaboration. ICT made more impact on education than most teachers appreciate. It goes much further than the specialist ELT software we have installed in our computer labs. All students are not able to be online, by any means, but the percentage of those using ICT equipments is increasing diversely. Use of Internet provides a window from the classroom into a real world of English, and incidentally, promotes learners autonomy by giving students confidence to operate in that world.

Ramesh Chandra Shukla in his exceptionally insightful research paper has observed that now, globalization has broken down the walls that were built as barriers segmenting the world into sharp divisions. Modern society is 'global society', and the phenomenon of globalization has touched and transformed not only the world community but also its very culture and psyche. Globalization has invariably made its mark on the language of the world. Language is power, the feature that proclaims supremacy for the human race closely linked with culture and society. It has been used as a weapon by the conquerors to subdue and strengthen their authority on the conquered. To silence them into submission in "colonialism" whether as indirect rule or the exploration and settlement of continents, brought with it the English language, English literary form, and English culture assumptions (Bruce King). The process of globalization has endowed the English language with an eminence that has eclipsed many other languages with time starting from the sixteenth century.

The role of ethics is to enable to us to be reflective to reflect upon and understand the nature of good human life. In this age of IT, it has become mandatory to safeguard our ethical responsibilities. The ethical actions of a person can be described in general terms as those actions that are performed within the criterion of which is regarded as socially, morally and legally acceptable within the framework of a particular society or nation.

Dr. Sunil Kumar Jha and ***Dr. Rashmi Gupta*** in their joint research paper examine the unlimited potentials that remain mostly untrapped in ICT that can better be optimally utilized in the process of planning, organizing, coordinating and controlling and controlling of ELT class. Many changes have taken place in practising and using ICT for English language learning and teaching; gone are those early days of the microcomputer when both the teacher and the taught did not have a great deal of choice in the range of software. ICT has gone up to that extent to make available to the taught in the classroom workstations for independent study. The files in the computers are present to them digitally so that they may work through their exercises at their own pace, independently of the teacher. ICT tools are today in a position to enhance learning rather than teaching strategies.

Ms. Ruchi Banger observes that through books, English has been taught for a long time but, with the change of time, new ideas regarding training have been developed. It has enriched the training style and made a better environment for the persons desiring to learn the language. In the modern time, TV, Internet, radio and cinema are being used as tools for learning language by drawing attention and interest of the persons. Though internet, TV and radio, including newspapers, have been in our life for a long time yet they had not been introduced as aids in learning English language. This approach is rather new but quite effective in the sense that its impact on our mind is deeper.

She further aims at illustrating the fact that each and every medium, for teaching English language to learners, has its own special importance in its own respect. So, if used effectively, after understanding the need of learners and by acquiring suitable solutions regarding problems in teaching through these elements, learners may get a positive atmosphere and acquire the language in its broader aspect and meet their needs.

Lt. (Dr.) Satendra Kumar in his extremely discerning research paper says that language is manoeuvring the mind of the people through the media. It is the most powerful tool of the media to reach the audience. The media circulate words, sounds and images that surround us. They tell us who is famous—from movie stars to scientists—and give reasons for it Fictional presentations such as books, movies and TV dramas tell us what people do and are like. Newscasters, textbooks, and even advertisements tell us that we are part of a society that extends far beyond what we can see. All this is possible because of the existence of language; without it, media wouldn't have existed too. Language is the soul of the media. Without it, the media won't be able to survive and prosper.

Dr. Priyamvada Agarwal in her research paper observes that many developments in language teaching have evolved from a growing awareness of the different mediums with which we can work. Available technologies are Interactive whiteboards, pod casts, wikis, interactive practice materials, electronic translators, CD-ROMs, electronic dictionaries to word processing, email and the World Wide Web, etc., which make it possible to present language in forms other than speech and print too. Unmatched and unique opportunities are now available in the field of education because of Information and Communication Technology (ICT). It goes without saying that ICT can exercise a sizeable effect on the way teachers teach and how learners learn, thereby providing more ways and opportunities to achieve excellence in both teaching and learning. Inclusion and use of ICT in schools at the elementary level in America and Europe have given wide exposure to children. The only idea behind that is to help children achieve excellence when they grow up.

Consequently, good English language teachers should embrace or at least recognize the constant changes in the field of English language teaching. Additionally, they should always try different teaching methods, use a variety of classroom activities, and strive to seek out new ideas. The new ICT has broken down old barriers of time and space. It has made it possible to generate, store, transmit, retrieve and process information and knowledge at increased speeds and with increased efficiency and flexibility. As a consequence, new ICT has opened up almost unlimited possibilities, for teachers and students in terms of information flow and human communication.

Senthil Kumar Devarajan in his tremendously insightful research paper observe that with so many interesting topics on the Internet, the students can be easily motivated and involved in many communicative activities which are connected to their real life needs. This allows and enables them to become independent learners and help them enhance their second language learning and also equip them to meet their academic and professional needs.

He aims at exploiting materials related to films, job opportunities and using chat rooms for balloon debates and engage the students in groups in doing certain learner-friendly and challenging tasks/activities that will invoke students' involvement in not only the four skills of LSRW but also various critical thinking skills such as predicting, hypothesizing, concentrating, planning, evaluating, ordering, associating, sequencing, discussing, concluding, etc.

Sudhir Narayan Singh and ***Narender Kumar Chauhan,*** in their joint research paper scrutinize the need of ICT in effective English Language Teaching and its various advantages. The growth of ICT has brought about drastic changes not only in language teaching but in each and every sphere of the life also. In the modern era of Liberalization, Privatization and Globalization (LPG) where Cross Cultural Communication (CCC) is challenging all the established norms and values of the past, everything is in its transitional phase. Today ICT is regarded as primary and vital resource for ELT development.

ICT and ELT both are very interrelated terms like pestle and mortar because ICT provides the basic opportunities to understand the language from its basic core along with some latest teaching aids like videos, animations, graphics, sounds and ICT also provides the platform where techniques and ideas can be exchanged on global level without wasting time and money. Because of its techno-friendly nature it is a language of global acceptance and has popularly been welcomed by the technocrats, professionals, corporate houses and the global business community. Authors strongly feel that ICT and its integration in ELT classes is the need of the day, and it must be implemented religiously if we want to have a holistic development and see India as a developed country in the coming years.

Dr. Vikas Raval, in his research paper, examines that in 1995, Dr. Bernie Dodge developed an instructional activity that he called a webquest. He briefly traces the history and increasing popularity of the webquest instructional strategy. His original definition left much room for interpretation. As a result, there are many different ideas about what constitutes a webquest. He examines the webquest instructional strategy in the light of selected learning theories: constructivism, Robert M. Gagné and his nine instructional events, cooperative learning, theory of scaffolding and constructivism. He has also informed research findings of the webquest project carried out at the college level. He further points out the needs for research in this area of growing interest.

Vikrant Sehgal, in his extremely intuitive research paper outlines a study that explores what factors EFL learners consider to be important when making presentations. He has surveyed 304 undergraduate students at a large private university in India. A 30-item questionnaire was used to discover what components are considered to be important to learners in doing effective English presentations. Descriptive statistics and principal component analysis were used to analyze the results of the data. The results indicate that the participants consider the following three factors as the major criteria for effective English oral presentations: clarity of speech and voice quality; correctness of language; and interaction with the audience. Based on the outcome of the study he further delineates the pedagogical implications for oral presentations in EFL.

Suruchi Dubey in the highly technical article says that teaching students about the computer and other technological tools as a part of the normal curricula together within the aim of developing their abilities to use these tools to complete language activities, will prepare them in using the technology. Hence, at present, literacy does not simply mean the ability to read and write a particular language, it also involves abilities and practices related to the particular media through which texts are transmitted. Literate people have a set of skills, knowledge, values, understandings and relationships that allow them to use language for reading and writing on the job, at home, in school, travelling purpose and so forth. Hyper media provide a number of advantages for language learning, such as, authentic learning environment created just like in the real world because listening is combined with seeing, skills are easily integrated because varieties of media make it natural to combine reading, writing, speaking and listening in a single activity, and teachers as well as students have a great control over their learning since they can not only go at their pace but even on their own individual paths.

The present book, I hope, will certainly prove to be an immensely valuable asset for the students, teachers and research scholars who want to be fully acquainted with the application of World Wide Web in English Language Teaching. I look forward to the book successfully addressing the issues raised in the anthology and suggest remedies for the challenges being faced in ELT nowadays. The healthy, critical comments and suggestions from various corners will be welcome.

List of Contributors

1. ***Afsha Jamal***, Asst. Professor, Vikas College of Engineering & Technology, Vijayawada, Andhra Pradesh.
2. ***Ashu Tomar***, Lecturer, Dept. of English, Bharat Institute of Technology, Partapur By-Pass Road, Meerut, U.P.
3. ***Dr. Anju Bala Agrawal***, Reader, Department of English, R.C.A. Girls' P.G. College, Mathura.
4. ***Dr. Ashok K. Saini***, Deptt. of English, Urdu & Other Languages, State Council of Educational Research & Training, Uttarakhand, Narendranagar Tehri Garhwal.
5. ***Dr. Ashok Singh Rao***, Assistant Professor of English & Head, Faculty of Arts, Science and Commerce, Mody Institute of Technology & Science (Deemed University), Lakshmangarh (Sikar) Rajasthan.
6. ***Dr. K. Sandhya***, Reader in English, Maris Stella College (Autonomous), (Acharya Nagarjuna University), Vijayawada, Andhra Pradesh.
7. ***Dr. Priyamvada Agarwal***, Lecturer, Regional Institute of Education (NCERT), Ajmer, Rajasthan.
8. ***Dr. Rashmi Gupta***, Sr. Lecturer, College of Engineering Roorkee, Uttarakhand.
9. ***Dr. Sudhir Narayan Singh***, Assistant Professor, Department of English and Communication Skills, The Technological Institute of Textile and Sciences Birla Colony, Bhiwani, Haryana.

10. ***Dr. Sunil Kumar Jha***, Lecturer, College of Engineering Roorkee, Uttarakhand, India.
11. ***Dr. Vikas Raval***, Asst. Professor in English, Nirma Institute of Technology, Ahmadabad, Gujarat.
12. ***Kavita Chauhan***, Lecturer, Humanities, NRIITM, Gwalior, M.P.
13. ***Lt. (Dr.) Satendra Kumar***, Assistant Professor & Head, Dept. of English, Govt. P.G. College, Lansdowne, Pauri Garhwal,Uttarakhand.
14. ***Narender Kumar Chauhan***, Head Librarian, The Technological Institute of Textile & Sciences, Birla Colony, Tosham Road, Bhiwani, Haryana.
15. ***Ramesh C. Shukla***, Joint Director, State Council of Educational Research & Training, Uttarakhand, Narendranagar, Tehri Garhwal.
16. ***Ruchi Banger***, Lecturer, NRI College of Engineering and Management, Jhansi Road, Gwalior, M. P.
17. ***Senthil Kumar Devarajan***, Lecturer in English, Shinaz College of Technology, Ministry of Manpower, Sultanate of Oman
18. ***Suruchi Dubey***, Department of Humanities, Krishna Girls Engineering College, Kanpur, Uttar Pradesh.
18. ***Vikrant Sehgal***, Associate Professor, Asia Pacific Institute of Information Technology, SD, Faridpur Road, G.T. Road, Karnal Side, Panipat, Haryana.

Contents

1

English Language Teaching @ World Wide Web: Position and Proposition

— Dr. Ashok K. Saini

Computer Assisted Language Learning (CALL) has drawn the interest of Indian language professionals, and many have required innovative and alternative ways of using computer technology to boost students' learning and to improve students' English dexterity and proficiency. Teachers are one of the key persons to implement innovation for educational enrichment. They nevertheless, necessitate developing technological literacy as well as academic knowledge when applying technology. For successful execution of the information and communications technology (ICT) into language teaching, it is significant to understand how and why teachers use ICT, and to explore the issues and barriers that teachers come across when trying to integrate ICT into their teaching. In acknowledging the trend toward using the computer technology in language instruction, language teachers will realize that they will soon likely need to undertake a range of fresh job responsibilities such as putting their courses online, evaluating CALL materials and websites, taking part in campus wide CALL projects/inter-institutional partnership, and incorporating and managing multimedia language laboratories.

It is indicated that features manipulating technological integration by faculty are diverse. Further, it also states that the barriers include organizational and pedagogical concerns, technical and logistical issues, and personal problems such as fear. Rogers' theory of innovation adoption (1995) consists of five attributes:

1) Relative advantage,
2) Compatibility,
3) Complexity,
4) Trial ability, and
5) Observability.

Rogers found that 49 to 87 per cent of the variance in the adoption rate of innovation could be explained by these five attributes. Other variables are:

1) Types of innovation decisions,
2) Communication channels,
3) Nature of social system, and
4) The extent of change agents' promotional efforts.

Park incorporated seven variables from three perspectives in his study. This showed that computer experience, subjective norm, self-efficacy, relative advantage, and complexity are important predictors of the level of web-assisted teaching. Time and support, however, indicated no significant effect, which contradicts Park's qualitative findings. Limited time and heavy workload may inhibit teachers from implementation. Teachers want to know if they can integrate the computer technology with education in ways that effectively link with the content of curriculum as well as the different components and stages of the learning process. In one study, teachers expressed a need for understanding the potential of technologies and the appropriate pedagogy for technology integration with regard to the fit of each with their personal philosophies of teaching and learning. Teachers need opportunities to expand their knowledge to try out innovative methods, to exchange ideas with experts and their peers, and to refine their skills so they may more quickly respond to the new developments in their fields.

Interdisciplinary panels can work out problems simultaneously, allocate panel members to expand from their colleagues' ideas and encourage the sharing of materials. Teachers are not only concerned about where to retrieve information and resources and how to obtain knowledge and skills about technological innovation, they are also concerned about how to integrate new technology into instruction and how to make the most of it. Most one-time workshops immediately teach teachers skills using an explicit software programme without demonstrating good and appropriate teaching strategies and without changing teachers' behaviour. Consequently, teachers are likely to feel inadequate and incompetent with respect to technology integration, and they may feel uncertain about whether it will improve learner knowledge.

There are a variety of administrative challenges and intricate problems being faced by teachers in all areas together with language teaching in computer technology application. Understanding organizational culture is essential for institutional change (Finley & Hartman, 2004). Three barriers that keep college leaders from ascertaining an environment that allows teachers to take advantage of technology resources comprise:

1) The needs for appropriate planning and budgeting for instructional technology,
2) Organizational structures and communication, and
3) Faculty rewards and incentives.

These comprise improved technological use due to social and economic manipulation, flexible approaches to teaching and learning on demand, a new and different picture of competition in higher education, and the potential of technology use to improve teaching and learning. Since higher education is organizing students for future markets, teachers should be equipped with the necessary knowledge and skills to meet the needs of the students in the millennium and to follow along with the trends of a global knowledge economics society. Contemporary studies have highlighted many benefits of continuous professional development:

1) Guiding teachers' understanding of technologies and the potentiality of technology for meaningful instruction.
2) Facilitating teachers' acquisition of technological literacy and skills.

3) Assisting teachers' knowhow for retrieving information and garnering resources and tools.
4) Improving teachers' abilities for monitoring student progress.

This is to understand how and why teachers execute the ICT into their language instruction, and to explore the issues and barriers that teachers encounter when trying to incorporate modern technology into their instruction. To recognize how and why EFL teachers integrate ICT into instruction, the basic interpretative qualitative study design (Merriam, 2002) is employed. The process, strategies, and data analysis of this qualitative research are all inductive. The qualitative results can provide rich, contextual understanding of certain findings, and strengthen a detailed/in-depth understanding of a certain problem. Participants were located through the researcher's professional networks. The majority of teachers e-mailed were referred to the author by other teachers based on their use of computer technologies as a teaching tool.

Teachers who extensively use computer technology include those who have taught CALL courses in their institutions or who have publications on the use of computer technology. These teachers may also have their own websites or may have received grants for conducting national projects or institutional research related to technology submission into teaching. This intends to discover and understand the meaning that the use of ICT has for the participants; data were gathered to build concepts and theories instead of being tested in a positivist study. Therefore, the data are analyzed to identify whether there are recurring patterns or common themes among these contestants.

Indeed, teachers only use Internet resources as a source of supplementary materials. Teachers think class time is limited and they feel they do not teach enough during the class period. They want students to have more opportunities to learn and obtain more knowledge and skills, and they expect students to practise more after class, especially for skills such as pronunciation learning. As classes at Indian educational institutions by and large are very outsized, outsized class can obstruct language teaching, and these teachers agree that the Internet provides a good tool for teachers to expand students' learning outside their classroom. This flexibility not only applies to expanding where the students can learn but also provides the flexibility for engaging a broader spectrum of students, such as different proficiency levels and students who are away from class because of unrestrained delicate tribulations.

Modern technology provides good practise for students' listening grasp. Students like to use the Internet because they get to discuss things with it. By using the Internet, the teacher provides many opportunities for students to learn beyond the classroom and after class. It is self-directed learning for students, unlimited by time and space. In addition, the fixed time in the classroom may not be suitable for those who don't feel well or who are physically drained. Teachers use the Internet resources most to develop their students' listening proficiency. They have established that language learning frequently starts from listening. In the past they often had to rely on reading as an instructional method due to large class sizes. As a result, students often did not get many chances to listen and speak.

Teachers assimilate ICT into curricular areas other than listening. Most teachers classify their current instructional phase as experimental. Teachers are interested in incorporating the available Internet tools and resources to create online learning activities on their own. Language teachers are increasingly experimenting with English for academic purposes, courses with blended teaching, to see if this is an effective method for teaching foreign languages. For one model in blended teaching, every other week students alternately complete online lessons or attend classes. Teachers have already begun using blended teaching in their institutions for the convenience of evening and weekend students.

Most teachers make an effort of innovative teaching to amplify students' awareness in learning and boost their impetus. Innovative teachers would use any strategies, attempt several methods, and relate several media to be creative in their teaching. So, most teachers stated that they use ICT to endow teaching with diversity. The computer technology is a tool to offer diversity for students. On the other hand, some teachers recognized the style in using contemporary technology in instructional practices but still doubted whether such innovations would affect students' comprehension.

Teachers straightforwardly entertain benefits of numerous bona fide materials offered on the World Wide Web. Audio-visual aids are important for language teaching and learning. Hyperlinks allocate the assimilation of graphic, audio, visual and text materials, which facilitate teaching culture and have brought convenience for language teaching and learning, such as listening and reading. The Internet provides good resources for listening and speaking teachers. While traditional textbooks may be out of date after only a year or so and getting an update may be slow, Internet broadcasts are current, authentic and multimedia. The benefits of ICT use are as:

a) Autonomous learning,
b) Real,
c) Comprehensible,
d) Easy to use, and
e) Providing cultural understanding.

Consequently, convenient teaching materials to accompany online materials might be good. Hence, we necessitate extra knowledge about ICT use and more training about sharing online. Self-governing learning has been an issue in education in India for a long time, and has caused excited argument. This is because in the past, enthusiastic competition for higher education kept Indian students under pressure to study. When students only value learning as a means to an end, gaining access to higher education, they may be less likely to pursue any type of self-directed learning on their own. Because the Internet allows ubiquitous instant access to ICT, many teachers look forward to its use in promoting students' autonomous learning.

Teacher training is crucial for technology integration into language instruction. Those who obtained a technology-related degree felt that it is much easier for them to know where the resources are and to know how to use them. Teachers like to take advantage of computer technology to assist their instruction, but the barriers are education and resources. Currently, most institutions regularly offer workshops for teachers to familiarize with the course management software they purchase or design. Teachers can use these tools for editing their materials and publishing them online. They encourage teachers to put their materials online to prepare for the long-term goal of institutional development. These innovative teachers are able to make use of these facilities and integrate ICT into their current instructional practices in various curricular areas.

Once teachers discovered that ICT can provide resources and tools for them to enrich their instruction, they immediately started applying them. Teachers take advantage of various types of resources and tools to assist their instruction and enhance students learning since we are not native speakers of English. ICT provides good resources for teachers teaching listening and speaking skills. The idea that there are abundant resources and tools on the Internet, so there is no reason why teachers should not take advantage of them, influence their use of information and communications technology. Teachers extremely and appallingly take the assistance of ICT. With the Internet, we upload multimedia materials to our websites for our students to retrieve. It's simple, fast, convenient and provides the best materials. Class sizes are usually large in Indian educational settings, so the use of hardcopy documents has long been a burden for institutions, teachers and the environment. The advantages of electronic documents as concluded are:

i) Teachers can save paper for notes and handouts.
ii) Teachers can share good materials without having to make lots of copies.
iii) Providing links to some materials rather than supplying the materials themselves may circumvent possible copyright infringement.

Teachers' outlook of ambiguity will hinder them from using technology. The unanticipated impenetrability from technologies has been a concern for most teachers. However, there are still limitations and we have problems with hardware and hackers that are difficult to control. The server doesn't have enough capacity for teachers to put their language learning materials online, and the network often goes down unexpectedly. The network also tends to crash when many students try to turn in assignments on a due date. Teachers can't rely on the university network too much, because its stability is sometimes beyond their control. Other feelings of uncertainty include worthiness of time, money investment and efforts.

Institutional support in the variety of commitment to funding is crucial for curricular reform. Availability and maintenance of infrastructure are only one aspect. The online courses still need to be developed and published. Most institutions have provided minimal financial support so far, providing incentives and grants to teachers for developing e-learning courses. The teachers developing these courses are doing so in addition to their regular course loads.

There are encouragements for faculty who are interested in creating online learning materials in addition to their regular courses. Faculty who do not already use ICTs as part of their teaching can't afford to create online learning materials. Compared to the endeavour and time language teachers spend the funding is insufficient and only a few teachers apply for it. While there are assistants to help edit files and create web pages for faculty, in reality, the amount of support these assistants provide is dependent on their individual knowledge and skills. Unless the assistants are fairly knowledgeable, language teachers who do not comprehend how to use the Internet or its tools may have difficulty getting the indispensable steps accomplished.

Faculties like to be acquainted with the use of ICT if it pertinent to definite course content or what teaching methodologies they can use. This is an area in which extra discourse would be particularly helpful. To learn technological skills is not enough. It is needed to have pedagogical knowledge for ICT integration in teaching. One desires to know the proper teaching methodologies. Language teachers like not only to advance their technological literacy but also to empower their pedagogical strategies in application of modern technologies. Teachers who lack technological literacy and knowledge prefer a teacher development programme, which essentially focuses on technology integration in language teaching.

All the way through information on technology in frequently held programmes or workshops, teachers keep abreast of modern technology upgrades, and they learn from other teachers in the field. Such programmes present opportunities to substitute ideas with other teachers who have related interests, and offer opportunities for teachers to work together. Those tools are generally for teachers in all disciplines, not specifically for language teachers. They provide Breeze using PowerPoint. PowerPoint is not suitable for language teaching because there is no real interaction.

ICT assimilation in teaching is primarily in the experimental phase, and teachers use ICT to try out innovative methods in their teaching. Internet resources are used as a source of supplementary materials and several have started trying blended teaching for a change of curriculum. While teachers have unique strategies for dissimilar curricular areas, most use online resources to develop their students' listening skills. They take advantage of the Internet to provide authentic, updated, and multimedia instructional materials. Their ICT integration in teaching aims to enhance students' motivation and interest and to assist students in developing autonomous and lifelong learning.

On the other hand, there are a variety of issues, barriers, and challenges being encountered by the teachers, or even contemporary language teachers. As a consequence, teacher utters the need for support, predominantly continuing professional development, to confront and accept the challenges ahead. Thus it clearly shows that only when we begin to provide effective continuing professional inputs, will we be able to expect fruitful realization of the potential of ICT to improve the quality of learning at educational institutions. Therefore, Indian educationists and policy makers should develop long-term and adequate funding for ICT integration in teaching, including ongoing professional development for teachers.

Educational institutions in India should place emphasis more on technology integration in the classroom than in distance learning. Administrators should try to understand and meet the needs of language teachers so that they can provide essential and suitable support for language teaching. They require efficiently and carefully measured budget for indispensable expenses on hardware and software. While Indian technical and professional institutions place great emphasis on the language proficiency of students and language education, they should also attend to the requirement of language teachers for comprehension, skill, and teaching strategies using modern technology and for boosting student learning.

Works Cited

Browne, C. & Gerrity, S. (2004). Setting up and maintaining a CALL laboratory. In S. Fotos & C. M. Browne (Eds.), *New perspectives on CALL for second language classrooms* (pp.17-1198). Mahwah, New Jersey: Lawrence Erlbaum Associates, Publishers.

Buckley, D. P. (2002, January/February). In pursuit of the learning paradigm: Coupling faculty transformation and institutional change. *Educause Review*, 29-38.

Cavanaugh, T. & Cavanaugh, C. (2000) Interactive PowerPoint for teachers and students. In B. Gillan & K. McFerrin (Eds.), *Faculty Development* (pp.496-499). (ERIC Document Reproduction Service No. ED444497).

Chen, H. J. (2003). *Seminar on Multimedia English Teaching*, Chungtai Institute of Health Sciences and Technology, 16-33.

Chen, J., Belkada, S. & Okamoto, T. (2004, May). How a Web based course facilitates acquisition of English for academic purposes. *Language Learning & Technology*, *8*(2), 3349. Retrieved October 22, 2005, from http://llt.msu.edu/vol8num2/chen/default. html

Chun, D. M. & Plass, J. L. (1997). Research on text comprehension in multimedia environments. *Language Learning & Technology, 1* (1), 6081. Retrieved October 11, 2005, from http://llt.msu.edu/vol1num1/chun_plass/default.html

Crystal, D. (2003). *English as a global language.* Cambridge, UK: Cambridge University Press.

Davies, G. (2003). Perspectives on offline and online training initiatives. In U. Felix (Ed.), *Language learning online: Towards best practice* (pp.193-214). Lisse, the Netherlands: Swets & Zeitlinger.

Epper, R. M. (2001). The new economy meets the ivory tower. In R. M. Epper & A. W, Bates (Eds.), *Teaching faculty how to use technology: Best practices from leading institutions* (pp.118). Westport, CT: The American Council on Education, ORYX Press.

Ertmer, P. A. (1999). Addressing first–and second–order barriers to change: Strategies for technology integration. *Educational Technology Research & Development, 47*(4), 47-61.

Finley, L. & Hartman, D. (2004). Institutional change and resistance: Teacher preparatory faculty and technology integration. *Journal of Technology and Teacher Education, 12*(3), 319-337.

Fotos, S. (2004). Writing as talking: Email exchange for promoting proficiency and motivation in the foreign language classroom. In S. Fotos & C. M. Browne (Eds.), *New perspectives on CALL for second language classrooms* (pp.109129). Mahwah, New Jersey: Lawrence Erlbaum Associates, Publishers.

_______________ . & Browne, C. (2004). The development of CALL and current options. In S. Fotos & C. M. Browne (Eds.), *New perspectives on CALL for second language classrooms* (pp.314). Mahwah, New Jersey: Lawrence Erlbaum Associates, Publishers.

Johnson, D.W. & Johnson, R.T. (2004). Cooperation and the use of technology. In D. H. Jonassen (Ed.), *Handbook of research on educational communications and technology* (2 nd ed.) (pp.785-811). Mahwah, New Jersey: Lawrence Erlbaum Associates.

Koehler, M. J., Mishra, P., Hershey, K. & Peruski, L. (2004). With a little help from your students: A new model for faculty development and online course design. *Journal of Technology and Teacher Education, 12*(1), 2555.

Kuh, G. & Vesper, N. (1999, April). *Do computers enhance or detract from student learning?* Paper presented at the annual meeting of the American Educational Research Association. Montreal, Canada. (ERIC Document Reproduction Service No. ED429592).

Liddel, P. & Garrett, N. (2004). The new language centers and the role of technology: New mandates, new horizons. In S. Fotos & C. M. Browne (Eds.), *New perspectives on CALL for second language classrooms* (pp.27-40). Mahwah, New Jersey: Lawrence Erlbaum Associates, Publishers.

Lin, H. C. (2003). Effectiveness of online poetry learning for EFL learners. *Proceedings of the Eleventh International symposium on English Teaching/Fourth Pan Asian Conference,* Taipei, Taiwan, 440-448.

Moore, Z., Morales, B. & Carel, S. (1998). Technology and teaching culture: Results of a state survey of foreign language teachers. *CALICO Journal*, *15*(13), 109-128.

O'Connor, P. & Gatton, W. (2004). Implementing multimedia in a university EFL program: A case study in CALL. In S. Fotos & C. M. Browne (Eds.), *New perspectives on CALL for second language classrooms* (pp.299-316). Mahwah, New Jersey: Lawrence Erlbaum Associates, Inc.

O'Dowd, R. (2003, May). Understanding the "other side": Intercultural learning in a Spanish English email exchange. *Language Learning & Technology*, *7* (2), 118-144. Retrieved September 24, 2004, from http://llt.msu.edu/ vol7num2/odowd/default.html

OppBeckman, L., & Kieffer, C. (2004). A collaborative model for online instruction in the teaching of language and culture. In S. Fotos & C. M. Browne (Eds.), *New perspectives on CALL for second language classrooms* (pp.225-251). Mahwah, New Jersey: Lawrence Erlbaum Associates, Inc.

Park, B. (2003). Faculty adoption and utilization of Web-assisted instruction (WAI) in higher education: Structural equation modeling (SEM). Unpublished Ph.D. dissertation, The Florida State University, Tallahassee, Florida.

Pascarella, E. & Terenzini, P. (1998). Studying college students in the 21st century: Meeting new challenges. *Review of Higher Education, 21*, 151165. Pennington, M. C. (1999). Computeraided pronunciation pedagogy: Promise, limitations, directions. *Computer Assisted Language Learning*, *12*(5), 427-440.

Reeder, K., Heift, T., Roche, J., Tabyanian, S., Schlickau, S. & Golz P. (2004). Toward a theory of e/valuation for second language learning media. In S. Fotos & C. M. Browne (Eds.), *New perspectives on CALL for second language classrooms* (pp.255-278). Mahwah, New Jersey: Lawrence Erlbaum Associates, Inc.

Repman, J., Carlson, R. D., Downs, E. & Clark, K. (2000). Power Web searching techniques for teacher educators. In B. Gillan & K. McFerrin (Eds.), *Faculty development* (pp.492-495). (ERIC Document Reproduction Service No. ED444497).

Rogers, E. M. (1995). *Diffusion of innovations.* (4th ed.). New York: The Free Press.

Shih, YC. D. (2003). Online English language learning: A Texas Taiwan connection. *Proceedings of the Eleventh International symposium on English Teaching/Fourth Pan Asian Conference,* Taipei, Taiwan, 507517.

Susser, B. & Robb, T. N. (2004). Evaluation of ESL/EFL instructional Web sites. In S. Fotos & C. M. Browne (Eds.), *New perspectives on CALL for second language classrooms* (pp.279-296). Mahwah, New Jersey: Lawrence Erlbaum Associates, Inc.

Toyoda, E. & Harrison, R. (2002, January). Categorization of text chat communication between learners and native speakers of Japanese. *Language Learning & Technology*, *6* (1), 82-99.

Verdugo, D. R. & Belmonte, I. A. (2007). Using digital stories to improve listening comprehension with Spanish young learners of English. *Language Learning & Technology*, 11(1), 87-101. Retrieved January 1, 2007 from http://llt.msu.edu/vol1num1/verdugo/default.html

Warschauer, M. (2000). The changing global economy and the future of English teaching. *TESOL Quarterly, 34*(3), 511-533.

Weasenforth, D., BiesenbachLucas, S. & Meloni, C. (2002, September). Realizing constructivist objectives through collaborative technologies: Threaded discussions. *Language Learning & Technology*, *6*(3), 58-86.

Zhao, Y. (2003). What teachers need to know about technology? : Framing the question. In Y. Zhao (Ed.), *What should teachers know about technology? : Perspectives and practices* (pp. 114). Greenwich, Connecticut: Information Age Publishing.

2

Exploiting Internet Resources for ELT in ESL/EFL Classrooms

— Senthil Kumar Devarajan

Introduction

The growth and development of information technology has influenced every aspect of our life. It is very difficult to find an area which has not been revolutionized by the application of computer technology in some form or the other–be it engineering/architecture, medicine, defence or education. The power and pervasiveness of this technology has become an integral part of education which has generated the rapid growth of Computer Assisted Language Learning (CALL). And, in every field of education the Internet has a major role to play.

The magnitude and variety of information and resources on the Internet is so unlimited that Teeler and Gray (2000) name it a "vast virtual library". The Internet provides every individual unlimited access to vast amounts of authentic material on any topic of one's interest, and offers opportunities to interact 24 hours a day with native as well as non-native speakers from different parts of the world. In this context, Johnson (1985: 217) rightly remarks that the Internet has a global scale which facilitates communication, action, interaction among individuals across the world. Thus the useful resources on the Internet could be fruitfully exploited for our EFL/ESL learners to engage in many communicative activities in a congenial and stimulating environment. This paper, with its pedagogical motives, aims at evolving and illustrating some good classroom teaching practices using some pieces of interesting material from the Internet.

Before we get down to discuss the actual classroom practices, it would be in the fitness of a good perspective on the paper to talk about some motivating reasons to use Internet resources for the purposes of ELT.

WHY USE INTERNET MATERIALS IN ELT?

To begin with Dudeney's (2000: 1) remark, Internet is not merely a source of authentic material in English, but also home to encyclopedic information about all sorts of topic you may want to engage within the classroom, and of professional knowledge for teachers, i.e. bibliographies, chat groups, articles, courses and conferences. Students can be involved in improving their ability to read, write, communicate, research and publish on the Internet as a new form of literacy. This is motivating for the reasons rooted in Warshauer's (1996) research which suggests that electronic discussions tend to provide more equal participation among students, and these students use more formal and complex language, both lexically and syntactically, in the discussion. Evidence in Blake's (2000) research also shows that ESL/EFL learners are able to successfully negotiate meaning with other speakers, native or otherwise, in computer-mediated communication. Furthermore, it also empowers the students to become autonomous learners who can find the information they need, and also collaborate with others and help construct new knowledge. And, more importantly, the Internet can inject vitality into teaching and motivate students as and when they communicate in a medium that is multidimensional, flexible, rapidly changing, and connected to their real-life needs.

These motivating reasons for the use of Internet resources in ELT lead us to a small discussion of some interesting web-based activities.

Some Internet-based Activities

Now an unlimited range of materials is quickly, cheaply and readily available from the comfort of our desks or homes. To the busy teacher, the Internet can be an infinite resource file of texts, visual stimuli, listening material, vocabulary, information, video files, live TV and radio, newspapers from around the world. The list is endless. Let us talk about some of them:

> "As films always fascinate people, it would be a good idea to involve our learners and finding out from the web what films are going to be released shortly and get them to read reviews of the films and draw up a list of which ones they would go to and why. A good starting point for this activity could be the Internet movie database at www.us.indb.com."

Solving a mystery can be a good activity for those who are interested in problem solving. Students can be prepared by starting a mystery of their own, e.g., there are three men in a cabin in a forest. They are all dead. How did they die? (It was a cabin of a crashed aircraft...). Then use the www.case.com creatively.

Using a travel sites could be another interactive activity. Learners could be divided into groups and each group may be explained that they have a competition for a weekend in London. Groups will research places to stay and things to do, and then agree between themselves on an itinerary. They can go to http://directory.excite.com/travel/destinations/europe/england/london. Comparing news can be used as yet another communicative activity. We can ask our students to find a couple of newspapers from yahoo or ipl.org (Internet Public Library). Then they compare the coverage of a current issue in different countries, record their observations and share with the rest of the class.

Another useful activity could be exploring job opportunities. Students work with job ads from a newspaper/website. Then they do a personality quiz at www.ncsu.edu/careerkey and are given a list of jobs that suit them. They can print out and discuss. And finally they can write their CVs and applications for the job of their choice.

Giving online advice can be used as one more communicative activity. We can involve one of the many online columns such as "teenadvice online" at www.teenadvice.org. The class can be divided into groups and each group can be given three to four titles from the advice site with the explanation to them that these are real problems, written by teenagers who want advice. The student in different groups discuss the titles and guess what the problem is by focusing on the identity of the people involved, their relationship, the exact problem and the possible advice to be given. Then students go online to the site to check their guess against their real queries. Next, they can discuss their reaction to the problems. Finally, when offline, students from different groups can share the problems that they looked at, and discuss similar problems they might have had.

Many such similar interactive activities could be planned like creating your own newspaper using www.crayon.com, specific lexis can be reviewed related to, for example, houses by using www.forgottenhouses.freeserve.co.uk/mframe.html, etc.

After a good deal of discussion on Internet-based activities, it is now time to move to another section which includes three sample classroom application procedures, dealing with reviewing films, exploring job opportunities and participating in balloon debates.

Lesson Plan 1

Summary: Reading reviews and giving opinions

Level: Undergraduate and above

Time: 90 mins. (30 minutes on the Internet)

Language work: Reading, note-taking, discussing and giving a short presentation

Sites: http://www.imdb.com

Requirement

Hardware: A computer per two-three students, Internet connection

Software: Any web browser, word processor

Knowledge: Surfing the web and using a word processor

Preparation

Start with a small warm-up asking about students' favourite film, who was the leading actor/actress in the film?, the type of film (action, comedy, tragedy), etc. Check that there is a relevant list of forthcoming films on the website before the lesson. Put the students into groups of two to three at each computer and explain to them that they are going to see a list of forthcoming films in their area. And they to have to choose a film which they wish to find out more about. Each group has to select a different film. Also tell them about the sample location.

Online

The students load the list and choose the film. They read the information about the films, go through the review, watch the trailor, and make the notes in word processor. Then they edit their notes to make a suitable text for presentation to the rest of the class.

Offline

The spokesperson from each group gives the group's presentation trying to persuade, with good reasons, the other students to see the film. At the end of all the presentations, the class votes on which film they would be interested in seeing.

Follow-ups

The students could go and see a film when it opens or watch on DVD earlier and then write their own review on it. Then they can compare their opinions with the previous review that they read about it. Parallel activities of writing reviews can also be done with other events taking place locally, such as concerts.

Lesson Plan 2

Summary: Exploring job opportunities and applying for it

Level: Intermediate and above

Time: 90 mins. (30 minutes on the Internet)

Language work: Writing CVs and application

Sites: http://www.yahoojobs.com

Requirement

Hardware: A computer per two-three students, Internet connection

Software: Any web browser, word processor

Knowledge: Surfing the web and using a word processor

Preparation

As a small warm-up, elicit from students about their career objectives, how they are going to pursue them, what are some of the skills that are needed in the profession of their choice and how confident are they to take up respective responsibilities, etc. Then tell the students that they are going to do a job hunt exercise on the net and do a personality quiz at www.ncsu.edu/careerkey to find their suitability for the job. Accordingly they have to write a CV and application for the job.

Online

Students visit the job website and explore various job possibilities and select a job that matches with their background and inclinations. Then they do a personality quiz and print the result, i.e., a list of jobs that suit them. From this list they go for the best option.

Offline

Students use the word processor, and write a good application and CV for the job. After that the groups can exchange their work and study the variety in the work.

Follow-ups

On the basis of their application and CV, job interviews can be conducted by a panel of teachers, which could be recorded and discussed for their effectiveness in the class.

Lesson Plan 3

Summary: Balloon debate

Level: Intermediate and above

Time: 60 minutes

Language work: Giving opinions, agreeing and disagreeing, supporting and contradicting

Requirement

Hardware: A computer per two-three students, Internet connection

Software: Web browser

Knowledge: Surfing the web

Preparation

Explain the task to the students that they are going to participate in a balloon debate where they will get the theme or topic for discussion from which they have to choose only one aspect. And they have to present their arguments and counter-arguments in defence of their topic using the chat rooms. Any of the following topics, as suggested by Penny Ur (1981:108) could be given for this debate:

i) The person most worth preserving from death is: a politician / a sportsman / a writer / a television personality/ a scientist.

ii) The best place to live is: a flat / a caravan / a castle / a cottage/ a tent.

iii) The best hobby to have is: stamp-collecting / hiking / theatre-going / carpentry.

iv) The most worthwhile subject to study is: English / Science/ History / Literature / Psychology.

v) The best profession to have is: policeman / explorer / teacher / politician / nurse.

Online

All the groups will enter chat rooms and initiate the debate on their topic. Then they will give arguments and counter-arguments on the opinions received from the other groups, on their topic. This exercise of attacking/refuting others' points of view in order to defend their stand will continue till the ideas are exhausted and a kind of winning situation is reached.

Offline

After the debate is stopped, the groups will review various arguments and vote for the winning team.

Follow-ups

As a follow up task, students may be asked to complete all the notes and write a good essay on the topic.

Conclusion

This paper has illustrated as to how the Internet provides unlimited resources and enormous opportunities of ELT to language professionals and educators. The paper claims that these resources can be fruitfully used if interesting materials are selected and interactive approaches are utilized properly. This way students can be easily motivated to communicate in an exciting medium that is flexible, multimodal, constantly changing and moreover, connected with their real-life needs. This will enable them to become independent learners in enhancing their language proficiency, general knowledge and critical thinking skills, thereby equipping them to succeed in their academic as well as occupational ambitions.

Works Cited

Blake, R. "Computer-mediated communication: A window on L2 Spanish inter-language". *Language Learning and Technology.* 2000: 4(1), 120-36.

Dudeney, G. *The Internet and the Language Classroom.* Cambridge: CUP, 2000.

Felix, U. "Web-based language learning: A window to the authentic world". R. Debski and M.Levy (ed.) *WORLD-CALL: Global Perspectives on Computer-assisted language learning.* Lisse, Netherlands: Swets & Zeitlinger, 1998: 85-98.

Galloway, I. and O'Brien, D. "Learning Online: Choosing the best computer-mediated communication activities". *The Language Teacher.* 1998: 22 (2), 7-9.

Johnson, D.G. *Computer Ethics.* New Jersey: Prentice Hall, 1985, rep.2001.

Kramsch, C. "Language Teaching in an Electronic Age". G.M. Jacobs (ed.) *Language Classrooms of Tomorrow: Issues and Responses.* Singapore: SEAMEORELC, 1997.

Penny, Ur. (1981). *Discussions that work: Task-Centered Fluency Practice.* Cambridge: CUP.

Sandholtz, J.H., Ring staff, C., and Dawyer, D.C. *Teaching with Technology: Creating Student-Centred Classrooms.* New York: Teachers College Press, 1997.

Teeler, D. and Gray, P. *How to use the Internet in ELT.* England: Pearson Education Ltd., 2000.

Warschauer, M. "Comparing face-to-face and electronic discussion in the second language classroom". *CALICO Journal.* 1996: 13 (2), 7-26.

3

Integration of Information and Communication Technology in English Language Teaching Classrooms in India

— Sudhir Narayan Singh & Narender Kumar Chauhan

Introduction

This paper discusses the need of Information and Communication Technology (ICT) in effective English Language Teaching (ELT) and its various advantages. The growth of ICT has brought about drastic changes not only in language teaching but in each and every sphere of life also. In the modern era of LPG (Liberalization, Privatization and Globalization) where CCC (Cross Cultural Communication) is challenging all the established norms and values of the past, every thing is in its transitional phase. Today ICT is regarded as primary and vital resource for ELT development. ICT and ELT both are closely interrelated terms like pestle and mortar because ICT provides the basic opportunities to understand the language from its basic core along with some latest teaching aids like videos, animations, graphics, sounds, and ICT also provides the platform where techniques and ideas can be exchanged on global level without wasting time and money.

English, being the second language in terms of a number of people communicating in it, because of its techno-friendly nature, is a language of global acceptance and popularly welcomed by the technocrats, professionals, corporate houses and the global business community. Authors strongly feel that ICT and its integration in ELT classes is the need of the day, and it must be implemented religiously if we want to have a holistic development and see India as a developed country in the coming years.

In the modern era of LPG and CCC where the dynamic change is the only constraint, English Language is still growing at the most rapid pace, and it has already established itself as the fastest growing and the most flexible 'Global Language' at the very beginning of the twenty-first century. Due to the advent of the ICT towards the very end of twentieth century, English language is acquiring the status of the 'International Language of Business and Profession'. Information and Communication Technology was the phrase coined by Stevenson in the year 1997 in a report which he submitted to UK government. Further in the year 2000, information and communication technology was promoted by the new national curriculum documents for the UK. In addition to subjects included in Information Technology (IT), ICT encompasses areas such as telephony, broadcast, media and all types of audio and video processing and transmission (rubble.ultralab)

Defining ICT Information and Communication Technology

Before proceeding further, it would be essential to understand the meaning and definition of the term ICT Information and Communication Technology. According to the *Oxford Advanced Learner's Dictionary,* 'ICT' is "the study of the use of computers, the Internet, video, and other technology as a subject at school" (O.A.L.D.: 768). A few more definitions will be of a great help in clarifying the concept of ICT. Some of the definitions are selected here for the suitability of the study:

a) A generic name for all the technologies involved in communicating with computers.

b) Is the catch-all phrase used to describe a range of technologies for gathering, storing, retrieving, processing, analysing and transmitting?

c) Information and Communication Technologies (ICT) is an umbrella term that covers all technical means for processing and communicating information.

d) Technological fundamentals for increasing the efficiency of various communication devices, technical analysis and studies of an efficient cooling.

Thus it would be safe to draw a conclusion from the above mentioned definitions that information and communication technology is a comprehensive term covering all those technologies used in reducing time in the communication, minimizing barriers to the communication, and enhancing effectiveness and efficiency in the process of communication. All the technical and even semi-technical devices used in the process are subject to the consideration for the study of the information and communication technology. Information and communication technology is willingly welcomed by Indian academia and industry. While announcing a new three years ICT-enabled Bachelor's Course in Three-Dimension Animation Programme, Professor Shambhu Nath Singh, Director, School of Journalism and Media Studies, of the world's largest open university, Indira Gandhi National Open University (IGNOU), New Delhi, expressed his favour saying that such educational programmes like "3D animation and Visual effects will enable students to have the technical skills along with the technology edge which will help them to be job ready animation pro..." (*The Tribune*, New Delhi, May 19, 2010: 2).

Information and Communication Technology and English Language

English language is absorbing information and communication technology because of its techno-friendly and flexible nature. In the technical sphere, no other language in the world is used and accepted as widely as English. Second only to Mandarin Chinese, English is currently the most widely spreading language in the world, in terms of the number of people who speak it, but second to none in terms of the number of non-native speakers and the number of people learning it. It is spoken by more than 350 million native speakers, and between 700 and 800 million non-native or foreign users. It is currently the primary language used on the World Wide Web, in the political and business arenas. It is the official language of air transport and shipping; the leading language of science, technology, computers, and commerce; and a major medium of education, publishing, and international negotiation. For this reason, scholars frequently refer to its latest phase as 'World English'. English language comes to our aid in our commercial transactions throughout the globe. English is the language of the latest business management in the world. English is a means not only for international commerce; it has become increasingly essential for inter-state commerce and communication. With regards to the popularity and to the monopolistic dominance of English language over any other language of the world in the field of information and communication technology M. F. Rice aptly observes:

"The diffusion of ICTs within societies is varied, with some institutions and sections of society having greater access to ICTs than others. These divisions are reflected in the content of ICTs. For example, the English language, which is understood by only 10 per cent of the world population, accounts for approximately 80 per cent of internet content." (Rice, M.F. 2003: 72).

Though English is absorbing information and communication technology like anything yet it would be sheer injustice to draw a conclusion that it carries its importance in English Language Teaching only. ICT is influencing a varied range of sectors and it has been identified by many international development institutions also as crucial element for economic development. For example, the World Bank has collaborated with the International Financial Corporation to promote access to ICTs, an initiative which it describes as one of its most successful. In 2006, the United Nations launched an initiative called Global Alliance for Information and Communication Technologies and Development *(The World Bank).*

English Language and Its Growth in India

Let us have an overview of the journey of English language and its rapidly increasing importance in India. English entered India as a 'Foreign Language' but it would be unfair to use the term 'Foreign Language' for it as English is popularly accepted by Indians as the 'Second Language'. As the result of the ceaseless efforts of literatures like Ram Mohan Roy, Rabindranath Tagore, S. Radhakrishnan, Jawaharlal Nehru, Mulk Raj Anand, Khushwant Singh, R. K. Narayan, Jayant Mahapatra, Keki N. Daruwala, Henry L. Derozio, Asif Karim Bhoy, Amitav Ghosh, Muhammad Fakhruddin and literati like Sarojini Naidu, Toru Dutt, Kamala Das Suraiya, Anita Desai, Arundhati Roy, Kiran Desai, Shashi Deshpande, there emerged an 'Indian English Language' and in this way journeying from a 'Foreign Language', then 'Second Language', finally English enjoyed the status of 'Indian English Language' towards the later half of the twentieth-century India, which was later to be considered as 'Hindlish' or 'Hinglish' during the last couple of decades. In a languages' hub like India, English is also flourishing as a 'Linking Language'.

Parliament has also recognized English as an 'Official Language' in addition to Hindi. People going from the northern to southern part of India for education or business mostly communicate in English, which has become a link language. In a few states of India where people are showing zero tolerance to Hindi, in order to cash some cheap personal interests or political ideology, constantly posing threat to the life and property of Hindi-speaking people, English is serving as a sole means of survival and also as a 'Lifeline Language' to those Hindi-speaking people struggling to survive in the extremist states of their own country. All these facts of history and present developments in India underline the increasing importance of learning English in addition to vernaculars. Even the uneducated and semi-educated citizens of India are aware of the emerging demands of English in India. In support of this need and the awareness of the parents, it would be better to have a pulse of the 'illiterate and semi-literate' but aware parents from an article published in *The Times of India*:

> "Education alone is not enough nowadays. The medium of education is equally important if you want your children to succeed. (Adarsh Pant, A Bookseller proudly talks about his daughter studying in the English-medium St.

Anthony's High School in Malad), 'She even tells me stories in English that she learns at school. It makes me very happy to know that she can now converse in a language that is still foreign to me and my wife'".

"And regarding the importance of Information and Communication Technology as well as English Language Teaching both: Knowledge of computers is so important these days and, to understand all that, knowing English is important. (36-years-old Sharad Lokhande of Chembur, a vendor,) 'I studied till the sixth standard and my wife is illiterate...'" (*TOI*, May 19, 2010 p-10)

The above statements from popular English daily are sufficient enough to feel the role and importance of English as well as information and communication technology in the twenty-first century India. In order to train a person for the effective use of any language, these four sequential basic skills are required. These skills are popularly known as (LSRW):

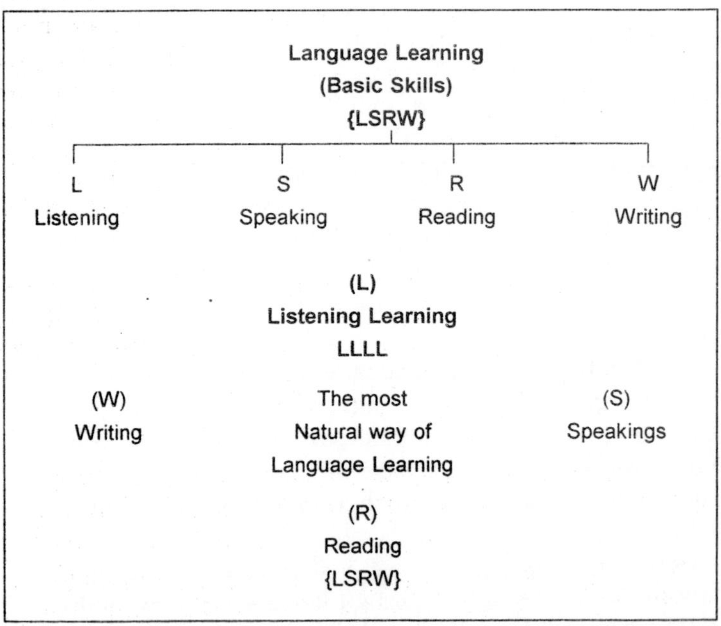

Figure 1

Why LSRW Skills are said to be the Most Natural Way of Language Learning

Justifying the Sequence of LSRW

To make this concept of LSRW more explicit, it would be better to discuss it with the help of an example. Suppose a baby takes its birth in a family. Soon after the birth, the language learning process begins. At the very beginning, it simply listens to the various sounds produced by various family members and then it tries to correlate all the sounds produced in its environment. As a language learner, the baby plays the perfect role of an effective and active listener so it would be safe to draw a conclusion that 'Listening' is the first and the most important of all the skills of language learning.

After a few months (positively seven to twelve months), the baby begins to utter and identify some verbal sounds and in this way, the perpetual course of 'Speaking' begins. A two-to-three year-old baby begins identifying the letters of the alphabet of the native language and practises some phonetic sounds and even morphological words with their meanings. In this way, the skill of 'Reading' is developed. A few more months of training and the baby is ready to write some terms of the mother tongue and herein lies the commencement of the forthcoming skill of 'Writing' which is to be followed by a bundle of skill-sets in the remaining part of the life including non-technical, semi-technical, technical and soft skills. This example justifies the sequence of LSRW and validates this sequential learning as the most natural way of language learning.

Blind people are supposed to be very good singers, not because they have a good mouth or vocal chords but because they have good ears. This popular saying emphasizes the importance of listening in language learning. Technology is providing a variety of hearing aids in order to enhance effective listening and also to help those to shoot the troubles and encounter the problems of those people who are hard of hearing. Speaking is also one of the most important skills to be developed and it cannot be ignored at any cost. For the improvement and the enhancement of speaking skills, ICT is providing a number of tools related to speech therapy to be monitored by trainers and surgeons for the effective interventions in speech-related problems. Reading and writing are equally important skills to be nurtured with care

English Language Lab and Information and Communication Technology

The very concept of an English Language Lab couldn't have been possible without the help of ICT. Advanced and well-equipped ICT integrated language lab is offering new ways to English language teaching in India. Meticulously designed language learning software specially prepared by expert and experienced organizations like the British Council, and integration of computers in ELT classrooms, are providing many more new and innovative ways of English language teaching and learning. Software like Sky Pronunciation Suit, Connected Speech, Issues in English, Tense Buster, Error Terror, Robotel, Sanako, Eyespeak, ACEN, MLS Easy Immersion, various translation-related software and digital dictionaries are now available and one can carry them even in windows-enabled cell phones. Most of them are easily accessible. In this way, experiences of ELT classrooms are changing drastically and English language teaching-learning experience is gradually becoming more and more pleasant day by day.

English Language Teaching Methodology and Information and Communication Technology

For the training of LSRW, ELT teachers adopt various teaching methods and among those various teaching methods available 'Grammar-Translation Method' is the oldest method of teaching English in India accepted from Greek, Latin and Sanskrit teaching which required mostly memorizing of grammatical forms. In this method, reading and writing come first whereas listening and speaking are not given much attention which is the unnatural way of language learning. Software like 'Error Terror', 'Tense Buster' and many more translation-related software are adding qualitative input to this method and so this method of ELT may revive again. The emergence of Direct Method was a reaction against Grammar Translation Method which was introduced in India in the early twentieth century. *Webster's New International Dictionary* defines Direct Method as "a method of teaching a foreign language, especially a modern language through conversation, discussion and reading in the language itself without use of the pupil's language, without translation and without the study of formal grammar. The words are first taught by pointing to an object or a picture or by performing action". Theoretical grammar has no place at all. Emphasis was given on listening, speaking and correct pronunciation whereas reading and writing are compromised. This method became the quickest method of learning English. ICT interventions can change this method by adopting teaching aids ranging from tape recorders, television, lingua-phones, projectors, computers, etc.

Software like Sky Pronunciation, Connected Speech, and Issues in English can really improvise this teaching method. During the1930s and 1960s, the British applied linguists and researchers like Harold Palmer and A.S. Hornby recommended the Oral Approach and Situational Language Teaching as a new teaching methodology for ELT classrooms involving systematic principles of 'selection', recommending a process by which lexical and grammatical contents are chosen, 'gradation', a process for the organization of contents, and finally 'presentation', a process and technique used for presentation and practice of items in course. It was a more systematic approach than the Direct Method. Oral Method and SLT begin with the spoken English. Material is taught orally before it is presented in the written form. It advocates a method of teaching from simple to complex.

The Audio-lingual Method flourished as a new method of ELT in United States towards the end of 1950s which drew its inspiration from the theory propounded by American linguists in the same decade known as structural linguistics, which laid emphasis on the systematic analysis of phonemic, morphological and syntactic systems underlying the grammar of a language. This method was more or less in the form of modifications of the Direct Method. Emerging out of the Second World War, this methodology came to be known as the Army Method and it stressed upon grammar and pronunciation by intensive oral drills and practices where it identified the language with speech that was further to be approached with structure. In this method, the aural training came first, then pronunciation, and so the training was followed by speaking, reading and writing. In spite of its scientific basis, during the 1960s this theory was challenged as it was found deficient in pedagogy principles. Audio-lingualism was defied in America and the fate of Oral Situational Language Teaching in Britain while at the same time theorists like D.A. Wilkins worked out a functional or communicative definition of language and devised communicative syllabi for language teaching. National Syllabuses published in 1976 found a rapid acceptance by the British Language Teaching specialists. This theory targets to communicate effectively, and permits judicious use of native language and translation if necessary.

Based on similarities and differences of sounds, structures of student's mother tongue, there evolved the Bilingual Method as another efficient method of ELT. Structural meanings and concepts were conveyed in the mother tongue of the students whereas practising was to be done in target language. This teaching methodology was carrying a major drawback of establishing a habit of learning everything in the target language through the medium of the mother tongue among the language learners. In recent years, the Central Board of Secondary Education (CBSE) is putting its emphasis on interactive English teaching and it is making classrooms more and more user-friendly and customer (learner/student), oriented. This methodology also recommends judicious distribution of course content, scientific distribution of available time and their effective implementations in classrooms.

ICT is supporting all these teaching methods and providing scope and opportunities for a number of innovations in ELT classrooms. ICT is revolutionizing ELT classrooms in India by its effective interventions in each and every teaching methodology. Audiovisual teaching aids are adding new dimensions and giving new shape to ELT classrooms in India.

There has been noticeable changes in the ELT classrooms from delivering oral talks, chalkboards, manually prepared aids, a few visual pictures, to transparency-projectors, transparency-slides, radio, televisions, computers, LCD projectors, PowerPoint Slide Presentations, PowerPoint Slide Shows, video-conferencing, tele-communications, educational movies, virtual classrooms, web-portals, web-blogs, uses of windows-enabled mobile phones, mobile learning, group discussion, debate, extempore, highly interactive lecture sessions and many more educational and social websites loaded with numerous teaching aids and information. All these powerful changes could have been possible only because of the advent of ICT and techno-friendly nature of English language, and its global acceptance as professional and technical language.

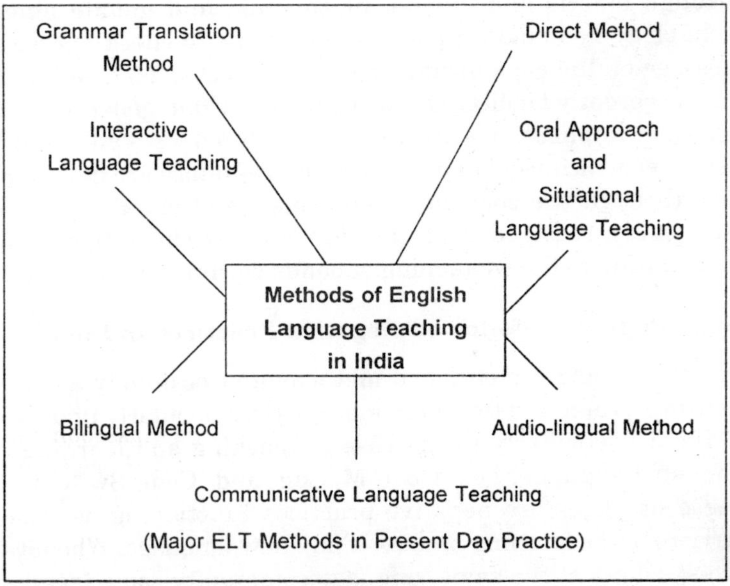

Figure 2

Information and Communication Technology Enabling Effective Intervention in Speech Therapy

ICT is also providing new ways of speech therapy where the latest technologies are readily available for the effective intervention in the sound process and speech mechanism of a language learner. Newly available tools, devices and equipments are helpful in ensuring more accuracy than ever available earlier. Phoneticians have begun to employ sophisticated instrumental techniques such as sound spectrograph and x-ray photography. Due to emergence of ICT new techniques are revolutionizing this major segment also. In recent years, x-ray photography is found hazardous to health and that is why it is being replaced by many more point tracking devices such as x-ray microbian and electromagnetic articulo graph. Describing the overall impact of ICT on inter-personal communication and its influence *Science Ray* describes:

"ICTs facilitate the ease of communication, which has many profound effects. In the business world, deals can be made through emails and video-conferencing, and mobile phone technology has made it possible for people to check and send message on the go, allowing us to be connected 24/7. Although this has greatly facilitated the business world in general, many negative implications are to be considered as well. Simple messages which used to be delivered face-to-face are now being sent through the cold impersonal means of email. This has effectively reduced socialisation within the office, thus contributing to the weakening of bonds within the workplace.[11]

Some Popularly Followed Negative Practices in India

Apart from above-mentioned methods and positively adopted measures, there are two more malpractices popularly practised in India particularly in the case of teaching and learning of English Language, i.e., 'Code Mixing' and 'Code Switching'. These practices are negative practices functioning as major barriers in the learning process of any new language. Whenever two speakers of the same language community come together communicating situation in any second language, first they converse in second language then, after a few minutes conversation, they adopt these practices. The sooner it becomes clear to them that their mother tongue is the same they start mixing codes of their first language frequently and after a few hours of conversation, they switch over to their first language and continue their further communication in their first language or mother tongue. These practices are negative and can hamper the growth and process of learning English or any other foreign language, and so they must be checked.

Establishing ICT Integrated ELT Classrooms in India: Challenges and Limitations

Effective implementation of information and communication technology in English language teaching classes in India is really a great challenge India being a country of villages, there are many limitations functioning as the barriers to the effective use of ICT in ELT classes in India. Almost 70-80 per cent education aspirants are yet to receive education in India in ICT integrated ELT classrooms. In response to the question "What are the opportunities and challenges that are being faced with respect to ICT integration in the education sector?" Prof. R. Govinda, Vice Chancellor, National University of Educational Planning and Administration, Ministry of Human Recourse Development (HRD), Government of India, answers:

> "We have only challenges. I don't think in India we have made much headway in ICT integration in education, with least in higher education and partially in school education. What is projected is only what the vendors want. If we do not have a proactive thinking as to how and where we want to take ICT in education, then the market will not only sell us but also tell us, what we should do with it. They will say that we are advising you but they will sell us. Higher Educational professionals, I think are least literates when it comes to use technology, as they do not understand the relevance of using technology" (Ravi Gupta, 2010: 16).

While delivering his speech at the Higher Education Summit on April 09, 2010, New Delhi as the keynote speaker, Professor V.N. Rajshekhran Pillai, Vice Chancellor, Indira Gandhi National Open University (IGNOU), stated his concerns in view of higher education very clearly:

> "The challenge in higher education is accessibility to large number of learners. But we also have to focus on Vocational Education that will give us skilled professionals. But in all the cases enhancing GER (Gross Enrolment Ratio) is not possible without the capacity building of the teachers for which ICT plays a crucial role. We need smart classrooms, employable graduates, on line capabilities of day to day functionalities of educational institutes, and of course quality research fellows who can take the knowledge network forward" (Ravi Gupta et al, 2010: 43).

Prof. Pillai's concerns regarding infrastructural deficiencies are really the biggest hurdle in the effective implementation of ICT-enabled ELT classrooms. Prof. S.V.S. Chaudhary, Vice Chairperson, National Council for Teacher Education (NCTE) also regretted the current situation of ICT in India saying that the "accessibility of ICT in education in India is still very poor." He also expressed his serious concerns on the "dire need of proper teachers' training in technology applications." He has no grudge in going up to this extreme, "otherwise we won't be able to get the best of the opportunities" (Ravi Gupta et al, 2010: 43).

One of the eminent panellists of the Higher Education Summit, April 09, 2010, Dr. B. K. Murthy, Director, Department of Information Technology, Ministry or Communication and Information, Government of India, commented:

> "We need to bridge the gap between content and ICT. To create a large National Knowledge Network, we are in the process of leveraging high bandwidth connections to all the institutions in education, governance, telemedicine to be interconnected and intra-connected as well" (Ravi Gupta et al, 2010: 43).

It being a very expensive and costly affair, and having its limited expansions, ICT enabled ELT classrooms are available only in metros and only a few financially sound learners are having an access to ICT-enabled classrooms. While discussing anything related to education visionaries must not adopt a myopic or narrow vision. To have a developed India, the socially deprived segment of society must not be ignored. Here is the other side of the coin: alarming as the biggest approaching challenge in ensuring the effective implementation of ICT integrated ELT classrooms for all and also undermining the vision of 'Education for All':

a) "I studied till the sixth and my wife is illiterate, but we work hard to ensure that our kids get the best education so that their futures are bright," says thirty-six years old Sharad Lokhande of Chembur who sells home ground masalas and idli batter from door to door and sends his three children to New Model English High School, Chembur. (*TOI,* New Delhi, May 19, 2010)
b) "My son's eighth standard results have been withheld since we haven't been able to pay his full fees. My wife is trying to make some arrangements while I am still looking for a job. It is getting difficult to get ends meet, but I am working hard at providing my son a good education and hoping he will lead a better life," says Naresh Hire, thirty-six, whose son studies in MK Trust School, Vikhroli. He recently lost his job as a watchman and his wife works as a maid. (*TOI*, New Delhi, May 19, 2010)
c) "We found one school, but it was very far from our home and the fee was similar to that of an English-medium in our neighbourhood. My husband and I then decided that it would be better to send our kids to an English-medium school," says thirty-seven-year old Hansa Maru, whose husband has since expired and daughter studies in Vikas High School, Vikhroli. (*TOI*, New Delhi, May 19, 2010)

It won't be an exaggeration to say that even at the end of the first decade of the twenty-first century, the ICT-integrated ELT classrooms are beyond the reach of more than 80 per cent ELT learners. Until and unless we create opportunities and its access for the last existing aspirant of ELT, the very purpose of ICT-integrated ELT classrooms will be defeated. What makes the situation more critical is non-availability of funds and lack of well-trained language lab staff and faculty members.

Suggestions and Recommendations

In order to obtain the effective output, authors would like to make the following suggestions:

a) *Prior planning to enable well equipped ICT-integrated classrooms* and have well trained teachers should be the first priority as it is to be implemented on a war footing. Planning of activities, or exercises should be made fool proof and complete in all aspects and then only should it be handed over to the implementing team and workforces. Planning should be part of a comprehensive strategic system guiding the day-to-day management towards achieving its vision.

b) *Establishment of a world class and state-of-art infrastructure* throughout the country and ensure its availability to reach the common learner. The main objective of the state-of-art infrastructure is to make effective use of the ICT and its resources which helps to understand and use the graphics, animation, sound and video effects to make the teaching learning process much more interactive and effective.

c) *Orientation and training* of ICT to those ELT teachers who are still practising chalk-board and chalk-and-talk method. The emergence of ICT has put forth the new challenges and responsibilities before language learners and teachers both because languages play an important role in understanding the concepts and providing the opportunities to exchange the ideas. Hence without proper training and orientation, the basic concept of any programme cannot be understood and followed easily. Since languages are the first to welcome the applications of ICT, as an intermediary of communication as well as information system.

d) *Implementation* is very important and is a key to the success of any programme; so it requires utmost care.

It requires some special techniques and tactics. This phase of implementation faces many more unforeseen challenges like the impact of new technology (may be positive or negative), devotion towards full absorption, its expenses, support, retrospective conversion of existing, cooperation, etc. So implementation should be done with accurate planning.

e) *Rigorous Follow-ups* is a very serious phase for any programme. It is human tendency that once a work is done, it is considered sufficient and in most of the cases, it is taken for granted that it needn't be followed up. But for the upgradation of any technology, it is a must to have a rigorous follow-up scheme and maintain the continuity constantly to achieve the objectives of having the ICT-integrated ELT classrooms.

f) Last but not least, these resources and ICT-enabled world class state-of-art classrooms must be cost-effective and within the reach of common man, otherwise we won't be able to ensure education for all. If only the rich and powerful segments of society have an access to the ICT-integrated ELT classrooms, the very purpose of education will be defeated. In order to ensure education for all, a major segment of ICT enabled ELT classrooms should be initiated from rural India, and these suggestions need be followed religiously.

Apart from all the above-mentioned discussions, the most urgent and important thing is the "will power and courage" not only to "accept new changes but to welcome them also." If this is possible, definitely it will prove a big leap towards achieving the vision and mission of having a developed India and sharing, and rather joining the dreams of visionaries like A.P.J. Abdul Kalam that will definitely come true in the near future:

"A developed India, by 2020 or even earlier is not a dream. It need not even be a mere aspiration in the minds of many Indians. It is mission we can all take up and accomplish....Ignited young minds, we feel, are a powerful resource. This resource is mightier than any resource on the earth, in the sky and under the sea. We must all work together to transform our 'developing India' into a 'developed India', and the revolution required for this effort must start in our minds" (Kalam, A.P.J. Abdul, and Y.S. Rajan, 2002: XV-XVI).

Works Cited

Bhandari, Shreya. Education Not Enough, English Needed Now, *Times of India*, New Delhi. May 19, 2010. en.wikipedia.org/wiki/Information_and_Communication_ Technology.

Event Report, "Digital Learning Higher Education Summit, April 09, 2010, New Delhi", *Digital Learning India,* (ed.), Ravi Gupta et al, Vol.06, May 2010.

"Global Information and Communication Technologies." *The World Bank.* About GICT. Retrieved 2009-10-21.

Govinda, R. (2010). "Higher Education: Technology for Educational Advancements", *Digital Learning India* (ed.), Ravi Gupta et al, Vol. 06.

http://rubble.ultralab.anglia.ac.uk/stevenson/ICTUKIndex.html (2008-09-19).

Jobs and Career, Course Watch, Bachelor's course in 3D animation, *The Tribune,* New Delhi, May 19, 2010.

Kalam, A. P. J, Abdul and Rajan, Y. S. (2002). *India 2020: A Vision for the New Millennium.* Penguin Books India.

Rice, M.F. (2003), 'Information and Communication Technologies and the Global Digital Divide Technology Transfer, Development, and Least Developing countries', *Comparative Technology Transfer and Society,* Vol.1, No.1, pp.72-78.

Science, Ray, *Technology and its influence on interpersonal Communication* http://scienceray.com/technology/information/technology-and-its-influence-on-interpersonal- communication. Retrieved 2010-04-24.

www.bfe.admin.ch//forschungelektrizitaet/01739/01744/index.html

www.smartstate.qld.gov.au/strategy/strategy05_15/glossary.shtm

www.syberworks.com/glossary/i/i.htm

4

Putting out the Information and Communication Technological Flames: It's Ethics

— Ramesh Chandra Shukla

I have crossed ocean
I have lost my tongue
From the root of the old one
A new one has sprung.

— *Grace Nichols*

Cross-cultural encounter muticulturism and hybridity are all phenomena closely associated with the concept of globalization or, in other words, the shrinking of the distances that have separated men and culture from others. Now, globalization has broken down the walls that were built as barriers segmenting the world into sharp divisions. Contemporary society is 'global society', and the phenomenon of globalization has touched and transformed not only the world community but also its very culture and psyche. The globalization has invariably made its mark on the language of the world.

"The globalization of languages can be viewed as a process by which some languages are increasingly used in international communication while others lose their prominence and even disappear for the lack of their speakers" (Manfred B. Steger). Language is the basis of civilization. Evolving from the earliest spoken word, it has developed to symbolize the culture, society, people and their ethos. It is the signifier of identity, the 'self' which, when asserted, correlates to the assertion of one's individuality. Language is power, the feature that proclaims supremacy for the human race closely linked with culture and society. It has been used as a weapon by the conquerors to subdue and strengthen their authority on the conquered. To silence them into submission in "colonialism' whether as indirect rule or the exploration and settlement of continents, brought with it the English language, English literary form, and English culture assumptions (Bruce King). The process of globalization has endowed the English language with an eminence that has eclipsed many other languages with time starting from the sixteenth century. British colonialism reigned over almost the entire Third World. It was somewhat natural that wherever they went, they took their language with them and used it as a medium of cementing their colonial rule, and so English "....came to represent the British Empire and symbolized the hegemony of colonizers" (Sudhakar Pandey).

After the Second World War, this position of Britain as a world power was lost to the emerging power of America. With time, America made tremendous advancement, and invaded the whole world. English or 'Amerilish' has defined and transformed the lingua franca of the world. In the present global scenario, English or Amerilish is gradually colonizing the entire world. Global English speaks with voices: British and American. The differences are essentially differences of accent, inflection; spelling and, above all, vocabulary (Bruce King). People have no or little time for formalities and long complicated rules. Everything, today, is preferred, simplified and easy the American way, even the language.

Nature of Ethics

Ethics is the study of values, virtues, rules or principles to live a good human life. How should one live a good human life or what ought to do in a particular situation is a fundamental question of ethics that everyone of us faces sometime or the other, and we try to answer it in some way. We happen to face the question on our own because it is a natural human inclination to improve upon the way we live; living a good human life, thus, is a goal that we all strive to attain.

However, we stumble many a time by the way to achieve the goal of living a good human life because we find it difficult to discover the correct path. But it is possible for a human being at any given moment of his life to reflect upon what he thinks or does. This is exactly where the role of ethics assumes vital dimensions. The role of ethics is to enable us to be reflective, to reflect upon and understand the nature of good human life. In this age of IT, it has become mandatory to safeguard our ethical responsibilities. The ethical actions of a person can be described in general terms as those actions that are performed within the criterion of which is regarded as socially, morally and legally acceptable within the framework of a particular society or nation. It relates thus to the question of what is good or bad in terms of human actions. According to Spinello (1995: 14) the purpose of ethics is to help us to behave honourably and attain the basic good that makes us more fully human.

David Hume on Sympathy

I propose that the source of the reflective understanding of good human life may align to the David Hume's conception of sympathy or humanity or fellow-feeling. He suggests that the sentiment of sympathy is universal because it is natural to be human and to have the sentiment of sympathy. It is, of course, not to be understood in the narrow sense in which it is now commonly used to mean something like compassion or pity. Richard Norman informs: "He means by it a capacity to be moved or affected by the happiness and suffering of others to be pleased when others prosper, and distressed when others suffer. He insists that sympathy, thus understood, is an independent human tendency which exists in its own right" (Norman, 53). Everyone, thus understood, what is, to some extent, affected by the happiness or suffering of others.

It is not about an impractical claim that everyone is always motivated by feelings of kindness and concern for others, or we have nobody who acts inconsiderately or cruelly towards others. Hume simply asks us to envisage a situation where someone is incapable of responding to people as of other human beings or toys or chairs. This cannot be true in the case of a normal human being. He does possess the feeing of sympathy itself which is not a morally admirable quality but the source of all moral qualities. For this sentiment of sympathy denotes not an object of approval but the source of moral approval. And this may further imply that since we have this capacity, we are inclined to morally praise or blame people in so far as they exhibit morally admirable or deplorable qualities. We respond favourably to personal qualities like benevolence, justice, cheerfulness, modesty, decency and politeness because they are either usefully agreeable to their possession or to others. In other words, they are directly or indirectly advantageous to possessor or others. The possession of such qualities promotes happiness and it is through sympathy with happiness, whether of the individual possession or of general sort, that we admire such qualities, and through the same mechanism, it is natural again that we blame people so far as they bring in suffering, the opposite of happiness.

The sentiment of sympathy, Hume goes to add, denotes a fellow-feeling. It takes one out of one's language of self-love. He maintains:

> "When a man denominates another his enemy, his rival, his antagonist, he is understood to speak the language of self-love and to express sentiments peculiar to himself and arising from his particular circumstances and situation. But when he bestows on any man the epithets of vicious or odious or depraved, he then speaks another language, and expresses sentiments in which he expects all his audience to concur with him. He must here, therefore, depart from his private and particular situation, and must choose a point of view common to him with others. He must move some universal principle of the human frame" (Hume, Section IX, 6). This universal principle is the natural human sentiment of sympathy and Hume wants us to call up.

Sympathy as a Normative Stance of Global Communication

We may apply the universal principle of sympathy to bring in the ideal of global communication for information resolution

It may be also kept in mind that no aspect of human life is exclusive in itself or value neutral. All aspects of life, social or personal, are interconnected. For example, we cannot say that a person's life has no bearing upon his relations with his family members or members of society in general. Or anybody may do anything in his life and claim that it would have no bearing upon the social fabric or the way he should live a good human life. The point being made here is that we must come out of value neutral stance that we may adopt in a communication process for protecting sectarian interests and recognize the need for a normative stance of any such process that we as a group may undertake.

The recognition of neutral sentiment of sympathy as a normative stance may strengthen other processes such as social, political or religious to attain the ideal of global communication for information resolution. The front page headline of *Sunday Times of India*, New Delhi on November 19, 2006, quotes Afghan President Hamid Karzai, "Karzai Pushes Pakistan To Do More Against Taliban" and as reported in the *Week*, May 13, 2007, Pakistan President Pervez Musharraf reacts, "The ones who do nothing against terrorism, like Karzai, are those who criticize the ones who fight like us." This example shows a small part of ongoing global communication as a means of finding a solution to a socio-political problem, which rests on the calculation of consequences to secure national or group interests—explicit interests of Afghanistan, Pakistan and Taliban and implicit interests of India, U.S.A. and, of course, the newspaper and the weekly magazine. And if the utility of a normative stance of global communication in the above-mentioned context is recognized, the headlines could be, "Karzai and Musharraf Resolve to Contain Taliban." Such a collective human response would accommodate a greater degree of uniformity, and it is not easy though Hume maintains:

a) Sympathy, we shall allow, is much fainter than our concern for ourselves, and sympathy with persons remote from us; much fainter than that with persons near and contiguous; but for this very reason it is necessary for us, in our calm judgments and discourse concerning the characters of men, to neglect all these differences and render our sentiments more public and social (Hume, Section V: 42).

b) Hume suggests here the adoption of criteria such as freedom, impartiality, conceptual clarity and information about all possible relevant facts to correct the opinion of sympathy, so that we may attach equal moral importance to the happiness or suffering of ourselves and others. Such an impartial fellow-feeling, therefore, is not a mere cosmic requirement but a life-thread of global communication.

The Concept of Privacy

In addition to ethics, the concept of privacy too has become a force to reckon with. Privacy can be defined as an individual condition of life characterized by exclusion from privacy (Neethling et al, 1996: 36). The concept follows from right to left alone (Stair, 1992: 635. Shank, 1986: 12). As such, privacy can be regarded as a natural right which provides the foundation for other legal rights. The legal right to privacy is constitutionally protected in most democratic societies. This constitutional right is expressed in a variety of legislative forms: The Privacy Act (1974) in U.S.A. and the Data Protection Act in England. Privacy is an important right because it is a necessary condition for other rights such as freedom and personal autonomy. Thus, we can say that there is a relationship among privacy, freedom and human dignity. Respecting a person's privacy is the acknowledgement of such a person's right to freedom and to recognize that the individual is an autonomous human being. The duty to respect a person's privacy is furthermore a prima facie duty. In other words, it is not an absolute duty that does not allow for exceptions. Two examples may be cited for better understanding. Firstly, the police may violate a criminal's privacy by spying or by seizing personal documents; secondly, a government also has the right to gather private and personal information from the citizens with the aim of ensuring order and harmony in society (Ware,

1993: 205). The right to privacy as an expression of individual freedom is thus confined by social responsibility.

Different Concepts of Private Information

Based on the above-mentioned definition of privacy, aspects which are of specific relevance for information based society must be emphasized. The first is the fact that the privacy as a concept is closely related to information. According to Neethling (1996: 35), privacy refers to the total of facts and information applicable to a person in a state of isolation. The fact is that the privacy is expressed by means of information that implies that it is possible to distinguish between different categories of privacy, namely, private communication, information which relates to the privacy of a person's body, other personal information, and information with regard to a person's possession. Each of these categories is briefly dealt with.

Private Communication

This category of privacy is concerned with all forms of personal communication which a person wishes to keep private. This information can be exchanged during an interview between a user and service provider which is an example of this category (*Privacy of the Body,* Westin, 1967: 351). This normally refers to medical information (Neethling, 1991: 35-36).This means that a person has the right to be informed about the nature of an illness and can be forced to make it known to others. The only exception is when the health and possibly the lives of others may be endangered by the specific illness – such as the case may be where a person is HIV positive and the chance exists that other people may contract the virus. This category of information is of specific importance for an information professional working in a medical library.

Privacy of Personal Information

Personal information of this category refers to only that specific person, for example, name, address and the financial information. This type of information is of relevance to all categories of information professionals.

Information about One's Possessions

This is an important aspect of the issue of privacy. It implies an explicit desire for privacy. This desire is important for the delimitation of privacy. In short, the desire for privacy implies that privacy will only be an issue in cases where there is a clear expression of a desire for privacy. For example, a personal conversation between two persons will be regarded as private as long as there is an expressed will to keep it private. The moment this will is relinquished, the information is no longer regarded as private. The same applies to the other categories of personal and private information too.

If a person makes a private telephone number (as a form of personal information) known to a company, it is no longer private information. It can even be seen as business information which may legally be traded in. This expressed will to privacy acts, therefore, as a very important guideline for the information professional regarding the delimitation of privacy. Here, it is also important to distinguish between privacy and confidentiality or secrecy. The confidential treatment of information is not restricted to the above-mentioned four categories of information, such as trade secrets.

Influence of Technology on Processing of Personal and Private Information

Definition of Information Technology

According to Van Brakel (1989: 240), information technology is the gathering, organizing, storage and distribution of information in various formats by means of computer and telecommunication techniques based on microelectronics.

Communication: Communication is what we try to do, speak to those near us. It involves:

a) *Thought:* First, information exists in the mind of the sender. This can be a concept, idea, information or feelings.
b) *Encoding:* Next, a message is sent to a receiver in words or other symbols.

c) *Decoding:* Lastly, the receiver translates words or symbols into a concept or information that he or she can understand.

Ethical Implications in the Processing of Information

The main ethical impact is in regard to accessibility and inaccessibility while its impact is on gathering, storage, retrieval and on the road to information too. Its impact goes on manipulation of information. By implication, it becomes easier to access a person's private information by more people. On the other side, a person cannot be included from necessary information in electronic format by means of its variety of security clues such as passwords. Technological manipulation of information refers, among others, to the summation of information (merging of documents), the repackaging thereof (translations and the integration of textual and graphical formats) by electronic means. The application of technology in the processing of information can thereof not be seen as ethically neutral. Brown (1990: 3) indicates that the ethical problems that are caused by the use of technology do not imply "That we should rethink our moral values". The impact of the use of technology on the privacy of people manifests itself in a variety of areas. These include the following:

a) *Electronic Monitoring of People in Workplace:* This includes personal and private information both are the justifications by companies for the use of such technology is to increase productivity. Stair (1992: 655), however, in the discussion of this practice, clearly points out the ethical problem relating to the use of these technologies. According to him, peoples' privacy in the workplace is threatened by these devices. It can also lead to fear and of always being watched.

b) *The Interception and Reading of E-Mails:* This leads to an ethical problem which has the concern with private information. It is technically possible to capture e-mail messages, and the reading thereof is normally justified by companies because they see technology infrastructure as a resource belonging to the company and not the individual. Secondly, messages are intercepted to check on people to see whether they use the facility for private reasons or to do their job.

Merging of Databases which Contain Personal Information

This is commonly known as data-banking (Frocht and Thomas, 1994: 24). It means the integration of personal information from a variety of databases into one central database. The problem is in the first place but from the integration of the information as such. In fact, the problem arises that the individual is not aware of personal information being integrated into a central database. The surprising thing is that the individual does not know the purpose for which the integration is effected, or by whom, or by whose benefit the new database is constructed and whether the information is accurate. Another notable threat to privacy is the rise of hackers and crackers who break into the computer system (Benjamin, 1991: 7).This coincides with a shift in ethical values and the emergence of cyber culture with the motto of 'Free Information'.

The Development of Software Securities

The development of such software securities that make the a coding of digital information virtually impossible also poses a serious legal as well as ethical issue because it can protect criminals.

Individual and Socio-Economic Effect

These can be distinguished as:

a) *On the Individual Level:* It is a loss of dignity and spontaneity as well as a threat to freedom and the right to privacy. On the basis of survey findings, it can be said that 79 per cent of the respondents indicated that they were wary of the use of technology for the processing of their personal information (Frocht and Thomas: 24).

b) *On Economic and Social Levels:* The biggest effect is the growth of large information business-like credit bureaus and telecommunication companies that specialize in the processing and trade of person-related information. This brings about a redefinition of the role of society in the personal and private lives of the individual, i.e. the use of personal information as a commodity.

Levels of Information Professional

There are the following three levels:

a) The information professional works with all categories of personal private profession.

b) Increasing use is made of technology with processing thereof.

c) A new trend of entrepreneur has emerged whose main function of business is the buying and selling of person–related and other personal information.

Main Ethical Issues

The ethical problems confronted by the information professional while handling different categories of personal information are dealt below:

a) *Deciding which Categories of Personal Information are entitled to gather:* This question is of utmost importance to the information professional working in all sectors and business.

b) *Confidential Treatment of Such Information:* Main ethical problems in concern (with specific reference to online searching) are as follows: Can personal details obtained from a reference interview be used for purposes other than for that which it was specifically gathered? Is it ethically correct to re-use a search strategy formulated for one user for another user? Is it appropriate to discuss the nature of a specific query with other people?

c) *Purposes for which Various Categories of Information may be Used:* The question is here whether an information professional may use any private information for any other reasons than the original reason given for the gathering thereof. Thing is there whether the person must be notified about the way in which personal information is going to be used.

d) *Accuracy of Information:* This issue says whether an information professional is working with personal and private information that can have a direct influence on the life of a person. An example is the processing of medical examination.

e) *Rights of a Person in Terms of the Use and Distribution of One's Personal Information:* This problem also relates to the above-mentioned issues and boil down to the question of consent of the user in terms of personal information. Some related issues are as follows: Does a user have the right to verify any personal and private information that is being held by an information professional, and if so, what are such person's rights regarding the correcting (in cases of the incorrectness thereof) of this information, and does the person have the right to know who is using that personal and private and personal information and for what purposes?

Applicable Ethical Norms

The following norms can act as guidelines as well as an instrument of measurement which must be formulated to address these ethical issues. They are discussed in brief:

a) *Truth:* Truth as an ethical norm has dual ethical application. First, it serves a norm for the factual correctness of information. As a norm, it guides the personal information relating to the accurate and factually correct handling of private information. Secondly, truth is an expression of ethical virtues such as openness, honesty and trustworthiness.

b) *Freedom:* According to this norm, a person has the freedom to make choices in terms of freedom of privacy and freedom from intrusion. As a norm, however, it may not become absolute. Therefore, the choice to privacy from intrusion may not restrict the freedom of others.

c) *Human Rights:* This norm is nearly related to freedom but can be regarded as a more correctly applicable norm.

Applied to privacy means the juridical acknowledgement and protection of a person's right to privacy. As an individual human right, it also protects the individual from unlawful interference from society.

Ethical Guidelines for Putting out Information Flames

Based on the above-mentioned norms, some practical guidelines for information professional can be formulated. Before formulating, two things must be kept in mind, namely, the recognition of a person's autonomy and freedom as well as the fact that the legal guidelines on privacy do not offer a complete framework for ethical actions of the professional information regarding the handling of personal and private information.

Once a person's private and personal information have been made known publicly, such information is no longer, according to the law, viewed as private. This implies that the information can legally be dealt with as trade information. Therefore, there is from a juridical perspective, no ethical sensitivity on the issues of autonomy and freedom of the individual in connection with his right to privacy. The second remark relates to the content of legislation itself. Immense growth in and development of IT give rise to the fact that legislators fall behind in tabling of appropriate legislation on the protection of personal privacy. Keeping in mind these two things, the following practical guidelines can be laid:

a) As an acknowledgement of the autonomy and freedom of the individual the information personal must act on the assumption the client regards as confidential all personal and private information that is handled by the information professional. This has the meaning that the information professional acknowledges the right of the client to control to a certain extent. Any personal and private information. This is based on the norm of freedom.

b) The client must, on a regular basis, have access to all private and personal information that is held and used by the information professional. The reason for this is to provide the client the opportunity to verify the accuracy of the information. It is then the responsibility of the information professional to see to it that necessary corrections are made and again verified by the client (Fouty, 1993: 290), based on the norms of human rights and freedom.

The merging of personal and other private information of an individual into a different database than the one for which it was originally collected must be done with necessary caution (Schattuck, 1995: 310). This is specifically applicable in situations where the client is not aware of such merging or the implications thereof. The appropriate action would not only be to inform the client about such a merging and the implications thereof., but also to give the client the right of access to the information on the central database, the opportunity to change the information where it is incorrect, and the right to know who is using the information as well as the purpose of such use based on the norms of human rights, freedom and truth.

The information professional must notify the client explicitly of the intended purpose of the use of all personal and private information. This implies the client's permission. Different avenues exist for seeking such information. Spinello (1995: 122) prefers the method of implicit informed consent. According to this principle, companies or information professionals who have collected information about a person must diligently inform that person about the various uses of the information. Clients must be given an opportunity either to consent to these uses or to withhold their consent. The burden is on the client to respond, and lack of response implies the consent. However, the client must be granted the opportunity to withdraw consent (Amidon, 1992: 67) based on the norms of freedom and human rights.

a) It is necessary that private information must be gathered. This is not only for logistic reasons but also to prevent the unnecessary violation of exposure of person's privacy based on the norm of freedom.
b) Personal and other private information, that is no longer necessary for the function for which it was collected, must be destroyed (Branscomb, 1995: 71) based on the norms of freedom and human rights.

c) When the description of a specific service or product to a person is refused on the grounds of personal information (e.g. creditworthiness), the reason for this denial must be made known to the person based on the norms of truth and human rights.

A person's information must be handled with the necessary confidentiality. This implies security and control of access to the information of the right to use it, as well as the right to change or add any information (Fouty, 1993: 290) based on the norms of truth and human rights.

A private policy must be formulated having the following elements—the categories of information that must be regarded as private and personal, the levels of confidentiality (e.g. who has access and use of which information), a clear explanation of the purposes of the use of the information and the detail of the procedures to ensure the accuracy of this information based on the norms of freedom, truth and human rights.

Works Cited

Amidon, P. (1992). "Widening Privacy Concerns". *Online,* 16 (4) pp.64-67.

Benjamin, L. (1991). "Privacy, Computers and Personal Information: Towards Equality and Equity In an Information Age" in *Communications and the Law*.13 (2). 3-16.

Branscomb, A.W. (1994). *Who Owns Information? From Privacy to Private Access.* New York: Basic Books (A division of Harper Collins Publishers).

Frocht, K.T. & Thomas, D.S. (1994). Information Compilation and Disbursement: Moral, Legal and Ethical Considerations" *Information Management and Computer Security*. 2 (2), 23-28.

Fouty, K.G. (1993). Online Patron Records and Privacy: Service Vs Security." *The Journal of Academic Librarianship*.19 (5). 289-293.

Spinello, R.A. (1995). *Ethical Aspects of Information Technology*. New Jersey: Prentice-Hall Inc.

5

Information and Communication Technology: A Boon for Twenty-first Century English Language Teachers

— Dr. Anju Bala Agrawal

ICT stands for new multimedia technologies, including computer, software and CD-ROM, the Internet, mobile phone, television, film and other technologies. Researches show that the use of ICT on students' language learning provides much evidence that ICT has a positive effect on motivation. It increases students' learning including language learning; achievement and enthusiasm in the use of ICT in their lessons. DFEE (The Department for Education and Employment in the UK, 1998:17) demonstrates:

> "ICT is more than a teaching tool. Its potential for improving the quality and standards of pupils' education is significant. Equally, its potential is considerable for supporting teachers, both in their everyday classroom role, associated with it, and in their counting training and development."

ICT dissolves the barriers of time and place, and it throws open the possibility to initiate any human activity. The choice of ICT for educational communication is due to its user-friendliness, speed, accuracy high degree of reliability, high storage capacity, integrity, consistency, logicality, diligence, versatility, low failure rate, durability and probability; above all, it has a special characteristic of 'interactivity' which gives the total control to the learner. Technological innovations have gone hand-in-hand with the growth of English, and are changing the way in which we communicate, work, trade, entertain and learn, and it is non-native users of English, frequently from Asian countries, who are arguably, at the heart of this. It is fair to assert that the growth of the Internet has facilitated the growth of the English language, and that this has occurred at a time when computers are no longer the exclusive domain of the dedicated few, but rather widely available to many.

Managing a language classroom is different from others and is a bit difficult for the teachers of English. It is necessary for the teacher to get the attention of students and to use various methods and different ways to instil the interest in students. The teacher should mould and make the students settle in the class with ease, and to be active and attentive in the classroom. As the students have different grasping levels of learning and come from diversified backgrounds, so the responsibility of teachers increases. They should handle them tactfully. Through interactive language learning sessions, the teacher can analyze abilities of learners that help to take good steps to develop their skills. The role of the teacher increases to that of a facilitator, mentor, instructor and counsellor. Pronunciation and accent variation can be taught only by ICT. The predominance of technology in the modern scenario allocates some new roles and duties on the modern teacher. The various tools offered by modern technology can encourage the conventional teaching method to an advanced, effective and mesmerizing teaching method.

The inclusion of technology in teaching communication stimulates students' interest in learning technical aspects of communication. The inclusion of technology in technological aspects of communication, various tools such as audio-video aids, web browsing, web lessons and quizzes increase the output of teaching. In addition to this, technology offers new ways of communication such as emails, fax, teleconferencing, etc. These modern ways of communication can be included in the teaching of communication skills in such a way that their linguistic knowledge as well as communicative skills is enhanced. Information and communication technology empowers teachers to effectively teach writing. From software packages that address different areas of language learning such as grammar syntax and vocabulary to the myriad platforms for self-expression, afforded by the Internet such as mails, chats blogs and so on, there are many ICT resources and tools that an English language teacher can draw on to teach the different stages of writing process.

The wider changes taking place in the society are providing a context for instructional development. Over years there is shift from oral to written, formal to non-formal, teacher-centred to student-centred and rigid to flexible forms of instruction. Nowadays, teaching learning method is not limited to chalk and board method. A teacher should incorporate innovative teaching strategies for effective learning. The use of ICT has great educational potential because of its various attributes like text, graphics, music interactive communication. Grammar can be taught effectively with the help of ICT-enabled instructional package.

Often the use of technology helps a great deal in bringing to life places that could only be described in words. Shakespeare could definitely be more interesting if one could show Stratford-on–Avon. Similarly, teaching of drama and poetry can be more interesting by computers and technology. Students become aware of the use of punctuations in writing and speaking, preserving the charm of the language with the ignorance of grammatical rules. Similarly, in the field of dramas, a teacher can use definite scenes to develop critical thinking and thus make students aware of the thoughts and situations of the protagonist in the drama, different accents, tone, intonation patterns, and rhythm of sentences used by characters of different and particular speech communities in the drama.

Equalization of higher educational opportunities has become an important goal of contemporary developing nations. Open universities are considered to be a great educational innovation of modern times. Developments in communication technologies have enhanced the potential and utility of open universities. The three main communication technologies (audio, video and computer) have broadened the horizons of open and distance learning imparted through open universities. Distance learning courses use a variety of teaching methods, strategies and technologies. Technology plays a key role in the delivery of distance education.

There are interactive video-conferencing (ITV) courses, online courses (taught using the Internet), tele-courses (videotaped lessons) and 'hybrid' courses that combine several different technologies with a traditional face-to-face component. The communication is interactive in that the student receives support and feedback from the teacher. The feedback may be immediate or delayed. A synchronous delivery does not take place simultaneously. In this case, the teacher may deliver the instruction via video, computer, or other means, and the students respond at a later time. For example, instruction may be delivered via the web or videotapes, and the feedback could be sent via e-mail messages. Distance learning technologies offer a myriad of benefits, including convenience, flexibility, effectiveness and efficiency.

Multimedia can enrich language learning in the classroom. Students can complete tasks through multimedia. They can produce and present a paper on some topic. They may be asked to produce a TV advertisement for or against it. They can work in teams and access the Internet and CD-ROMs. They can write their reports on computers. PowerPoint can be used for final presentations. Most of the students when working with multimedia like a story much better than the traditional printed story. Lancy and Hayes point out:

> "Interactive books motivated readers to spend more time reading on it than print books. Students could access the texts faster and understand the text accurately on screen."

Multimedia lab is also an effective tool in developing the ability to use English for performing in academic, social and professional situations in their own way. A batch of students belonging to various departments with various level of comprehension in English should be selected for the multimedia lab. The teacher should choose the activities and divide it according to the level of the students, as it is a mixed ability classroom. Either one or two students have to be given a computer. In case of two, then the same levels of students have to be paired as each pair is given a separate system. They cannot discuss with their neighbour, so the question of inferiority complex has no role to play.

As the activities in the multimedia lab are based on the level, students will enjoy the session. Depending on the level, students will be listening to small passages through headphones. Then to check their comprehension level, activities are given based on the passage they have listened to. The answers will be evaluated by the system. And the score will be made available to the students. Critical thinking can be achieved through multimedia. The teacher has to introduce the concepts of the students prior to the multimedia session. Then the activities will be given and evaluated. To develop the critical thinking, a project work, related to the topic, can be given to the students finally. This procedure will be followed for all the levels of the students.

The web can be a powerful tool for teacher educators, teachers and others to develop and share contents that meet cultural, linguistic and educational needs of the Indian education system. In the process of developing a techno-pedagogy for the 'new' learner in the 'new' environment, learning 'new' things and 'new' technologies, the first issue to be addressed is the development of content. Other salient features of e-content via multi-sensory learning experiences, digital convergence of text, image, audio, video, animation, etc., and to create the effects of multimedia, accessibility, reusability, interpretability, etc., are the content development among all academic endeavours.

The rise of the digital world has completely changed the teaching world. The following points can easily validate the important role that technology is playing in a language class. Tape recorders and cassettes have been around since the 1970s, and many schools and colleges rely on them with speakers to help learners develop listening skills. Some of the schools and colleges are now using CD players instead of tape recorders and cassettes. Listening materials are moving from tapes and CDs to podcasts and MP3 files on the PC. Most schools, colleges and universities have moved from blackboards and flashcards. Graded readers, and any other book-based materials, are becoming available as e-books and PDFs on the PC which can be downloaded for lower cost than printed books. The rise of Web2.0 has made teachers and learners work easy, i.e., teachers can create notes or content for their learners, and learners can also modify those notes before they use it.

Students can find a large amount of reading material on the Internet for people to read. Such material is easy to search. The Internet can promote readers' development. Some websites offer readers an opportunity to publish and to read book reviews, comments and discussions about stories, exchange opinions and even write their own stories online. This can promote argument, critical literacy, thinking and language skills. When we use the Internet in the classroom, students and teachers are brought into other parts of the world and they are considered as participants in much wider and more complicated learning communities than before. It leads students' learning into more globalized contexts, compared to the past. There are three main features of Internet; the first is "multimodality", which means participation of the work in the world and comprehension of the large quantities of available information. The second is "non-linear", meaning the skills and strategies for searching for relevant information and material. The third is the vast potential of communication with others. In this connection, Pacheler comments:

> "Using creatively e-mail, e-mail attachments and the Internet could meet new partners in learning and enhance students to make high standards in their work."

Students' autonomous language learning self-assessment can become widely available through the web rather than being tied to particular classes. Students can interact with the learners from all over the world. The use of e-mail is an easy, cheap and quick way of communication. People can respond to e-mail quickly. The use of email exchange to improve language skills is widely recognized, and a number of studies are devoted to finding "key pals" for students and promoting student-student correspondence. Students who have problems with reading and writing can be motivated via the use of e-mail pen pals in other schools and other parts of the world. When a scanner is used, students can attach pictures to the e-mail, giving more interest to the task. It could also help teachers to exchange ideas and experience of teaching.

Mobile learning is seen as the future of learning, and has the potential to blend with the fast paced lifestyles of the digital generation. Movable learning has also emerged as having specific affordances for countries like India where a vast majority of learners are located in rural areas. Mobile learning objects can be used offline on mobile phones ensuring learning even during the dead time. Text features in mobiles are extensively used by students. Learners get a chance to explore real life English through reading and writing text messages, predicative texts, etc., even in classroom text-related features of mobile such as SMS and predicative texts.

To conclude, the use of ICT on language learning has a positive effect on motivation, and its use can contribute to our language teaching and learning. A better understanding of motivational aspects of use of ICT can make it more effective and increase potential for ICT to be more widely used in language teaching and learning around the world. Nowadays children are more fascinated towards the computer. If a teacher designs an individualized programme for developing the language and literacy processes and improving the understanding and abilities while they work on computer publication and drawing applications, then gradually towards text work. Certain games can also be created. Such programmes increase reading and writing competencies of students.

We have to explore the potential of using the same material in different ways to maximize the student's learning process. For example, when using the smart boards, it saves a lot of time in giving a feedback to students, and the teacher can use the materials other than to teach the target language (in reading or listening materials) to introduce them to the day-to-day vocabulary and other information, phrases in English language, collocations in the language etc, without ignoring them, thinking that is not in the course book to teach. In my opinion, a teacher should be resourceful in introducing the language to the students, specially in means of communication which I believe is the main purpose of learning a language. Therefore, the teacher should explore using technology without just sticking to the course books.

Works Cited

DFEE, (1998). *Teaching: High Status, High Standards, Requirements for Courses of Initial Teacher Training Circular,* 4/98.

Lancy, D. and Hayes, B. (1988). Interactive Fiction and the Reluctant Reader. *English Journal,* 77 (7): 42-46.

Pachler, N. (1999). Theories of Learning and ICT, In Leask, M. and Pachler, N. (eds), *Learning to teach Using ICT in the Secondary School,* London and New York: Routledge.

6

Role of Digital Technologies in Transformation of Education in the World

— Ashu Tomar

ICT is an acronym that stands for Information and Communication Technology. Information and communication technology is an umbrella term that covers all technical ways for processing and communicating information. It is most often used to describe digital technologies including methods for communication, as well as techniques for storing and processing information. The term has gained popularity partially due to the convergence of information technology and telecom technology. Information and communication technology is defined as the combination of informatics technology with other related technologies, specifically communication technology.

Information technology is "the study, design, development, implementation, support or management of computer-based information systems, particularly software applications and computer hardware", according to the Information Technology Association of America. It deals with the use of electronic computers and computer software to convert, store, protect, process, transmit and securely retrieve information.

Today, the term 'information' encompasses many aspects of computing and technology, and the term has become very recognizable. Information technology is starting to spread farther than the conventional personal computer and network technology, and more into integrations of other technologies such as the use of cell phones, televisions, automobiles and more, which is increasing the demand for such jobs. When computer and communication technologies are combined, the result is information technology or "info tech". Information technology is a general term that describes any technology that helps to produce, manipulate, store, communicate and disseminate information.

Information and communication technology has become within a very short time, one of the basic building blocks of modern society. Many countries now regard understanding information and communication technology and mastering the basic skills and concepts of information and communication technology as part of the core of education, alongside reading, writing and numeracy.

Information and communication technologies (ICTs) are undoubtedly the most dominant technologies emerging in today's economic scenario globally. The economic potential of ICTs for development was starkly highlighted by the United Nations former Secretary General, Kofi Annan, in his remarks at a session of the United Nations Commission on Science and Technology for Development (UNCSTD) in 1997: "Recent developments in the field of communication and information technology are indeed revolutionary in nature. Information and knowledge are expanding in quantity and accessibility. In such fields as agriculture, health, education, human resources and environmental management or transport and business development, the consequences really could be revolutionary. Communication and information technologies have enormous potential especially for developing countries and in furthering sustainable development" (Annan, K. 1997). A society in which the information embedded in ICT systems is combined productively with the creative potential and knowledge embodied in people, called "Knowledge Society", is being propagated by various International agencies as a model for sustainable development.

Internet, video-conferencing, telephone, television, newspapers and cell phones—the world has never been so well-connected. It is amazing how a corporation in the US outsources its customer services to a third party service provider based somewhere in India. Similarly, distance learning courses offered by a university in Europe benefits students in China. One cannot deny that innovative communication technologies have certainly brought the world closer, irrespective of the differences otherwise.

Information and communication technologies facilitate the ease of communication, which has many profound effects. In the business world, deals can be made through emails and video-conferencing, and mobile phone technology has made it possible for people to check and send messages on the go, allowing us to be connected 24x7. Although this has greatly facilitated the business world in general, many negative implications are to be considered as well. Simple messages which used to be delivered face to face are now being sent through the cold impersonal means of e-mail. This has reduced socialization within the office, thus contributing to the weakening of bonds within the workplace.

Information technology (IT) today is the world's fastest growing segment, and the use of IT is so widely spread throughout the world economy that no single country can avoid investing in this, if it wants to improve the standard of living of its citizens. The flow of information has changed our lifestyle and at present information is the backbone of every system. Nowadays information is also vital for running our day-to-day activities smoothly. IT has made our lives simpler and people can work on the Internet without really having to go outside to their workplaces.

Countries must be able to benefit from technological developments. To be able to do so, a cadre of professionals has to be educated with sound information and communication technology backgrounds, independent of specific computer platforms or software environments. Technological developments lead to changes in work and changes in the organization of work. Required competencies are therefore changing. The use of information and communication technology cuts across all aspects of economic and social life. Technological developments in information and communication technology are very rapid. Technology quickly becomes obsolete requiring new skills and knowledge to be mastered frequently. Adaptation is only possible when based on a sound understanding of the principles and concepts of information and communication technology.

Information and communication technology allow users to participate in a rapidly changing world in which work and other activities are increasingly transformed by access to varied and developing technologies. Information and communication technology tools can be used to find, explore, analyze, exchange and present information responsibly and without discrimination. Information and communication technology can be employed to give users quick access to ideas and experiences from a wide range of people, communities and cultures. In the recent decades widespread incorporation of information and communication technologies into many tiers of business, political processes and structuring of the global economy has occurred. Information and communication technologies have increased international interconnectedness and speeded up the process of globalization.

Information and communication technologies have impacted societies on many levels. They have extended the reach of public administration, leading to a centralization of regional management into urban centres. They have led to new forms of employment in innovation and production of information and communication technologies, and a demand for highly skilled specialists. However, information and communication technologies have also enabled professionals in certain industries to be replaced by unskilled workers or even made entirely redundant.

Information communication technologies (ICTs) have impacted almost all the sectors of the world economy, though it is accepted that the rate of development of new technologies has been lower in developing countries, especially those of sub-Saharan Africa. The information communication technology (ICT) which involves the use of electronic equipment for storing, analyzing and distribution of information is gradually replacing at a faster rate the old system of information storage, analysis, distribution and processing among governmental and nongovernmental organizations while information communication technology also involves the transfer and flow of information, circulation of knowledge and ideas in the society using electronic means. It is also a conscious attempt to share information or ideas with others at a faster rate for the purpose of getting desired results.

Digital technology affects the lives of people the world over in many ways. ICT is a key factor not only at the macro level in the process of globalisation but also at the micro level where the increased use of mobile phones, for instance, has changed communication patterns all over the world. ICT provides new opportunities for those who are literate, have a good education and adequate resources. Disadvantaged and marginalised groups have little chance to automatically benefit from tools such as the Internet. This further increases social divides, widens the gap between rich and poor countries, regions, individuals and even between men and women.

The intrinsic value of ICT lies not in easing communications and information but rather in enabling growth and development. In a country like India, where a vast section of the population is below the poverty line, ICT offers a chance to empower these people and transform them into productive human capital.

Well-endowed human capital goes beyond having hard-working, dedicated and diligent manpower. With the emergence of highly competitive production economies, the key for rapid development lies in building a knowledge-based society. The challenge is to be able to use ICT for the creation of new knowledge for all human endeavours. Traditionally, a nation moves through three stages of economic development, from agriculture to manufacturing and then to services.

The information revolution is commonly talked about as a phenomenon that affects everybody, bringing fundamental changes to the way we work, entertain ourselves and interact with each other. Yet the reality is that for the most part, such changes have bypassed the majority of humankind, the billions of poor people for whom computers and the Internet mean nothing. However, in a growing number of instances, and as part of a quieter revolution, a variety of local organizations, aid agencies and government bodies are discovering that information and communication technologies (ICTs) can be used to extend the reach of the information revolution to the poorest of people living in the remotest corners of the world.

Under the right circumstances, ICTs have been shown to be capable of inducing social and economic development in terms of health care, improved education, employment, agriculture, and trade, and also of enriching local culture. Yet making this possible is by no means straightforward, as it involves more than the mere deployment of technology, and requires as much learning on the part of the promoters of the technology as on the part of its users. It is all too easy to introduce technology with great expectations; it is far more challenging to create the necessary conditions under which the technology can attain its full potential, requiring as it does the combined and coordinated efforts of a range of stakeholders with disparate interests.

All governments aim to provide the most comprehensive education possible for their citizens within the constraints of available finance. Because of the pivotal position of information and communication technology in modern societies, its introduction into secondary schools will be high on agenda. Information and communication technology permeates the business environment, it underpins the success of modern corporations and it provides governments with an efficient infrastructure. At the same time, it adds value to the processes of learning and in the organization and management of learning institutions. The Internet is a driving force for much development and innovation in both developed and developing countries.

Discussions of information technology in education typically emphasize the technology rather than the information. Widespread technology has meant that people encounter more information, in a greater variety of formats, than ever before. Technology is the portal through which we interact with information, but people's ability to handle information—to solve problems and think critically about information—tells us more about their future success than their knowledge of specific hardware or software. These skills—known as Information and Communications Technology (ICT) Literacy—comprise a twenty-first century form of literacy, in which researching and communicating information via digital environments are as important as reading and writing were in earlier centuries. ICT literate students master content faster, are better problem solvers, become more self-directed and assume greater control over learning. Beyond the classroom, ICT literacy is essential for being productive citizens in a knowledge-driven society, and employers want their employees to have these skills. As a result, college and university administrators are beginning to require them as competencies for graduation. This focus has led to campus-wide initiatives to improve students' ICT literacy.

Information and communication technologies are today playing a very important role in transforming the mode of imparting education. While the interactive white boards are increasingly becoming common in the school classrooms, popularity of online courses are helping the countries in improving access and quality of education. Application of technology in the mode of imparting education is thus not only helping a lot in bridging the rural-urban divide but also in improving the quality of life.

Building a creative economy to sustain the continued growth of India is critical to our nation's future and prosperity—and it all starts with an education system that encourages creativity. Over the years, the Indian education system has made enormous progress and is now among the largest in the world. However, it continues to face challenges. Schools and colleges have computers and Internet access but they have not been able to seamlessly integrate technology into the curriculum and classroom.

Technology is no longer a means to an end or a separate class where bright IT students learn how to code; it's a fundamental part of the education process. The world around India's student population has changed dramatically. When they enter a school that focuses primarily on rote-learning, the process doesn't align with the communication tools and techniques they are used to. Hence, some of them feel out of place, and potentially brilliant students are alienated. In fact, lack of effective student engagement is a key reason why truancy is on the rise and retention of students is a nagging problem. Since only 10 per cent of India's large and high potential students enrol into higher education, the economic impact of this phenomenon is huge. Every dropout costs the exchequer millions of rupees. In addition to this it's generally acknowledged that students often lack the communication and creative skills required to succeed outside their classrooms.

The Indian education industry is committed to advance education through technology. A shift is being witnessed which has the following impact on the education system:

a) Teaching needs to be engaging, online, accessible and interactive to capture the attention of a student. Institutions such as IGNOU are extending their reach by providing access to their programmes online and increasing enrolment locally and globally.
b) Students today spend a lot more time on devices like computers, mobile devices, and online services like YouTube and Facebook. They are comfortable with digital media, and are using these tools actively to prepare and create their school and personal projects, be it a history project or research paper or to upload their personal video, which they scripted, directed and edited themselves.

The smart classroom concept, a process where students learn their subjects through multimedia content, has been increasingly adopted by education departments across the country. This mode of learning is self-paced; hence learning becomes more measurable as progress is made at the student's pace. The government is investing in ICT projects to improve the quality of education, and to reduce the dropout rates in public schools. The emphasis of programmes initiated by the Department of IT is to integrate the new approach with conventional classroom system to increase its access to more learners and spread e-learning from teaching of IT-related subjects to other subjects in the school curricula.

ICT teaching will provide opportunities for students to apply their ICT literacy skills using teacher-created examples within specified contexts. The curriculum is structured to provide students with opportunities to apply their ICT literacy in other subject areas to acquire specific skills and knowledge.

Skills training will be provided to support teachers of the ICT curriculum. The training will support the use of individual software applications and learning resources. Training will concentrate on the management of ICT, emphasizing personal ICT skill development. Training will tend to be "just-in-time" for a specific teaching topic or to coincide with the arrival of a new piece of software. Internet-based training will emphasize the identification of information, with direct support for the existing curriculum in a range of subjects.

Assessment allows teachers to report students' level of ICT literacy and their ability to apply what they have learned in ICT and other subjects. Individual teachers share assessments of students' attainment with other teachers within their subject area to moderate their reporting of standards of attainment. The assessments provide the opportunity for teachers to amend their curriculum. Assessment strategies are the responsibility of individual subject areas.

The school's learning and vision for ICT is developed and shared by subject specialists who seek to increase student levels of attainment in their subjects, exploring new ways of learning and the management of learning. The vision belongs to all staff and to the school's local and global learning communities, as well as to students.

A learner-centred approach, supporting students' choice of preferred learning styles and learning environments, tends to dominate. Students are able to collaborate with other learners, infusing learning across subjects and utilizing a wide range of resources found by students. The use of ICT to investigate and explore new approaches to learning is accepted.

The individual subject areas infuse ICT into their plans and policies within the total school development plan and policies. The school's planning processes encourage collaborative approaches to learning and the management of learning by staff and students. Funding of ICT is broadly-based and integral to the annual budgetary cycle. The provision of funding covers all aspects of ICT, including professional development of school staff.

The whole school is networked to ensure access to multimedia and learning—rich resources via the school's Intranet and the Internet wherever students and teachers are, in or out of school. The computer labs and classroom computers are sufficient in number to allow ready access by students and staff in most subjects across the school. Software content is critically appraised to ensure that it matches the requirements of the curriculum supporting a wide range of multi-sensory learning styles. All staff help identify the software and learning resources required. A wide range of peripheral and remote working devices, including video-conferencing, is provided and integrated into the curriculum. Large and small group presentation facilities are readily available.

The curriculum provides the opportunity for students to utilize their ICT literacy skills in real problem solving by means of project work that offers new ways for students to demonstrate their learning. The curriculum seeks to use real contexts for learning, using school-based and externally available resources. ICT is used as a tutor to support specific learning goals. Teachers regularly review the curriculum for opportunities to incorporate the use of ICT.

Emphasis is placed on the professional development of teachers' subject skills and their capabilities to apply ICT in a range of contexts. The provision of school-based, in-service training to support the shared development of collaborative, cross-curriculum uses of ICT complements any external professional development provision. The school's programme of professional development has evolved to meet changing needs and new opportunities.

Students' assessments are not limited to specific subjects, with reports on attainment informing all teachers in planning, teaching and learning programmes of study. Students are responsible for maintaining personal portfolios of their work, demonstrating their attainment, over one or more years, using

ICT facilities and resources to complement paper-based records. The assessments inform whole school curriculum planning and resource allocations.

The school provides leadership to its learning community, providing innovative and creative access and opportunities to learning and the management of learning, maximizing the contribution of ICT to realize the school of tomorrow, today. The school sees itself as network-centred, providing a physical place to learn, as well as web-based learning spaces, accessible anytime, anywhere, by students and staff.

Emphasis is upon the whole learner in all aspects of their learning, with a focus on critical thinking skills and well-founded decision making. Every student is responsible for his or her own learning. Learning is experiential, with learning pathways and learning styles continuously changing to meet learner requirements. The use of ICT to investigate and explore new approaches to learning is expected.

The school and learning community use ICT to rethink creatively and to renew the learning environment of students and staff, including the development planning and policy-making processes. The plans for the school seek to support continuous change and renewal, striving to provide truly differentiated and individualized curriculum for all students, and seeking to maximize student achievement. ICT funding is seen as essential as funding for basic utilities like water and power. Effective, accessible and inclusive ICT ensures that learning environments are mission-critical to all staff, students and learning communities.

A whole school learning and ICT infrastructure provides ready access to innovative learning environments and contexts. School facilities and resources are designed and enabled to support continuous change and development of approaches to learning, the management of learning and technology.

The curriculum is enabled by an understanding of the learning needs of every student, informed on a continuous basis by management of learning systems. Students' ICT literacy skills are assumed to enable learning readily within a personalized curriculum. The curriculum uses as a matter of course virtual and real world, real-time contexts and modelling. Students are involved in solving real problems. Focus is placed on learning and the management of learning, with specific ICT training provided when it is required. Teachers' development is self-managed and informed by a well-founded personal vision and plan that supports the school's overall vision and the needs of the learners. Teachers accept their role as co-learners, learning together with their students. Teachers are committed to professional development as a continuous, critically reflective process.

There are general competencies and abilities common to all approaches to infusing ICT in learning and the management of learning. The focus of professional development will be on developing the confidence and competence of teachers, building upon their previous education and professional development in applying ICT to teaching.

Professional development in this stage will encourage teachers to collaborate in developing their subject curriculum and identifying innovative teaching methodologies. Opportunities for students and teachers to experiment to identify preferred learning styles and differentiated pathways are encouraged. Infusing ICT across the curriculum to enhance learning and the management of learning leads teachers to an understanding of how to transform their teaching practice as well as the learning of their students. General competencies include the following:

Understanding why, when, where and how ICT tools will contribute to learning objectives and choosing from among a wide range of ICT tools those that are most appropriate to stimulate students' learning:

i) Choosing ICT tools and teaching methods that integrate ICT into the whole curriculum.

ii) Choosing and recommending ICT tools and teaching methods appropriate to individual students' learning objectives.

iii) Emphasizing the quality of what students produce and the contribution to individual learning goals and levels of attainment.

iv) Planning a whole learning programme that allows a range of ICT tools and teaching methods to be used, as and when required.

v) Choosing tools and teaching methods that allow the teacher and student to manage their own learning.

Managing whole school and classroom-based environments, and teamwork to achieve learning objectives:

i) Managing learning environments that contribute to the use of different ICT tools and teaching methods.

ii) Understanding differences between students according to their competencies in using ICT, and having available strategies to manage differences as students progress.

iii) Managing difficulties that can arise when using ICT to minimize impact on planned lesson objectives.

iv) Creating learning situations such that students manage their own learning.

v) Infusing ICT-based and non-ICT-based media, such as books and video, into learning programmes.

vi) Assessing the levels of attainment of individual students when working collaboratively.

Infusing multimedia presentations into whole class, group or individual teaching, and learning to increase access to learning programmes:

i) Ensuring that the most appropriate media are built into learning programmes, that learning is accessible to all students irrespective of ability, special need, or preferred learning style.

ii) Varying the kind of presentation, documents or other media according to the main goals and the chosen teaching method.

iii) Analysing a presentation for legibility, structure, coherence with teaching objectives, and suitability for students.

Analysing multimedia learning environments:

i) Utilizing web-based learning spaces and environments.

ii) Including CD-ROMs, websites, video and audio, courseware.

iii) Assessing the contribution of different activities to learners and the lesson objectives.

iv) Analysing the specific contribution of ICT tools to individual student learning.

Supporting students to find analyse and synthesize information from disparate Internet and school-based learning environments:

i) Supporting individual students and groups of students to perform complex web searches.

ii) Supporting students in managing, criticizing, synthesizing, and presenting learning processes and products using ICT tools.

Utilizing a range of communication tools to collaborate with colleagues, with students and other learning communities beyond the school. *Using* ICT more proficiently, regularly taking part in professional development, and participating in teaching experiments and developments:

i) Participating in, and contributing to, group discussions on the use of ICT

ii) Using ICT tools (forums, conferencing, bulletin boards, email) to collaborate in the improvement of teaching and learning and management of learning processes

The kind of teacher activities described in this section on professional development cannot be obtained through short courses, seminars or workshops. These forums can be used as appetizers to inform teachers about infusing ICT into all teaching activities but teachers cannot be expected to achieve all this as a result of just a short course. Most effective for this kind of teacher development is teamwork and educational leadership within a school.

A good starting point for teacher development is to form a group of enthusiasts within a school. Later, this group can be extended to larger groups of teachers from different schools, and even teachers from different districts, states, or countries. Where teacher networks can be built on teachers from different schools as described under the applying approach above, such networks should preferably involve some teachers from each school from different subject areas. Because the way of working in a totally integrated way is so different from what most teachers are used to, it is most important to share experiences, adopt common goals and tasks, have involvement and equal input from all teachers, and have others to lean on and give support when things do not go quite as expected.

In higher education, organizations such as IGNOU train 2.8 million students every year with the use of technology. IGNOU offers distance education for various courses to 53 countries worldwide. The future looks bright for new levels of possibility and engagement for India's student population.

This is the decade of innovation, a time when new thoughts, new ideas and new technologies are expected to revolutionize life, as we know it. Innovation is expected to be a key driver for industry, defining its next growth phase. Innovation, however, cannot take place in a vacuum. It requires a nurturing environment, a particular atmosphere, where companies can harness their creative energies to come up with something completely novel and unparalleled. For innovation to become rampant, it must be ingrained in the DNA of individuals and organizations. A culture of innovation must exist, both within and beyond the boundaries of companies, where fresh notions can be given free rein. This requires an ecosystem where all stakeholders, including citizens, the government, industry and academia work together to ensure that innovation happens continuously and has a direct impact on society.

While the government has to provide an enabling regulatory environment and the industry guidance on the kind of innovation needed, it is academia, however, that must build the foundation for such innovation, foster it through special learning systems and target it at the people who matter. Skilled human resources, the flag bearers of the future of nations, need to induct into this innovation ecosystem right from an early age, which means school and university. Learners must be provided with global class content, courseware, tools and technologies that ignite minds and unleash innovative thinking.

Over the last few decades, technology has proved to be the biggest growth catalyst for individuals and enterprises. The transformational role played by technology and the Internet in the lives of people and businesses has become part of twenty-first century. Information technology and the explosion of the 'net' have changed every facet of life. It has altered the way industry and governments work and impacted on the way services such as healthcare and education are delivered. Of all the sectors, technology has possibly proved itself to be the most useful in education. With high-tech campuses, a new era in learning and teaching has been ushered.

Technology is providing fodder for the mind. It is making available information that learners require in real time. It is empowering them in ways unheard of before. Today, students can interact with faculty, ask questions, get their doubts cleared and exchange notes with peers, all at the click of a few keys on their notebooks, PCs or even cell phones. The technology enabled campus has arrived and given wings to learners. They can now fly at the speed of light, explore unchartered terrains and learn as they go. Schools and universities that have unlocked the power of technology to bring countless benefits to learners know the importance of these living, breathing, connected campuses. They know that technology is crafting the pathway to innovation and helping shape talent for the new age.

Technology-enabled campus is an ideal, pervasive campus, which is state of the art, and enabled by "borderless networks". Diverse technologies co-exist in a technology enabled campus. An example, several networks like wireless personal area network (WPAN), wireless local area network (WLAN), wireless metropolitan area network (WMAN) converge on the campus. These networks seamlessly connect and this requires them to be inter-operable. Such a pervasive campus enables the creation of connected communities, where distance education, edutainment and health care are provided to people residing in the areas surrounding the campus. The aim is to use technology and learning to benefit society and build well rounded individuals aware of their social responsibilities.

A technology enabled campus is also a green campus, where every effort is made to preserve the environment, lower the energy consumption and harness the power of green computing and green communication. Typically, such a campus will be designed in a way that minimizes the carbon footprint. It will use smart approaches to cut energy usage and make life easier and better. Another crucial element of a connected campus is a set of affordable, robust, collaborative systems and tools. One such example is the synchronous learning technology, which provides real time, anywhere anytime education to students, bringing them face-to-face with professors and industry leaders from across the world. This two-way, bi-directional, interactive learning technology is proving to be critical in instances where the learners and faculty are separated by vast geographic distances. In a world where shortage of competent and experienced faculty is being considered a huge challenge to education, synchronous technology has appeared as a panacea. Using it, reputed global universities can make available their faculty to other institutions where this expertise is lacking.

In the future, we are going to see several collaborative endeavors between institutions of higher learning, where content will be beamed to students across the world and professors sitting in one part of the globe will deliver lectures remotely to learners in another time zone. Interestingly, it will be possible to deliver such learning to students in their local language, through the use of real time translators. Teachers would have more flexibility to address student queries and learners would be able to get answers to all their questions. The campus of the future will be fully connected, completely digital, offering students a rich multimedia experience. At the same time, it will connect with other similar institutions of learning seamlessly and efficiently.

For the technology enabled campus to become more prolific and be adopted by a larger number of institutions, the cost of technology, including bandwidth, has to come down further. At the same time, such campuses must have their share of researches that will enrich them with industry relevant skills and know-how. In emerging countries such as India, technology has to become more affordable, robust, reliable, scalable and available. There is also a requirement for educational applications that will run on high bandwidth 3G and 4G networks of the future. The good news is that India is currently at a take off point, with a large number of educational start ups expected to build numerous applications that will make learning more meaningful, effective and enjoyable for learners. The recently incorporated NIIT University (NU) is an example of a future focused, connected digital campus.

New communication technologies have brought about a revolution in the contemporary world. These technologies have added a new dimension to our lives and they have the capacity to change the way the world thinks about communication.

Works Cited

Alabi (2004). "Evolving Role of ICT in Teaching, Research and Publishing". *Nigerian Tribune*, Friday, 30 April, pp 30-31.

American Association of School Librarians & Association for Educational Communications and Technology (1998). *Information Literacy for Student Learning: Standards and Indicators.*

Anaya, G. (1999). College impact on student learning: Comparing the use of self-reported gains, standardized test scores, and college grades. *Research in Higher Education, 40*(5), 499-526.

Annan K., *Secretary General of the United Nations* (1997), in United Nations Commission on Science and Technology for Development. "Inter-Agency Project on Universal Access to Basic Communication and Information Services", 3rd Session, Geneva, 12 May, E/CN. 16/ 1997/ Misc. 3.

Hinson, R.A., G. Adika and S. Buatsi (2004). *International Journal of Information Technology.*

Jishnu, Latha and M. Anand (2001). "India's Great Digital Hope." *Business World* 2.

Singh, Kamal (2004). "Tarahaat: Employing Best Practices to Bridge the Digital Divide". *Development Alternatives Newsletter* 14(7): 5-6.

7

Relevance of ICT in ELT: Concept, Position and Scope

— Dr. Ashok Singh Rao

Introduction

Information and Communication Technology (ICT) allows users to participate in a rapidly changing world in which work and other activities are increasingly transformed by access to varied and developing technologies. The purpose of ICT in education is generally to familiarise students with the use and workings of computers, and related social and ethical issues. ICT has also enabled learning through multiple intelligence as ICT has introduced learning through simulation games; this enables active learning through all senses. ICT tools can be used to find, explore, analyze, exchange and present information responsibly and without discrimination. ICT can be employed to give users quick access to ideas and experiences from a wide range of people, communities and cultures.

ICT permeates the business environment, underpins the success of modern corporations, and provides governments with an efficient infrastructure. At the same time, it adds value to the processes of learning, and in the organization and management of learning institutions. The Internet is a driving force for much development and innovation in both developed and developing countries. Countries must be able to benefit from technological developments. To be able to do so, a cadre of professionals has to be educated with sound ICT backgrounds, independent of specific computer platforms or software environments.

Technological developments lead to changes in work and changes in the organization of work, and required competencies are therefore changing. Gaining in importance are the following competencies:

a) Critical thinking,
b) Generalist (broad) competencies,
c) ICT competencies enabling expert work,
d) Decision-making,
e) Handling of dynamic situations,
f) Working as a member of a team, and
g) Communicating effectively.

A secondary ICT curriculum should contribute to the building up of teams of professionals with these new competencies. The uses of ICT cuts across all aspects of economic and social life. Technological developments in ICT are very rapid. Technology quickly becomes obsolete requiring new skills and knowledge to be mastered frequently. Adaptation is only possible when based on a sound understanding of the principles and concepts of ICT.

Internet and Its Services

The Internet is a global system of interconnected computer networks that use the standard Internet Protocol Suite (TCP/IP) to serve billions of users worldwide. It is a network of networks that consists of millions of private, public, academic, business and government networks of local to global scope that are linked by a broad array of electronic and optical networking technologies. The internet carries a vast array of information resources and services, most notably the inter-linked hypertext documents of the World Wide Web (WWW) and the infrastructure to support electronic mail.

Most traditional communications media, such as telephone and television services, are reshaped or redefined using the technologies of the Internet, giving rise to services such as Voice over Internet Protocol (VoIP) and IPTV. Newspaper publishing has been reshaped into Web sites, blogging and web feeds. The Internet has enabled or accelerated the creation of new forms of human interactions through instant messaging, Internet forums, and social networking sites.

The origins of the Internet reach back to the 1960s when the United States funded research projects of its military agencies to build robust, fault-tolerant and distributed computer networks. This research and a period of civilian funding of a new U.S. backbone by the National Science Foundation spawned worldwide participation in the development of new networking technologies, and led to the commercialization of an international network in the mid-1990s, and resulted in the following popularization of countless applications in virtually every aspect of modern human life. As of 2009, an estimated quarter of Earth's population uses the services of the Internet.

Information

Many people use the terms Internet and World Wide Web, or just the Web, interchangeably, but the two terms are not synonymous. The World Wide Web is a global set of documents, images and other resources, logically interrelated by hyperlinks and referenced with Uniform Resource Identifiers (URIs). URIs allow providers to symbolically identify services and clients to locate and address web servers, file servers, and other databases that store documents and provide resources and access them using the Hypertext Transfer Protocol (HTTP), the primary carrier protocol of the Web. HTTP is only one of the hundreds of communication protocols used on the Internet. Web services may also use HTTP to allow software systems to communicate in order to share and exchange business logic and data.

World Wide Web browser software, such as Internet Explorer, Firefox, Opera, Apple Safari and Google Chrome, let users navigate from one web page to another via hyperlinks embedded in the documents. These documents may also contain any combination of computer data, including graphics, sounds, text, video, multimedia and interactive content including games, office applications and scientific demonstrations.

Through keyword-driven Internet research using search engines like Yahoo! and Google, users worldwide have easy, instant access to a vast and diverse amount of online information. Compared to printed encyclopedias and traditional libraries, the World Wide Web has enabled the decentralization of information.

The Web has also enabled individuals and organizations to publish ideas and information to a potentially large audience online at greatly reduced expense and time delay. Publishing a web page, a blog, or building a website involves little initial cost and many cost-free services are available. Publishing and maintaining large, professional websites with attractive, diverse and uptodate information is still a difficult and expensive proposition, however. Many individuals and some companies and groups use web logs or blogs, which are largely used as easily updatable online diaries. Some commercial organizations encourage staff to communicate advice in their areas of specialization in the hope that visitors will be impressed by the expert knowledge and free information, and be attracted to the corporation as a result. One example of this practice is Microsoft, whose product developers publish their personal blogs in order to pique the public's interest in their work. Collections of personal web pages published by large service providers remain popular, and have become increasingly sophisticated. Whereas operations such as Angel fire and GeoCities have existed since the early days of the Web, newer offerings from, for example, Facebook and MySpace currently have large followings. These operations often brand themselves as social network services rather than simply as web page hosts.

Advertising on popular web pages can be lucrative, and e-commerce or the sale of products and services directly via the Web continues to grow. In the early days, web pages were usually created as sets of complete and isolated HTML text files stored on a web server. More recently, websites are more often created using content management or wiki software with, initially, very little content. Contributors to these systems, who may be paid staff, members of a club or other organization or members of the public, fill underlying databases with content using editing pages designed for that purpose, while casual visitors view and read this content in its final HTML form. There may or may not be editorial, approval and security systems built into the process of taking newly entered content and making it available to the target visitors.

Communication

E-mail is an important communications service available on the Internet. The concept of sending electronic text messages between parties in a way analogous to mailing letters or memos predates the creation of the Internet. Today it can be important to distinguish between internet and internal e-mail systems. Internet e-mail may travel and be stored unencrypted on many other networks and machines out of both the sender's and the recipient's control. During this time it is quite possible for the content to be read and even tampered with by third parties, if anyone considers it important enough. Purely internal or intranet mail systems, where the information never leaves the corporate or organization's network, are much more secure, although in any organization there will be IT and other personnel whose job may involve monitoring, and occasionally accessing, the e-mail of other employees not addressed to them. Pictures, documents and other files can be sent as e-mail attachments. E-mails can be cc-ed to multiple e-mail addresses.

Internet telephony is another common communications service made possible by the creation of the Internet. VoIP stands for Voice-over-Internet Protocol, referring to the protocol that underlies all Internet communication. The idea began in the early 1990s with walkie-talkie-like voice applications for personal computers. In recent years many VoIP systems have become as easy to use and as convenient as a normal telephone. The benefit is that, as the Internet carries the voice traffic, VoIP can be free or cost much less than a traditional telephone call, especially over long distances and especially for those with always-on Internet connections such as cable or ADSL. VoIP is maturing into a competitive alternative to traditional telephone service. Interoperability between different providers has improved and the ability to call or receive a call from a traditional telephone is available. Simple, inexpensive VoIP network adapters are available that eliminate the need for a personal computer.

Voice quality can still vary from call to call but is often equal to and can even exceed that of traditional calls. Remaining problems for VoIP include emergency telephone number dialling and reliability. Currently, a few VoIP providers provide an emergency service, but it is not universally available. Traditional phones are line-powered and operate during a power failure; VoIP does not do so without a backup power source for the phone equipment and the Internet access devices. VoIP has also become increasingly popular for gaming applications, as a form of communication between players. Popular VoIP clients for gaming include Ventrilo and Teamspeak. Wii, PlayStation 3, and Xbox 360 also offer VoIP chat features.

Data Transfer

File sharing is an example of transferring large amounts of data across the Internet. A computer file can be e-mailed to customers, colleagues and friends as an attachment. It can be uploaded to a website or FTP server for easy download by others. It can be put into a "shared location" or onto a file server for instant use by colleagues. The load of bulk downloads to many users can be eased by the use of "mirror" servers or peer-to-peer networks. In any of these cases, access to the file may be controlled by user authentication, the transit of the file over the Internet may be obscured by encryption, and money may change hands for access to the file. The price can be paid by the remote charging of funds from, for example, a credit card whose details are also passed—usually fully encrypted—across the Internet. The origin and authenticity of the file received may be checked by digital signatures or by MD5 or other message digests. These simple features of the Internet, over a worldwide basis, are changing the production, sale, and distribution of anything that can be reduced to a computer file for transmission. This includes all manner of print publications, software products, news, music, film, video, photography, graphics and the other arts. This in turn has caused seismic shifts in each of the existing industries that previously controlled the production and distribution of these products.

Streaming media refers to the act that many existing radio and television broadcasters promote Internet "feeds" of their live audio and video streams (for example, the BBC). They may also allow time-shift viewing or listening such as Preview, Classic Clips and Listen Again features. These providers have been joined by a range of pure Internet "broadcasters" who never had on-air licenses. This means that an Internet-connected device, such as a computer or something more specific, can be used to access on-line media in much the same way as was previously possible only with a television or radio receiver. The range of available types of content is much wider, from specialized technical webcasts to on-demand popular multimedia services. Podcasting is a variation on this theme, where—usually audio—material is downloaded and played back on a computer or shifted to a portable media player to be listened to on the move. These techniques using simple equipment allow anybody, with little censorship or licensing control, to broadcast audio-visual material worldwide.

Webcams can be seen as an even lower-budget extension of this phenomenon. While some webcams can give full-frame-rate video, the picture is usually either small or updates slowly. Internet users can watch animals around an African waterhole, ships in the Panama Canal, traffic at a local roundabout or monitor their own premises, live and in real time. Video chat rooms and video conferencing are also popular with many uses being found for personal webcams, with and without two-way sound. YouTube was founded on 15 February 2005 and is now the leading website for free streaming video with a vast number of users. It uses a flash-based web player to stream and show video files. Registered users may upload an unlimited amount of video and build their own personal profile. YouTube claims that its users watch hundreds of millions, and upload hundreds of thousands of videos daily.

Electronic Mail

Most commonly abbreviated email or e-mail is a method of exchanging digital messages. E-mail systems are based on a store-and-forward model in which e-mail server computer systems accept, forward, deliver and store messages on behalf of users, who only need to connect to the e-mail infrastructure, typically an e-mail server, with a network-enabled device for the duration of message submission or retrieval. Originally, e-mail was always transmitted directly from one user's device to another's; nowadays this is rarely the case.

An electronic mail message consists of two components: the message header, and the message body, which is the email's content. The message header contains control information, including, minimally, an originator's email address and one or more recipient addresses. Usually additional information is added, such as a subject header field.

Originally a text-only communications medium, email was extended to carry multi-media content attachments, which were standardized in with RFC 2045 through RFC 2049, collectively called, Multipurpose Internet Mail Extensions (MIME).

The foundation for today's global Internet e-mail service was created in the early ARPANET and standards for encoding of messages were proposed as early as 1973 (RFC 561). An e-mail sent in the early 1970s looked very similar to one sent on the Internet today. Conversion from the ARPANET to the Internet in the early 1980s produced the core of the current service.

Network-based e-mail was initially exchanged on the ARPANET in extensions to the File Transfer Protocol (FTP), but is today carried by the Simple Mail Transfer Protocol (SMTP), first published as Internet standard 10 (RFC 821) in 1982. In the process of transporting e-mail messages between systems, SMTP communicates delivery parameters using a message envelope separately from the message (header and body) itself.

Technologies and University Teaching

Despite the technophile discourse extolling the virtues of

computers and of ICTs as teaching or tutoring tools, a review of the scientific literature unearths few systematic researches carried out in this field. These can be classed into three categories of varying importance. The first touches upon the effectiveness of resorting to different forms of ICTs as a means of favouring or of sustaining learning. This type of research leads to the question of how teachers define the nature of knowledge, the process of knowledge construction by students, and the role of both the teacher and teaching materials in the midst of this process. The second deals essentially with the analysis and identification of teacher or student attitudes towards hardware and software environments. The third refers to the identification of the degree of penetration of ICTs in university teaching.

The Epistemologically Determined Nature of ICTs as Teaching Material

For a few years now, a number of works on the integration of ICTs as teaching material in university have tended to establish a more or less explicit relation between resorting to interactive environments and a constructivist epistemological stance. There are three broad principles that together define the constructivist view of learning.

The fundamental principle is that each person forms their own representation of knowledge, building on their own individual experiences, and consequently that there is no single "correct" representation of knowledge (von Glaserfeld, 1994). The counter view, that there is a single "correct" representation of knowledge, is labelled by constructivists as objectivist. The second principle, normally attributed to Piaget, is that people learn through active exploration, and that learning occurs when the learner's exploration uncovers an inconsistency between their current knowledge representation and their experience. Bruner was the first to espouse a detailed theory of instruction based on this principle, in his discovery learning theory (Bruner, 1962). The third principle, normally attributed to Vygotsky, is that learning occurs within a social context, and that interaction between learners and their peers is a necessary part of the learning process. Vygotsky (1978) describes those capabilities that are beyond the learner on their own, but are able to be carried out with the assistance of more knowledgeable peers, as capabilities in the zone of proximal development.

These works on the integration of ICTs as teaching material that sustains a "constructivist revolution" in university implies two postulates. The first postulate is that teachers share a constructivist or socio-constructivist representation of the teaching-learning relation. The adoption of "new technologies," in so far as they make the learner responsible and eventually favour learner and learner-teacher interaction, are assumed to be the result of a significant rupture between the teacher and traditional or behavioural approaches to teaching.

The second implies the primacy of teaching material over epistemological orientations. Because ICT material allows or involves an interaction, it is assumed that learning will be its product. Thus this material guarantees the constructivist nature of learning and the collaborative dimension of teaching (Choi and Yeom, 1996; Marton, 1994). As an aside it is interesting to note that this representation of the role of educational material is quite similar to the discourse held by the Ministry of Education of Quebec over the last twenty years (Government of Quebec, 1979).

The Concept of Computer Literacy

For Mcmillan (1996) the concept of computer literacy is theoretically fuzzy and changing in that the definition of the concept is more or less precise depending on whether it occurs at the level of the definition of "operational" abilities or at the level of political discourse. As most contemporary authors do, he tends to centre the definition of computer literacy on a few competencies or abilities, identifiable as "open" behaviours (Bradley, 1996; Reid, 1997; Stein, Craig & Scollary, 1997). The characteristics are the following:

a) The individual knows how to use word processing software, an email and a browser for Internet navigation.

b) The individual is capable of registering or of downloading information on a diskette (or some other external saving unit) so as to recuperate and print it elsewhere.

To these behavioural "competencies," Stein, Craig & Scollary (1997) add a cognitive dimension, one that is also recognized by the Australian National Board for Employment, Education and Training (NBEET, 1995): the ability to use ICTs to identify and search efficiently for specific information in order to build knowledge and develop critical and creative thinking.

Types of Technology

In English, technology includes cameras, audio equipment, computer technology, video equipment, overhead projection devices, scanners, printers, CD equipment—almost any device that can access, present, manipulate and communicate words, sounds and images to enable us to create meaning.

Many of these texts blend the written, spoken and visual, so students can express ideas in exciting and powerful ways. The choices available to the creators and users of texts are expanding rapidly so English teachers need to start helping students to make informed choices.

Multimedia texts challenge readers and viewers to integrate information and ideas in new ways. Making meaning from the interplay of words, sound and vision involves a sophisticated set of skills, skills that have not necessarily been highly valued in the past:

> "...for hundreds of years western culture has privileged the verbal (print and oral) as the pre-eminent mode of conveying meaning and producing knowledge. However, with the arrival of the new communication and information technologies, the reign of the verbal has been at least interrupted, if not overthrown."

Hypertext heralds a different way of accessing texts since, even more than with traditional print or screen texts, the reader or viewer actively creates an individual text through choices made. We can choose to jump from link to link in different ways, creating many possible texts from one set of material. Adults often comment ironically on the almost irresistible lure of hypertext links that invite us to flit from site to site, searching for the better, brighter site that surely waits just one screen away. We need to explore the same issue with students to ask what effect this has on our understanding and how we judge when it is better to resist or go with the lure.

Use Computer Technology in English

There are two kinds of reasons for using computer technology in English. First, there are the benefits to teachers and students from including computer technology in any learning area.

To us, technology can:

a) Allow for the easy production, storage and retrieval of prepared materials such as certificates and work required sheets.

b) Free up communication with other teachers.

c) Help teachers to find information easily.

d) Assist good teaching but not replace it!

Secondly, there are the challenges and opportunities presented by computer technology that make it an increasingly important part of English in particular. These include:

a) The emergence of new kinds of texts and the consequent need to teach students to create and use these texts effectively.

b) Changing social practices associated with communicating via computers and the consequent need to teach students how to make judgements about appropriate use of different avenues of communication.

c) The pervasiveness and power of texts created through computer technology and the consequent need to teach students to be critical readers and viewers of such texts.

Attitudes about Computers

Most of the research is about teacher and/or student attitudes with reference to information science, understood in its widest sense and, more particularly, about individual-computer interaction. The majority of research projects are on the constructs of anxiety and of stress in interactive situations with computers (Brown, 1996; Hudiburg, Ahrens and Jones, 1994; Hudiburg, Brown and Jones, 1993; McBride and Nagle, 1996; Ngin and Simms, 1996). This body of research flows from a relatively recent trend, mostly found in the US and less so in England and in Germany. It is a trend identified with social psychology and with the psychology of work, whose major object of study is the impact of changes brought to work environments, notably at the time of major technical modifications. Although this field of research is relatively young in that it deals with the implications of the implementation of computer technologies in different working or educational environments, it reflects a well-established tradition in the psychology of work and, notably, in ergonomics.

Compared with other teaching tools: audio tapes, textbooks, and the basic blackboard, video is a relatively new option for the language teacher. The technology became affordable only in the late 1970s, and it was several years before video materials designed specifically for language learning were developed. In the twenty years or so since then, video has become an even more widely available teaching aid, although its penetration into everyday classroom practice and course/ syllabus design hasn't been as deep as many had anticipated. The development of video materials for ELT use can be seen as having gone through three main stages.

Issues Involved in Using Computer Technology in Classroom

Developing a Whole School Approach

This involves considering how students will be taught basic skills; what kinds of priority will be given to students in accessing computers; security and privacy implications of the use of computer technology; Intranet development and use.

The teaching strategies needed to accommodate the computers. As students' access to information improves so that they can go beyond what the teacher or school provides, and can locate information much closer to its source, the relationship between teacher and student inevitably changes. Some students may have a much stronger practical knowledge base and operational understanding of computer technology than their teacher does. Recognising this, we need to work out how to acknowledge and use their skills and bring our own teaching expertise and critical awareness to bear in choosing appropriate ways of working with computers. Questions arise such as: Can we use peer-tutoring to help students develop basic skills? How are computers best used within a writing programme? What is the most time-effective way to use computers for research?

Where to Place the Computers in the Colleges/Classrooms

Where do they need to go to become a natural part of learning programmes, and not an add-on? How can we ensure the most effective access to computer technology by the greatest number of students?

The Technical Assistance Needed

What happens in the event of a breakdown? Who will help you to troubleshoot? What kinds of routines might help to minimise technical difficulties and keep the learning programme going smoothly when they inevitably occur?

Classroom Dynamics

How do we ensure that students use the computers in a collaborative way? What balance of computer and other activities is appropriate at any one time to keep the class communicating and functioning well?

Skills, Attitudes and Knowledge of Computers and Computing

What kind of PD is needed and what is the best way to get it? How do we help students to develop the specific skills needed in English, such as effective use of spell-checking programmes and critical viewing skills?

Moral, Ethical and Equity Questions

When the Internet opens up information resources far beyond the schools' own, how do we ensure that students are protected from exploitation but not limited? What kinds of ethical questions do we need to investigate with students?

Techniques

Because the video courses written specifically for ELT are usually accompanied by fairly detailed teacher guidelines, the remainder of this discussion will focus on general techniques for using video materials. These techniques can be applied to specially written or authentic video materials, and aim to introduce a greater degree of variety into classroom practice and to create a more productive interaction between the learners and material. It should be stressed that these techniques are far from new, and the following is simply a brief overview of some of the methodological alternatives available.

Moving from the development of support and supplementary materials to the mechanics of using video, there are several ways in which the information transmitted can be broken down and re-assembled to good effect. One such technique is silent viewing. The students view a sequence, for example, of a couple checking into a hotel or ordering a meal in a restaurant, and they attempt to generate an appropriate dialogue for the scene. The actual dialogue can then be used as a model from which to adapt the students' efforts.

Alternatively, if the students have already heard the dialogue, they can use the silent re-viewing to reproduce the conversation. The reverse technique is to play the sound only, and have students discuss what the scene might look like. The teacher may also make good use of the freeze-frame option, particularly if the material is proving to be difficult, to check comprehension and to answer unanticipated questions. In some viewings, particularly "reviews" of the video after the pre-planned activities have been done; students should be encouraged to indicate if they want a pause in the viewing to pick up on points of confusion or general interest. This goes some way to lessening the degree of teacher-centredness (produced by the fact that the teacher has the controller.

Advantages and Disadvantages of ICT in English Language Teaching

The impact of the use of information and communication technologies (ICT) on the way English is taught has brought not only advantages to it, but also, some disadvantages concerning:

a) Availability of technologies to be used

b) Reliability of materials

c) Employment

Therefore, teachers and students of English can have access to the most up to date sources and information rapidly. Information can be found either on the Internet or by using specialized software. Many focused exercises can be found on the net completely for free and software can be bought via Internet or in any store.

Works Cited

Coutrer. *Mastering Office 2000*, New Delhi: BPB Publication.

Elliat, Andrew. *Universal Letter Writer*, England: Clarion MCMXCV, Surrey.

Forouzan, Behrouz, A. *Data Communication and Networking*, New Delhi: TMH.

Gupta, C.B. *Business Communication*, New Delhi: Sultan Chand & Sons.

Hahn, Harley. *The Internet*, New Delhi: TMH.

Hornby, A.S. *A Guide to Patterns and Usage*, New Delhi: Oxford University Press.

Introduction to Computer Science, New Delhi: Pearson Education.

Leech, Geoffrey. *English Grammar for Today*, New Delhi: Longman.

Murphy, and Reynolds. *Essentials of English Grammar*, New Delhi: Cambridge University Press.

Norton's Peter. *Introduction to Computers*, New Delhi: TMH.

Quirk & Greenbaum. *University English Grammar*, New Delhi: Longman.

Rajaraman, V. *Introduction to Computer*, New Delhi: PHI.

Sharma, R.C. & Krishna Mohan. *Business Correspondence & Report Writing*. New Delhi: Tata McGraw Hill.

Sinha, P.K. *Fundamentals of Computers*, New Delhi: BP Publication.

Sklar, Joel. *Principals of Web Design*. New Delhi: BPB.

Taxali, R. K. *PC Software for Windows*, New Delhi: TMH.

Young, M. L. *Internet Millennium Edition*. New Delhi: TMH.

8

Information and Communication Technology: Its Impact on Language Learning

— Dr. K. Sandhya & Ms. Afsha Jamal

Gone are the days instructors teach while students listen and understand! About two decades ago, shortly personal computers were introduced, people thought that computers would revolutionize education and computer-based teaching, and learning would become the saviour of education. The change has already taken place. The area of language learning is no exception. In India, it has materialized late, but it is not too late to adopt technology-based language learning and specifically ICT-based English language learning/teaching. Several educational institutions have adopted technology for imparting knowledge including languages. Hence, Technology in general and Information and Communication Technology (ICT) in particular have enabled self-learning among all areas of the world.

Further, technology has provided plenty of opportunities for both teachers and students. They are privileged to have internet access, a few computers and appropriate guidance. Video-teleconferencing is introduced in the classrooms. Students get benefited from this facility. Synchronized collaboration applies between desktop computers hooked to a projection system so that many people in the same location can participate. All the desktops are connected through the Internet. An instructor sits at a desktop workstation and communicates with a "classroom" of students, each of whom has a workstation in front of him and a connection to the Internet.

Another feature of it is that the students no longer have to be in the same room; they can interact with other students and teachers in different locations.

Thus, the instructor controls the students' machines and enables them to work on exercises, look for information, or communicate with other, remotely located students involved in a group project. In addition to presenting previously prepared information to the student machines, the instructor also provides new information to all students by preparing it in advance for delivery, by typing it in, or by using voice and, eventually, real-time digital video. The network represents a new environment for learning and teaching. Every teacher and student requires access to the information represented on the Web in order to be competitive in their work and in their lives.

The Human Development Report of the United Nations Development Program or UNDP (2001) states, "ICT is a pervasive input to almost all human activities. It breaks barriers to human development in at least three ways: by breaking barriers to knowledge, by breaking barriers to participation and by breaking barriers to economic opportunity."

The rapid advances in ICT create new effects such as storing information, retrieving information, handling, distributing and utilizing information. The advancement of ICT according to Ocampo (2002) is intertwined with globalization and together creates a new paradigm called the network age. Therefore, school counselors utilize computer technology to fully participate in eradicating institutional and environmental barriers which impede students' academic success.

The skills needed to fully integrate ICT in the counseling programs according to Tinio (2003) include digital-age literacy consisting of:

a) Functional,

b) Scientific,

c) Technological and

d) Information literacy.

Correspondingly, the advent of multimedia computer technology has increased the potential of career interventions, particularly at-risk youth. The interactive and computer-mediated situations allow the students to look for better ways to solve problems related with learning, reading and other skills.

This perspective is based on the three major premises, namely:

1) Individuals act toward things and people on the basis of the meanings that things have for them;
2) The meaning of such things are derived from, or arise out of the social interaction that individuals have with one another, and
3) These meanings are handled in, modified through, an interpretive process used by individuals to deal with the things and other people they encounter themes are generated on the uses and application of ICT in school counseling, namely:
   i) Storing, encoding and preparing of materials/documents related to counselling,
   ii) Retrieving, distributing and utilizing data/information related to counselling, and
   iii) Other uses on entertainment, leisure and recreational activities.

Learning in an Outcome Alert Environment

A successful teaching and learning programme in an outcome focused environment integrating technology in English need to:

a) Promote ground-breaking and student-centred approaches to learning.
b) Widen individual and group learning programmes as a consequence of recognizing the variety of students needs and learning styles.
c) Develop a balance of exclusively open-ended tasks.
d) Establish the use of technology in the learning outcomes for students.

e) Endow with opportunities for integrated learning or cross-curricula links.

f) Ensure that the technology improves the teaching and learning programme and learning effectiveness.

g) Obtain an enquiry-based and problem-solving approach to learning.

h) Offer occasions for students to assess and contour technological breakthroughs.

Further, the employer-centred workplace of predefined jobs and career paths has given way to a worker-designed environment where individuals pursue their own assignments and must effortlessly combine technical skills with an intellectual toolbox enriched with experiences, roles, team building and knowledge.

Information and communication technology (ICT) literacy is the term specified to digital literacy, technological literacy, and twenty-first century skills. ICT Literacy reflects the need for students to develop learning skills that enable them to think critically, analyze information, communicate, collaborate, and problem-solve, and the essential role that technology plays in realizing these learning skills in today's knowledge-based society. The following six fields are critical to students' achievements in the workplace:

1) *Communicate Effectively*: Students need to possess a range of skills to convey themselves not only through paper and pencil, but also audio, video, animation and design software.

2) *Analyze and Interpret Data*: Students must be able to analyze and interpret the accumulation of data.

3) *Understand Computational Modelling*: Students must possess an understanding of the power, limitations, and underlying assumptions of various data representation systems, such as computational models and simulations, which are increasingly driving a wide range of disciplines.

4) *Manage and Prioritize Tasks*: Students must be able to manage the multi-tasking, selection, and prioritizing across technology applications that allow them to move

gracefully among teams, assignments and communities of practice.

5) *Engage in Problem Solving*: Students must have an understanding of how to apply what they know and can do to new situations.
6) *Ensure Security and Safety*: Students must know and use strategies to acknowledge, identify, and negotiate twenty-first century risks.

The four key principles which help teachers to implement technology are:

1) *Separate the role of the teacher:* It is important to understand the respective roles played by the teacher and the technology in the learning process.
2) *Teach in a principled way:* Whenever a new technology emerges (such as, say, pod casting), it is important to go beyond the 'wow' factor and think about the pedagogical reasons for using it.
3) *Use the technology to complement and enhance* what the teacher does.
4) 'It's not what it is; it's what you do with it' (Jones 1986). So it is not the interactive whiteboard per se which could improve the learning experience, but how it is used.

Hence, using technology in teaching language learners has distinct advantages that relate not only to language education but preparing students for today's information society. Computer technologies and the Internet are powerful tools for assisting language teaching because Web technology is a part of today's social fabric, meaning language learners can now learn thorough writing e-mail and conducting online research.

Language Lab Systems

For some time now, the language lab has been expanding beyond its historical focus on audio, in order to take advantage of the new technologies and to respond to the needs of today's teachers and learners (Scinicariello, 1997). Language departments are exploring a computer-based alternative to the traditional means of multimedia delivery. Audio and video can now be digitized and placed along with software on video-capable file servers.

Thus, the language lab is basically introduced to provide in-class and independent access to analog audio, by and large in the form of audiocassettes. One of the features that augment this traditional audio component in language labs are the capacity to "bookmark" challenging segments of a tape (so students can return to them later) besides the capacity of response analyzers to automatically generate student test scores following completion of an exercise or test. A few systems are set up so that both tracks of an audio tape can be accessed for the practice of simultaneous interpretation.

In this system, different segments of a video or audio clip may be accessed by multiple users simultaneously from their computers. Another advantage is that it is no longer necessary for single computer stations to have a dedicated videodisc player or other peripherals; students at any networked station in the lab may access multimedia resources directly on the server. This server-based set-up means that teachers and learners in remote locations with network access can use instructional materials. Smart classrooms, which are set up to display video, videodisc, and computer output to a room full of students, allow faculty to incorporate networked lab resources into their regular instruction.

Though offering a myriad of pedagogical benefits, there are also a number of limitations that educators need to bear in mind in their attempts to employ the technology as a teaching aid. Being aware of possible pitfalls in conducting Internet-based lessons; teachers would then be able to invest in proper planning to ensure that the learning experience for their students is a meaningful and stimulating one. Students often go straight to the Web without waiting for guidance from a teacher or librarian. This results in students having a difficult time navigating the Web and locating appropriate information relevant to the tasks in their homework. It is a time-seeking task.

Students may also not distinguish between genuine websites and sites that contain biased and erroneous information but masquerade as being reliable. Institutions are thus faced with the challenge of teaching the students not just the power of having a wealth of information at one's fingertips in the Internet but also proper evaluation skills.

Besides being aware of the strengths and shortcomings of conducting Internet-based lessons for students, teachers face practical constraints that might otherwise hinder the desired implementation of these lessons. Time is one barrier to the extensive use of the Internet as students may be unable to spend a specific block of time on the Internet due to limitations in availability of computers with Internet access.

In the knowledge based economies of today, it is critical to be able to search for and retrieve information from the Web. Locating appropriate information on the Internet requires a variety of skills such as the ability to use Internet tools (e.g. search engines), having knowledge of search techniques (e.g. browsing through an information tree) and ability to execute the search

Effective use of the Internet to glean relevant information requires the ability to understand how information is organized, critical thinking skills that allow the searcher to make informed choices, and a working knowledge of Internet notations. One needs to have abilities such as searching for information, scanning and skimming information, and strategies such as planning, monitoring and evaluating in executing the search.

Therefore, the Internet has been useful in the educational domain as a stockpile of gigantic amounts of rich information. Thus it is imperative that students be taught a wide range of internet literacy skills from verifying the authenticity of content hosted by the Internet to seeking for information by using various search strategies and techniques. This helps to ensure that the true potential of the Internet as a learning aid is properly tapped to inject greater vigour into teaching practices in schools.

Especially, the students of engineering colleges require an ever-increasing range of skills to maintain relevance with the global environment of the new millennium. Communication skills are a vital component of this, recognized by academia and industry alike. Indeed, communication skills are considered a salient element in the make-up of the new global engineer. Since professional and result oriented companies always seek for the employees who can communicate persuasively and effectively. Communication skills were cited as the single most important decisive factor in choosing managers. A lack of sufficient communication skills serve only to be disqualified in the placement interviews.

The art of communication has evolved over the years. It goes back in time to the Biblical era, mythological times and even to the pre-historic period. People had learned to express themselves even before they evolved fully into their present form. It has been a long yet fascinating and rewarding journey through time from sounds, grunts, actions, signs, gestures and gesticulations to the world of reading, writing and sophisticated methods of communication.

In the process of civilization, human beings have learned to interpret sounds, understand actions and use signs and gesticulations to communicate. Messages are conveyed through sounds, cries and drumbeats. The spoken word added a new dimension to the world of learning. Sages and saints of yore learned to pass on the sacred verses and holy texts through word of mouth. Thereafter, human beings learned to use symbols and pictures to convey messages. This in turn led to the invention of writing. Early writings are engraved on stones and palm leaves. Further, the invention of printing brought about a great revolution in human civilization. Various inventions made possible the recording of the spoken word or ideas and led to the evolution of different languages likewise.

Gradually, the emergence of new media TV has added new dimensions to the world of communication. Advancements in technology have further enabled storage and retrieval of oral and written records in an effective mode. The claim for universal education has resulted in an augment in the number of students from all occupations joining educational institutions.

In this direction, the Kothari Commission [1964] named after its chairperson, D.S. Kothari, manifested an important event in the history of education in India. The commission was setup by the Government to counsel on the national prototype of education at all stages and in all aspects. The commission powerfully felt that education, especially science-based education, in unity with Indian culture and values can single-handedly give the basis influential to the nation's growth, safety and welfare.

Hence, the Kothari Commission recommended consolidation of advanced research centres with an aim to achieve international principles in research areas especially in the field of sciences. To attain these, the commission undertook the responsibility of making pertinent suggestions for civilizing sectors of education such as scientific education and research.

Thus, English was adopted as the medium of instruction for natural sciences that resulted in the rapid growth of university education, especially in urban areas, according to a report released by the study group appointed by the Ministry of Education, Government of India.

The success of Indian Education Policy can be measured by the content of the recent address of Dr. ManMohan Singh, the Prime Minister of India.

> "Of all the legacies of the British Raj, none is more important than the English Language and the modern school system. That is of course, if you leave out Cricket! Of course, people here may not recognize the language we speak, but let me assure you that it is English! In indigenizing English as so many people have done in so many nations across the world, we have made the language our own. Today, English in India is seen as just another Indian language."

Thus, realizing the need for improving communication skills particularly in English, engineering colleges are requested by K.C. Reddy, Chairman of Andhra Pradesh State Council of Higher Education (APSCHE) to open an English Language Training Centre (ELTC) in the colleges to vernacular students.

In his view, English is to be taught throughout four-year the engineering course.

The B. Tech Course comprises various fields of specialization viz, civil, mechanical, chemical, electronics and communication etc. English is extensively used for academic and professional purposes in this discipline. The prerequisites of the professions and the demand for communicative competency require a call for a study of English offered in the engineering colleges of JNTU. English course at the undergraduate level of engineering studies requires equipping the learner's need for both educational as well as professional requirements.

Under a broad policy framework of providing new technological education required for the industrial growth of the country in general and more particularly for the State of Andhra Pradesh, "Jawaharlal Nehru Technological University" was established on 2 October, 1972, by an act of State Legislature. Rightly named after the ardent lover of science and technology, Pandit Jawaharlal Nehru, the first Prime Minister of India, the University was established with the noble objectives of strengthening and improving the standards of technological education and making it relevant to the rural and industrial development of the country. Technological advancements and infrastructure facilitate to determine the progress and prosperity of a nation. This is very true in the case of India, endowed with a huge population growing at a rapid pace and vast natural resources largely remaining unexploited. Realizing that promotion of technical education was the imperative need of the hour, "JAWAHARLAL NEHRU TECHNOLOGICAL UNIVERSITY", the first technological university of India, was established in Andhra Pradesh with its headquarters at Hyderabad. The singular objective was by way of emphasis on training and research in engineering and applied sciences. On its formation, the Government Engineering Colleges at Anantapur, Kakinada and Hyderabad, along with the Government College of Fine Arts and Architecture at Hyderabad, became its Constituent Colleges. It has become the backbone of the oldest engineering colleges of South India.

In the last four decades, JNTU produced highly professional and competitive engineers by infusing greater quality and content into the curriculum, and educating the students with appropriate skills suitable for a rapidly changing industrial scenario. To improve the quality of technical education, it has participated actively in a number of national programmes like Teacher Quality Improvement Programme, National Programmes and Expansion of Infrastructure Facilities for Emerging Technologies. Distance Education programmes in B.Tech in Civil, Electronics & Electrical, Mechanical and Electronics & Communication Engineering were started by the University, in the correspondence-cum-contact mode, in 1983.

JNTU (Jawaharlal Nehru Technological University) was originally 'The College of Engineering, Vizagapatam' at the time of its inception in 1946. It is now a sprawling campus of 110 acres, green with mango trees, in the fast developing port city of Kakinada, East coast of peninsular India. Kakinada has a rich political literacy and cultural heritage passed on through generations. This college became a constituent of the Jawaharlal Nehru Technological University w.e.f 02-10-1972 through an act of legislature along with other sister institutions under the control of the then Director of Technical Education, Government of Andhra Pradesh. Earlier, it was affiliated to Andhra University. The college became autonomous in the year 2003.

The Jawaharlal Nehru Technological University, Kakinada, (JNTUK) has signed a 'services agreement' with Social Media India Limited (SMIL) and Knowledge Base Technologies (KBT). The purpose of the agreement is to establish a total automation environment in the functioning of the day-to-day administrative, managerial and academic matters of JNTUK such as management of university website, affiliations, examinations and evaluation and student attendance.

Describing it as an historic agreement, JNTUK Vice-Chancellor, Allam Apparao, said it would facilitate both JNTUK and its affiliate college managements to reach the goal of attaining world-class status within 1,000 days.

"With the help of this agreement, JNTUK desires to provide opportunities to its students a platform to know the industry requirements, opportunities to obtain required skill sets, interface with industry, participation in various seminars, projects and to obtain placements of superior opportunities in various sectors like Oil and Natural Gas, Communications, IT and Infrastructure," he added.

The educational tasks include oral and written communicative comprehension of lectures and books, note-making, note-taking, paper presentation, participation in seminars, attending interviews and so on. The professional tasks include oral and written communication, involving business dealings, interacting with their superiors and subordinates for planning and execution of work and so on.

Apart from technical subjects, English communication course is introduced by JNTU to impart communication skills to the Engineering students to meet the rising demand of the skills front to relish success in placement interviews. The objective of the course is to improve the language proficiency of the engineering students in English language with an emphasis on Listening, Speaking, Reading and Writing (LSRW) skills and to develop the communication skills in both formal and informal circumstances. The course material for the prescribed syllabus is selected to interest the students and to serve the actual purpose.

The students who join the engineering colleges are usually high intellectuals. They come with different backgrounds and thus, bring along with them different levels of aptitude. With such existing conditions in a classroom, teaching should be satisfactory to meet the requirements of all the students.

In the second semester of third year B.Tech course, the students have to be well equipped for placement interviews. Hence, the study recommends the social interaction activities including conversation and discussion sessions, dialogues and role-plays, simulations, skits, improvisations and debates. Therefore, a learner-centred needs analysis of the learners should form the base for improving communication skills of engineering students.

Bringing in too much of the concept of a subject specification into the English classrooms rarely interests the student. Thus, the disappointed students of engineering colleges are likely to approach private or off campus courses to develop their communicational skills. With the fast growing requirements in the world of information technology, there is a demand for effective communication among the professionals to meet the desired skill.

In the technological institutions affiliated to Jawaharlal Technological University, besides theory, three periods are allotted to the practical course, English Language Communication Skills Lab per each branch once a week. The students are exposed to several topics related to learning English language through computer system. All the technological colleges impart practical knowledge with the help of English softwares.

The English Language & Communication Skills Lab monitors and guides students towards enhancing their skills through the softwares. The students listen to the recorded lessons and can even record their voices. The English Language Lab has facilities for the teachers to listen to individual students in turn, and to speak with them. Guidance is provided to all the students whenever necessary by the teacher sitting at the teacher console. The students would be in a position to judge his/her own performance. If the student is not satisfied, he/she can return to the same exercise – retry or again listen to the examples.

All other activities have preparation material installed in the systems. Teachers guide the students towards understanding and participating in various activities like Oral Speeches, JAMs, Mock Interviews, and Mock GDs etc. The feedback sessions are eye-openers which pave the way for further enhancement.

The following course content is prescribed for the *English Language Laboratory* sessions:

a) Introduction to the Sounds of English — Vowels, Diphthongs & Consonants.

b) Introduction to Stress and Intonation.
c) Situational Dialogues and Role Play.
d) Oral Presentations — Prepared and Extempore.
e) 'Just A Minute' Sessions (JAM).
f) Describing — Objects / Situations / People.
g) Information Transfer
h) Debate
i) Telephoning Skills
j) Giving Directions

A brief review of the above-mentioned topics is necessary to analyze how the technology is being useful in imparting practical knowledge to the engineering students through ICT.

Phonetics

Phonetics is a branch of linguistics, and it is the branch dealing with the medium of speech. It deals with the production, transmission and reception of the sounds of human speech. Linguistics is a systematic study of language. Language has a very important social purpose, because it is mainly used for linguistic communication. Thus, a language can be used in two ways for the purposes of communication: spoken and written.

Introduction to Stress and Intonation

Stress

It is an important feature of spoken English, and the use of incorrect word accentuation by Indian speakers has been found to be one of the most frequent causes of their being unintelligible to the speakers of English. A word in English has one or more syllables. In each syllable there is one sound, usually a vowel, that is more prominent than the rest. A syllable also corresponds to a chest pulse, a muscular movement, pushing the air out of the lungs. Vowels generally take the central position in syllables, and consonants take the marginal positions. Students are given practice in the division of sounds and the division of words into syllables. If an English word has more than one syllable, not all the syllables are equally prominent. Those that are more prominent than others are said to receive the accent.

Intonation

When one speaks, the pitch of the voice goes on changing, that is, the voice rises and falls, and each language has its own intonation patterns. The speaker divides his utterances into tone groups, each group having a nucleus, also called tonic syllable. It is on the tonic syllable that a noticeable pitch movement, that is a change in pitch of the voice, is initiated. If the voice falls, it is a falling tone. A rising tone is generally used in certain types of questions in English. Some sentences may have both the falling and rising tone. Thus intonation plays a very important role in conveying the meaning.

Situational Dialogues/Role Play

Students are instructed to start a conversation, respond appropriately and relevantly use the right body language by participating in role plays.

Presentation Skills

A presentation is a technique of communicating information, knowledge, facts and ideas in a subtle manner to a group of people. An oral presentation is a form of oral communication. It's a participative two-way communication process characterized by the formal and structured presentation of a message using visual aids. It is purposeful and goal-oriented, and communicates a message to an audience in a way that brings about the desired change in their understanding or opinion. It is flexible, changing as well as complex and varied. Thus, an oral presentation is:

a) *Purposeful:* The Presentation will be made with a definite purpose.

b) *Interactive:* It involves both the speaker's and the listener's.

c) *Formal:* It is a formal situation.

The following should be observed by the presenter when conducting an oral presentation:

a) One should understand the level of one's listeners.

b) Anticipate what they want to know.

c) One has to adjust to one's audience throughout the presentation.

d) Have a persuasive, informative, progressive presentation.

e) Make use of all materials available like environment, audio-visuals, notes and references.

f) Give listeners an assignment.

g) Be clear on central theme and key ideas.

h) Anticipate listeners' questions and use a variety of support for key ideas.

i) Arrange ideas for clarity impact.

j) Have a provocative message as speech is like this – any fool can start it, but to end it, requires considerable skills.

k) Go for starting statements, rhetorical questions, quotations, definitions, with a winning presentation.

l) Deliver your message like a professional.

m) Use action endings like gestures, body movements facial expression and eye contact.

n) Avoid vocal cues as certain potentially distracting, vocal cues might be contradicting the meaning conversed.

o) Avoid breathy, whining, or strident voice.

p) Avoid rapid-fire delivery as dull expressionless recitation.

q Avoid word-for-word copy of the talk, i.e., over use of notes, – as there is every danger of losing eye contact with listeners. So practise loud before delivery.

These points might help in dealing with challenges and opportunities in customer service, human relations, personal effectiveness and communication to face contemporary management challenges.

Just a Minute Sessions (JAM)

Just a Minute Sessions are conducted to check the communication skills of the students' construction of sentences, sequencing of thoughts, putting forth ideas, knowledge and so on in a stipulated timeframe. A topic is put forth to the student, and he is expected to make an oral presentation in a short period of time and speak within the stipulated time.

Describing Objects / Situations / People

Describing is something which involves recreating your experiences and impressions. Describing includes perceiving the subject of your description accurately. The subject of a description can be an object, situation and people. Tips for description:

a) Avoid using general, vague or abstract words in your description.

b) Be as specific as you can and give as many details as possible.

c) To write a good description, we should know why it is written and whom it is written for.

Information Transfer

Technology in every field of information means the macro information is being transferred as much as the micro is being, which we have at our fingertips. The information can be shown through texts, tables, maps, tree diagrams, bar graphs, pie charts, flow-charts and so on. Information in verbal form can be made clearer and easier to understand by presenting it in graphic or pictorial form. Pictorial representation has many advantages:

a) Allows quick and easy viewing of a large amount of data.

b) Quicker to locate required information in a graphic than in a written text.

c) Data relating to a long period of time or to large number of people can be effectively summarized.

d) Convenient to use in making comparisons involving amounts of data.

The different types of graphic representation that could be used to supplement writing are:

1) Tables
2) Bar charts
3) Maps
4) Graphs
5) Pie charts
6) Tree diagrams
7) Flow charts and
8) Pictograms.

Debate

A debate is a structured argument. It is one way of communication where an analytical and logical thinking comes into play. It is an art of knitting arguments and putting them forth in a constructive way. A debate makes one think about the two opposite sides of a subject and helps to decide. A debate can be in an argumentative form through letters, and essays. Usually, in a debate, a topic is thrown between two teams or two individuals. One team decides to go for the topic and the other goes against it. The topics are suitably selected as to have both pros and cons as the debate begins; the teams declare their stand and get into arguments and counter-arguments. At the end, an evaluation is made on the basis of the arguments put forth by both the teams, and a decision is taken on who the winner is.

Telephonic Skills

Telephoning skills have become an integral part of our day-to-day lives. Today's business communication is solely centred on telephonic skills. Telephonic conversation relies on two things:

1) Listening and concentrating on what we hear and so on
2) The tone and words of voice of the caller/Listener.

Giving Directions

Giving direction is a specific way of communication. One needs to be careful in giving directions and following instructions. Also while making suggestions, one has to take into account what others want. Suggestions which include the other participants in the conversation will be accepted more easily when they are put forth in a polite manner. Therefore, giving direction is also considered as partial information transfer.

Thus, practical English is being taught through technology in all the technical colleges affiliated to JNTU (Jawaharlal Nehru Technological University). Undoubtedly, technology has revolutionized society in many places around the globe, including how language instruction is taught and delivered. In particular, the Internet has become a means of expression where people can learn, share and collaborate in ways not possible years before. However, a great deal of success comes from preparing students to interact and learn in this online environment. Therefore, an extensive effort is needed to integrate technology in teaching. A refocused approach to teaching boosts the learners a long way in making technology and the Internet a more rewarding partner in the teaching and learning process.

Works Cited

Barrett, B. and Sharma, P. (2007). *Blended Learning: Using Technology Inside and Beyond the Language Classroom.* Macmillan.

Becker, H.J. (2000). Who's wired and who's not: Children's access to and use of computer technology. *Future of Children, 10(2),* 44-75. Los Altos, CA: The David and Lucile Packard Foundation. Retrieved charts from: http://www.gse.uci.edu/doehome/DeptInfo/Faculty/Becker/packard/saveall.html#top.

Bertelsmann Foundation & AOL Time Warner Foundation, (2002). CEO Forum, (2001); NCREL, (2002); ISTE, (1999); *ETS: International ICT Literacy Panel, 2001; Partnership for 21st Century Skills*, 2003, 2005).

Blumer, H. (1969). *Symbolic Interactionism: Perspectives and Methods.* Englewood Cliffs, NJ: Prentice Hall.

Bruce, B., & Levin, J. (1997). "Educational Technology: Media for Inquiry, Communication, Construction and Expression." *Journal of Educational Computing Research*, 17(1), 79-102.

Carroll, J. B. (1999). "Expert Internet Information Access." *Journal of Educational Computing Research* 20 (3): 209-222.

Dr. Manmohan Singh. *In Acceptance of Honorary Degree from Oxford University, July 8, 2005.* (http://pm India. nic.in/visits/content asp? id-44.)

Government of India Report of the Kothari Commission. Ministry of Education: New Delhi. (1964) (http://www.qub.ac.uk'schools/school of English/imperial/India/educate,htm.)

Government of India: The Wood's Dispatch Report. Ministry of Education: New Delhi. (1854). (http://www.qub.ac.uk'schools/school of English/ imperial/India/educate, html.) http://jntuk.edu.in/atozindex/ constituent/http://jntuk.edu.in/ http://www.cdac.in/html/edu/acb/ IICT/jntu.htm

Integrating Learning Technologies into the English Learning Area. The Department of Education. *Internet Sunday,* 2 May, 2010.

JNTUK signs services agreement with two companies Kakinada, Thursday, June, 11 2009. http://jntuk.edu.in/atozindex/constituent/

Jones, C. (1986). 'It's not so much the program, more what you do with it: the importance of methodology in CALL' System 14 / 2, 171-178

Kay, K. & Honey, M. *Beyond Technology Competency: A Vision of ICT Literacy to Prepare Students for the 21st Century.* The Institute for the Advancement of Emerging Technologies in Education. Charleston, W.V.: Evantia.

Laboratory Manual for English Language and Communication Skills for 1 B.Tech—Regulation 09, Sphoorthy Engineering College Nadergul (vill.) Saroornagar.

Macaulay, Lord. (1935). *Speeches - by Lord Macaulay with his Minutes on Indian Education*, Oxford University Press, Oxford,

Ocampo, P.D.S.2002. Enhancing Philippine science and technology thru ICT. Preface. *Transactions of the National Academy of Science and Technology*, 24:v-vi.

Randall Davis Utopia or Chaos? The Impact of Technology on Language Teaching. eslrandall[at]yahoo.com English Language Institute, University of Utah (Salt Lake City, Utah, USA)

Ravi Kanth Reddy. R. Making English Accessible Education Plus. *The Hindu*, Monday, Nov. 12, 2007.

Scinicariello, S. (1997). Uniting teachers, learners, and machines: Language laboratories and other choices. In M. Bush & R. Terry (Eds.), *Technology-enhanced language learning* (pp.185-213). Lincolnwood, IL: National Textbook Co.

The Study of English in India A Report of The Study Group appointed by the Ministry of Education, Government of India. (http:// en.wikipedia.org/wiki/English_Medium_Education# The_Post_Colonial_Indian

Tinio, V. (2002). *Survey of information and communication technology utilization in Philippine public high schools.* Retrieved on May 5, 2010 from www.digitalphilippines.org/research

Tricia Doyle. *Western Education in Nineteenth Century India.* 4 June 1998. (http://www.qub.ac.uk'schools/schoolofEnglish/imperial/India/educate, htm.)

Trimble, Louis (1985). *English fort Science & Technology, A Discourse Approach.* Cambridge: Cambridge University Press.

9

Effective English Language Teaching through ICT: Unifying the Diversity

— Kavita Chauhan

Globalization and technological changes—a process that have accelerated in tandem over the past fifteen years—have created a new global economy powered by technology, fueled by information and driven by knowledge. (U.S Department of Labour, 1999)

What is ICT?

Technology and tools that help people to communicate with one another, one by one, or in group is ICT. Information technology uses computer, which has become indispensable in modern society to process data and save time and effort. Telecommunication technologies include telephone and the broadcasting of radio and television, often through satellites. Networking technologies, of which the best known is The Internet, also extended to mobile phone technology, Voice over IP telephony phone, are still in their infancy.

Graham Daevis began his career as a teacher in French and German in secondary education in 1960; he moved to higher education in 1972 and taught German at Ealing College until 1990, when he became the Director of Language Centre. He has lectured and run ICT training courses for long. Teaching in 22 different countries in 1982, he wrote one of the first introductory books on computer language learning.

An ancient Chinese proverb states that one picture is worth a thousand words. Pictures and other visual aids

> maps, slides, films, graphs, models certainly do make an impact, though they seldom replace word altogether.
>
> — (Ellison John Kahn, 1991: 509)

Visual aids enable a speaker to communicate information more quickly, and listeners to absorb it more readily. A simple formula emerges:

Words + visual aids = quick comprehension + long lasting impressions.

Learning and teaching levels through ICT rose at regular intervals. ICT has measurable beneficial effects on the learner. The benefits of ICT are:

a) It helps to cover different types of tasks.

b) With the help of ICT, we can teach languages to learners.

c) It can help to improve behaviour in classroom and help to enhance language learning. There have been a wide range of applications by which we can easily switch tasks or action buttons within presentations, which link to the other activities.

d) It can engage better and motivate more effectively. It helps in delivering repetitions and memorization activities.

e) ICT enhances pupils' grammar skills and listening skills too.

ICT supports in special education needs. It can enhance teaching and learning in special education needs. It aims to explore the following issues relating to how ICTs enhance learning and it will explore how ICT enriches the learning opportunities and potential of students who have SEN, especially in the following area:

a) Physically Disabled Students.

b) Visual Impairments

c) Hearing Impairments

d) Autistic Spectrum Disorder

e) Dyslexia

f) Learning Disabilities

g) Emotional and Behavioural Difficulties

Information and communication technology supports special educational needs. ICTs can enhance teaching and learning in special educational needs. This study aims to explore the following issues relating to how ICTs enriches the learning opportunity and potential of students who have SEN, especially in the above-mentioned areas.

a) ICTs can help disabled people but it is not a magic world.

b) ICTs can help disabled pupils to provide access to learning.

ICTs can provide support for learning. It can help disabled pupils and teachers and promote their skills. It may be essential for access for some pupils. It also helps in written works; pupils and helpers need training and support.

Communication aids in computer access devices, switches access utilities and specialized software—software with alternative input options, word list and word prediction facilities. ICT made more impact on education than most teachers realize. It goes much further than the specialist ELT software we have installed in our computer labs. All students are not able to be online, by any means, but the percentage of those using ICT equipments is increasing diversely. ICT-based activities help in providing information, which is easily accessible to learners. One of the features of the computer is to store and retrieve information. When students need to check the spelling or meaning of a word or need to find a grammar rule, they make use of the dictionary and grammar programme on the computer. Use of Internet provides a window from the classroom into a real world of English, and incidentally, promotes learners' autonomy by giving students confidence to operate in that world.

Information and communication technology helps students in preparing homework. Students can work through traditional library-based research; and include pictures they had found on the web, and even submit the project or presentation on powerpoint. The computer is an ideal tool for drilling: it is, in fact, more consistent and more patient than a living teacher does. One can improve pronunciation power with listening to a programme designed to help students to recognize and produce the individual phonemes of English language both in isolation and in the context of word.

The purpose of information and communication technology (ICT) is to enhance an effective blended learning model of English-speaking teaching for pupils in primary schools. English conversational material, which integrates ICT into classroom learning, developed by David Goldberg, was adapted as the instruments in this study.

ICT is the new mode of learning and communicating teaching activity. It facilitates online content creation and collaboration by entailing various social and communication tools that support teacher-student, student-student and teacher-teacher interactions.

The aim of my study is to provide ample knowledge to language teachers rather than generalizing with regard to the computer, as just another teaching tool provided for the teachers to adopt the dual role of content developer and coach.

Today we are living in the twenty-first century. The present age is different from the previous one as today's age is the technological age and it vast influence is the major feature that marks our present age. Technology is useful in the present era, in some cases, it is harmful too. Technology education is one such field and my study is going to focus on information and communication technology (ICT). Education can be understood itself through language education and particularly English language education.

Learning through programme is a different perspective; for easy learning it is better to break it down into small pieces, then organize systematically and logically for transmission. Programmes are considered like machines as they control the behaviour of the learners and provide quality output.

The study of ICT popularly known as "networking" is concerned with the science and technology for building communication network of communication links. In networks that offer only store-and-forward services, the technology has been driven more by an effort to develop best-effort data transport that would work under diverse conditions. Among the best-effort transport technologies, the Internet protocols have by far the largest installed base. In ICT, instruments used to communicate information are radio, television, computer, digital lab, and Internet.

Radio

Radio is another kind of learning instrument. It was usually used as a means of communication in times of war and disaster, then became a means of entertainment. Radio is used mainly for non-formal teaching. Through radio, we can educate the peasant by informing them about the latest technology for agriculture, and it helps in teaching language and music. In spite of luxury, radio became an important or necessary instrument for people. Through radio, we come to know about child care, women's health, hygiene, balanced diet, latest information, sports, etc. In India radio became a part of the school curriculum in several states, Gujarat being one of them. With the invention of television, the charm of radio has diminished. However, it is getting popular with the FM broadcast.

Radio plays a vital role in communicating information. Information reaches even the most remote place of the country. It imparts language education, provides entertainment, and disseminates information to both literate and illiterate listeners. It helps in imparting a wide variety of educational, cultural and entertainment items, aimed at a board spectrum of classes of people.

The broadcast for farmers and workers try to use a style that is supposedly understood by less literate groups. Radio plays a major role in language. The newsreader introduces standard pronunciation values to the phenomenon, words, phrases, and sentences.

It also helps in developing an individual's imagination, in creating pictures in the mind while listening to words. Besides getting information and entertainment, in language classes radio helps in correct pronunciation, the intonation, the pitch of voice, etc.

Television

Television is like, the radio considered as another instrument for learners. It also helps in the field of teaching and in education. Television acts as a magic eye for learners as it can stimulate several situations and manipulate creativity. Video-conferencing facilitates in bridging the gaps between the haves and have-nots in education today. With addition to television, we can also use slide projector, OHP, films, tape recorder, videocassette and LCD and OHP all used as substitutes for chalkboard.

Television is the audiovisual non-literacy medium. It is advantageous in providing visuals to reinforce the information being presented in spoken form. Even in this field, language education plays a vital role, because additional cues compensate for dialectal difference between speakers and listeners. Telecasting information through TV is beneficial to the illiterate and literate people. Television provides a ground for additional cultural learning, and also facilitates to entertain and educate the viewers. Television aims to enlarge both knowledge and understanding. Critics call it the idiot box due to some mindless programmes, which promote mindless viewing.

Television provides a lot of information. It gives quick and exact information in different fields. It uses advance technology. It provides educational information regarding wildlife, civil war, science, cultures, etc. We can bring this information into the classroom through videotaping various television programmes for later use

Language Laboratory

Language laboratory is another kind of programmed learning, which use listening programmes. Today's laboratories are based on digital laboratory and these provide multimedia exposure to learners. Learning through this laboratory is termed as advance learning. Laboratories still treat learners as isolated entities whose learning behaviour can controlled.

The prime objective of the language lab is to facilitate efficient teacher-student interaction, to correct phonetic accents and dialects, to effectively use for business and official communications. To ensure an effective mode of communication internationally, English was, and is, the most accepted language. To harness this communicative skill advance emerging technologies have developed an internationally accepted multilingual software combining ICT known as the language lab software. To acquire a language lab there are four basic requirements: listening, reading, speaking and writing (LSRW).

Uses of ICT

a) Develops observational assessment practices.
b) Supports the documentation of learning.
c) Supports the foundation stage profile.

According to some practitioners, using ICT will develop or promote speaking and listening skills of children and self-reflection among them. Informational communication technology plays a big role in providing multimodal communication tools or instruments to children. Teachers record voices of the children and this recording frequently helps the children to give a more coherent response.

ICT Equipment

a) *Talking button*: Small boxes with 30 seconds worth of recording time available at the press of a button. Very easy for small children to use.
b) *Digi Blue Camera*: Hand-held video camera, specially designed for small children. They record five minutes at a time.
c) *Voice Changer*: Tubes which electronically change the voice in several ways

d) *Virtual Learning Environment*: Shared web across a local authority so that all schools and setting can upload and share files.

e) *To Create a Story Programmer*: It helps young children make multimodal stories, which they can e-mail easily.

Digital language lab software provides all students, no matter wherever they are seated in a classroom, equal opportunity to hear and too be heard by the instructor. With the use of this lab, learners can talk freely and lose their inhibitions while talking in front of their peers. The language lab helps the learners to listen individually, and ultimately increases the attention span of the learner to listen and analyze the content of the lesson. The language lab helps the students to develop the following qualities in them:

a) *Self-pacing:* This will help students to work through the lesson at a pace suited to their capability.

b) *Developing Listening Skills:* Until you are good listeners, you cannot be a good speaker. Digital lab helps students to develop good listening skills and aids the process of communications. Students are able to listen to the correct language pattern. While listening to the lesson they develop the correct pronunciation.

c) *Developing Good Speaking Skills:* The digital lab provides a variety of voices to student to converse, and is used as a model voice subject for the rest of the class.

d) *Developing Reading Skills:* Learners have the ability to read the text and record their voices with the master stimulus. Students can retrieve and hear their recorded voices together with the model voice.

e) *Developing Writing Skills:* Learners can write the text they read and type the text they read.

Language can help to think and speak, and with the help of these lab learners students can improve phonetic skills and develop effective communication skills. They can develop confidence to carry out a simple conversation and be able to conduct focused discussion.

"The English language is nobody's property of the imagination: it is the property of the language itself."

— *Derek Walcott*

Introduction of Computers in the Field of Education

When computers were introduced to education, they made a significant place in the teaching learning process. Traditionally it is considered as an instrument of numerical processing. It makes possible to capture systematically their operation and manipulations. The speed with which a computer works and provides result sets us thinking about harnessing this potential for language processing or, what we today call, word processing.

Now computers also help us to correct errors while typing a text. We can check our spelling mistakes through the computer. Nowadays computers have several features, which help us in checking our grammar and spelling mistakes. We can also store dictionary and grammar detecting applications. Our computer compares every word, spelling, and grammar of the sentence and points out about the mistake in that sentence. This helps a lot to the new user of the language and helps those who are regular users.

The computer can also store the data, which we want to store, and is easily accessible. It is easy to educate the people through the computer by creating the interest of the person in that area. We can use computers to develop language skills and to teach the contents area.

Information and communication technology (ICT) includes radio and television, as well as newer digital computers and the Internet. ICTs are said to be helpful in expanding education, strengthening the relevance of education to the increasingly digital workplace, and raising educational quality, among others.

Internet

Internet refers to the worldwide inter-connection of packet networks that all use. IP (internet protocol) is the network layer protocol, and TCP (Transmission control protocol) and UDP (User Datagram Protocol) are the most commonly used protocols at the transport layer. The IP protocol can operate over any link layer that can transport IP packets.

The Internet has a wide range of information about all sorts of topics, which we want to discuss in classrooms, and at the same time a source of professional knowledge for teachers. For accessing all sorts of information through the Internet one must have, some practice and experience to know how to surf the Internet. We have some tips about the ways to search the Internet.

It helps all sorts of individuals to induce and deduce ideas, to analyze errors, to abstract concepts, to analyze perspectives, to gather information, to work in teams, etc. The information on the Internet is the latest, extensive, and easily accessible. Information is available on the Internet inexpensively and without a great deal of effort. Sometimes students are unable to comprehend material available on the Internet due to its complexity or their disorientation in countless links. To overcome this confusion we should focus our attention, think critically and analyze the various amounts of information.

The Internet is nowadays considered as the greatest innovation in the ICT field. The Internet can make information more attainable and understandable by more people. It is a vast store of information from which society and its people can have is knowledge of language. It helps in communicating information in an understandable way.

Meaning is the key to effective communication and logical origination is the key to meaning.

The words you choose to say something are just as important as the decision to speak.

— *Anonymous*

Teleconferencing

Teleconferencing refers to interactive electronic communication among people located at two or more different places (Rao, V. Rama, 2010). There are four types of teleconferencing:

a) Audio-Conferencing
b) Audio-Graphic Conferencing
c) Video-Conferencing
d) Web-Based Conferencing

Audio-conferencing means to exchange the voice over a telephone network. When images such as graphs, diagrams or pictures are exchanged along with voice messages it is called *audio-graphic*. *Video-conferencing* means exchange of voice and graphics as well moving images. This kind of technology makes a use of satellite link or television network. *Web-based conferencing*, involves transmission of text, graphics and video and visual aids via the Internet, which requires a computer with a browser. Communication can be both synchronous and asynchronous. It is used in both formal and informal communication.

TELECOLLABORATION

The organized use of web resource and collaboration tools for curriculum appropriate purposes is called telecollaboration. Judi has defined telecollabration as an "educational endeavor that involves people in different locations using internet tools and resources to work together. Much educational telecollaboration is curriculum-based teacher designed, and teacher coordinate. Most use email to help participants communicate with each other. Many telecollaborative activities and projects have websites to support them" (Harris, Judi, 2010).

English is the dominant language of the Internet. As estimated, 80 per cent, online content is in English (Anzalone, Stephen, 2001). In most of the countries, English is the second language. It is imperative that teaching and other learning material will be developed in locally meaningful content in local languages so that the people of different cultures will also take advantage in an equal stake and voice in the global communities of learning online. The bulk of the educational material in ICT is in English language. There is a need to develop original educational content and to convert print-based content to digital media.

While school and universities may already have agreements that expressly authorized the use of certain materials for classroom purposes, these agreements may not be broad enough to accommodate telecommunication transmission, video tape-recording, or the distributing of course-related material beyond the classroom settings (Anzalone, Stephen, 2001).

CONCLUSION

Education through ICT is a complex, multifaceted process that involves technology. It helps in institutional readiness, teacher competencies, and long-term financing, among others. ICT addresses four broad issues on education: effectiveness, cost, equity and sustainability. There are challenges among policy makers in developing countries when making decision about the integration of ICTs in education.

The purpose of ICTs is a diverse set of technological tools and resource used to communicate and to create, disseminate, store and manage information (Salomon, K., 2010: 5).

Introduction of ICTs in different fields is the most challenging task. It is the most powerful tool to attend educational opportunities. It is beneficial for those groups who are excluded from education due to cultural and social reason e.g., a person with disabilities, girls and women as well as persons who, because of reasons of cost or time constraints, are unable to enrol on campus.

These technologies include the computer (the Internet) broadcasting technologies (radio, television and telephony). ICT technologies prove that older technologies such as the telephone, radio and television, although now given less attention, have a longer and richer history as instructional tools (Bultrton, C., 2010).

Through ICT one can have asynchronous learning. Online courses material are available, teachers and learners are not solely dependent on books, and others study materials available in library with the help of the Internet and the World Wide

Web provides a wide range of subject material in each and every subject. One can surf the Internet anywhere or anytime. At one time, an unlimited number of people can access the Internet. It also facilitates access to persons—researches, business leaders, experts, mentors and peers all over the world.

Radio and television are used more frequently for open and distance learning, although print remains the cheapest, most accessible and therefore most dominant delivery mechanism in both developed and developing countries (Postashink, M. and J. Capper, 2010).

The use of ICT is to prepare people better for the next generation at workplace. Technologically literate can easily handle ICTs effectively and efficiently. ICT can improve or enhance the education to facilitate the acquisition of basic skills by enhancing teachers' training.

In developing countries ICTs in education plays a vital role in accessing and improving the relevance and quality of education. They greatly facilitate the acquisition and absorption of knowledge, offering developing countries unprecedented opportunities for businessmen and others. One of the greatest hardships endured by the poor, and by many others who live in the poorest countries, is their sense of isolation. The new communication technologies promise to reduce that sense of isolation and to open access to knowledge in ways unimaginable not long ago (World Bank, 1998).

Moving images, sounds and colour motivate the learners in the learning process. In radio, one can make use of sound, songs, drama and comic skills which enhance teacher training. Institutions like the Cyber Teacher Training Centre (CCTC) in South Korea takes advantage of the Internet to provide better teacher professional development opportunities for in-service teachers. The Government provided CCTC establishment in 1997, offering self-directed, self-paced web-based courses for primary and secondary school teachers. Courses include "Computers in the information society", "Education reform" and "Future society and education". Online tutorials are also offered, with some courses requiring occasional face-to-face meetings (Jung, 2010).

The potential of each technology varies according to how it is used. Hadded and Draxler identify at least five levels of technology used in education presentation, demonstration, drill and practice, interaction and collaboration (Haddad, Wadi, D. and Alexandra, Drexler, 2002: 9). Finally, we say that:

> Think like a wise man but communicate in the language of the people.
>
> — *W.B. Yeats.*

Works Cited

Anzalone, Stephen, "ICT to Support Learning in Classrooms in SEAMEO Countries: At What Costs?" Paper prepared for *SEAMEO* Conference, in Bangkok, March 26-9-2001.

Bultrton, C, "New Directions of ICT- Use in Education." Available online http://www.unesco.org/education/educprog//wf/dl/edict.pdf; accessed May 2010.

Cuban, L (1986), *Teachers and Machines: The Classroom Use of Technology Since 1920.* New York: Teachers College Press.

Ellison John Kahn, (1991). *Readers Digest*, "How to Write And Speak Better", London; New York.

Haddad, Wadi D. and Alexandra Drexler (2002), "The Dynamic of Technologies for Education," in Haddad, W. & Drexler, and A. (eds.) *Technologies for Education: Potentials, Parameters, and Prospects.* Washington DC: Academy for Educational Development and Paris: UNESCO.

Harris, Judi, "First steps in Tele-collaboration"; available from http://cc.utexas.edu/~jbharris/virtual-Arichitechture/Articles/First Step.pdf; accessed 6 May 2010.

Jung, I., "Issues and Challenges of Providing Online In-service Teacher Training: Korea's Experience; available from http://www.irrodl.org/content/v2.1/jung.pdf; accessed 5 May 2010.

Postashink, M. and J. Capper, "Distance Education: Growth and Diversity;" available from http://www.world bank.org/fandd/English/pdfs/0398/0110398.pdf; accessed 4 May 2010.

Rao, V. Rama, "Audio Teleconferencing- A Technological Prescription for Interactive Learning"; available from http:// www.clrec. Org/ rama; accessed 6 May 2010.

Salomon, K, "A Primer on Distance learning and intellectual property issues"; available from http://www.teletrain.com/copyright.htm#3. student%20 waives; accessed 4 May 2010.

U.S Department of labour (1999), *Future Work—Trend and Challenges for Work in The 21st Century"*. Quoted in *En Guage, 21st Century Skills*, North Central Regional Educational Laboratory; available from http: // www.ncrel.org / engage / Skills / 21 Skills.htm; accessed 31 May 2002.

World Bank, (1998), "The World Development Report 1198/99. Quoted in Blurton, C., *New Directions of ICT-Use in Education*.

10

Shifting Paradigms: Opening New Vistas in Teaching and Learning through Information and Communication Technology

— Dr. Priyamvada Agarwal

Language use is a multisensory experience. So use of new technologies can assume a natural place in language teaching. Many developments in language teaching have evolved from a growing awareness of the different mediums with which we can work. Available technologies are Interactive whiteboards, Pod casts, Wikis, Interactive Practice Materials, Electronic translators, CD-ROMs, electronic dictionaries to word processing, e-mail, the World Wide Web, etc., which make it possible to present language in forms other than speech and print. Unmatched and unique opportunities are now available in the field of education because of Information and Communication Technology (ICT). It goes without saying that ICT can exercise a sizeable effect on the way teachers teach and how learners learn, thereby providing more ways and opportunities to achieve excellence in both teaching and learning. Inclusion and use of ICT in school at the elementary level in America and Europe have given wide exposure to children. The only idea behind that is to help children achieve excellence when they grow up. This paper is an attempt to present the role and importance of ICT in enhancing excellence in both teaching and learning, and a brief introduction of a few new technologies, which can be integrated into pedagogies.

There is no such thing as accidental excellence. Sure, there may be flukes now and then, but significant, sustained excellence is never a matter of luck. It is a matter of preparation and training. Preparedness, whether physical or mental, precedes any significant accomplishment. When an opportunity presents itself, the level to which you rise to meet the challenge of the moment will depend entirely upon how well you have prepared for it. Every significant accomplishment begins with the belief and expectation that it is attainable. Our expectations are vitally important, because belief and expectations drive the choices that we make. Those choices, in turn, drive the actions that we take. Those actions determine our results. ICT is a means to prepare our students. The importance of ICT convinces us to endeavour to integrate ICT in teaching English to the learners, thereby helping them to actually attain the desired goals. At this point, talking about how computer, Internet or other audio visual aids can be used to enhance language teaching would be little out of place. I assume now everybody knows as to how the same can be used to make teaching and learning of language an engaging and interesting process with the help of different aids. Therefore at the onset I will discuss why we should integrate ICT in our teaching with the aim of attaining excellence, and then in brief a discussion about new technologies.

Why Should We Use ICT?

Technology is concerned with "designing aids and tools to perfect the mind" (Brown, A. L. 1994: 12). Exposure and interaction are two important factors which help us learn a language. To be able to learn a new language, we need to listen to the language in natural contexts, and have opportunities to genuinely interact with somebody in that language. Technology in the classroom can make that easy. ICT can improve learning outcomes. By incorporating ICT in education, changes may be introduced in both teaching-learning methods and in content. Students can enjoy learning actively, such as by bringing the outside world into the classroom or by interacting with peers, experts and others. Furthermore, the students will have the opportunity to learn different skills. Information and communication technologies can motivate and engage students in ways not previously possible in new dimensions in: exploring and experimenting, thinking and working creatively, reflecting and planning, and creating new learning possibilities, and ultimately achieving excellence. Use of ICT can transform learning. ICT can not only make teaching and learning more effective and efficient but can also create new learning environments, and extend the depth and nature of learning. A number of international studies have been done to assess the impact of technology on education. To name a few: Kulik's Meta Analysis Study (1994), Sivin–Kachala's *Review of the Research* (1998), *The Apple Classrooms of Tomorrow* (1994) Scardamalia & Bereiter's *Computer Supported Intentional Learning Environment Studies* (1996). It is well documented through research that in technology rich environment students:

a) "Learn more in less time".
b) They like their "classes more and develop positive attitudes".
c) They "experience positive effects on achievement in all major subject areas".
d) Students have shown better "depth of understanding, reflection".
e) Technology based teaching even "encourages progressive thought, taking multiple perspectives and independent thinking" (Schacter, John: 2010).

Education, being the fundamental right of children, doesn't simply mean education for all but it also implies quality education for all. The best education isn't for the best few but for all. The principle of quality education can be possible when access to education and equity in education are improved. ICT can aid improvisation. It can:

a) Technologies such as CD-ROM, radio and cable television, or a mix of technologies, can be combined with the Internet to expand its reach. For example, community radio can be used as a gateway to the Internet for its listeners in remote rural areas. Regional/ international cooperation can reduce the cost of access to the Internet. The development of ICT has provided improved tools for learning through a global network, and wireless technologies enable developing countries with little telecommunications infrastructure to connect to the network (Majumdar, S. 2005: 06).

b) Enhance the quality of teaching and learning. Teaching and learning "involve a process of engaging minds and opening up awareness for exploration and discovery" (Wright, C: 2000), through such acts as: explaining concepts, illustrating principles, giving examples, outlining procedures, etc. Fundamental and most central to this process are talking and communication through languages. Technologies augment this teaching-learning process in various ways. Human communication, or teacher-pupil interaction, is central to the process of learning. To the extent that technology can facilitate and enhance such communication, it has the potential to improve pedagogy and the quality of education (Wright, C: 2000). Technology, in general, and ICT, in particular, is an aid to teaching and a tool in the facilitation of learning; it is supplementary to the fundamental process of teaching and learning. ICTs can enhance the quality of education in several ways: by increasing learner motivation and engagement, by facilitating the acquisition of basic skills, and by enhancing teacher training (Haddad, Wadi, D., & Jurich, Sonia. 2002: 34-37).

Teachers make the most intensive and systematic use of pedagogy to promote effective and efficient learning as part of the process of education. Teachers need a comprehensive bank of pedagogical skills and teaching aids, along with many other professional/personal qualities. Technology can play a key role in promoting pedagogy for the facilitation of effective and efficient learning. ICT offers new and innovative modes of learner-centred learning culture at all levels of education. It can bring classroom without walls and has deep impact on learning environments. ICT integration can assist in ensuring the learner's ability to relate their learning to the real world. Technology has an important role to play in helping pedagogy create holistic understanding of learning and integrating various aspects of the teaching and learning. ICT-supported education can promote the acquisition of the knowledge and skills that will empower students for lifelong learning. It can help them achieve "21st Century Skills which includes digital age literacy (consisting of functional literacy, visual literacy, scientific literacy, technological literacy, information literacy, cultural literacy, and global awareness), inventive thinking, higher-order thinking and sound reasoning, effective communication, and high productivity" (En Guage: 2002).

ICT aids in active learning. Language being a skill can be best learnt in context. Active use of it in various activities helps learners learn as they do and, whenever appropriate, work on real-life situations, making learning less abstract and more relevant. In this way, and in contrast to memorization-based or rote learning, ICT-enhanced learning promotes increased learner engagement. ICT-enhanced learning is also "just-in-time" learning in which learners can choose what to learn when they need to learn it. Technology Aided Language Learning can be clubbed with classroom activities promoting simple useful language environment.

ICT aids in collaborative learning. ICT-supported learning encourages interaction and cooperation among students, teachers, and experts regardless of where they are. Apart from modeling real-world interactions, ICT-supported learning provides learners the opportunity to work with people from different cultures, thereby helping to enhance learners' teaming and communicative skills as well as their global awareness.

Innovative Technologies

a) Interactive White boards.

b) Pod Casts

c) Wikis

d) Interactive Practice Materials

e) Electronic Translators

Interactive White Boards (IWBs)

(SMART Boards) can transform language teaching by making board lessons much more dynamic, multimodal, and interactive.

a) Teachers archive and share all their SMART Board lessons. They can instantaneously re-visit and review lessons from yesterday, last week, and last month to help reinforce learning in a way that was never possible in the past.

b) They are accompanied with a set of softwares that can help in using charts, etc., in the classroom.

c) Most IWBs are set in such a manner that Internet can be used on them.

d) Audio and video facilities are available.

e) They are accompanied with learner response devices, which can help students to either vote or write text on board.

Scott Thornbury is of the opinion that "IWBs help solve" problems like lack of motivation, "by providing a change of focus, delivering interesting content, and offering multiple functions (including an interactive potential) that can keep learners (especially younger ones) engaged and entertained" (Thornberry, Scott, 2009). IWBs are a possible solution to "the delivery-of-lesson-content problem" (Thornberry, Scott, 2009). IWBs deliver content better, arguably, because:

a) They are networked,

b) They combine multimedia functions that were once distributed across audio, video and computer media.

c) They are visual, auditory, and kinesthetic.

d) They are relatively easy to use.

They also promote a "heads-up" classroom dynamic, and (if used to their full potential) "they allow learners to interact with the content themselves, e.g., by manipulating it, responding to it, and even creating it" (Thornberry, Scott, 2009). One report on IWB use in primary classrooms summarizes these advantages in the following terms: "The interactive whiteboard is an effective medium for teacher input to the whole class, and for reviewing the lesson. The teacher is able to present from the front, and is better positioned to observe pupils' response" (Smith, H. 2001).

Pod Casts

"Pod casting has now become popular as an alternative way of providing 'radio' type content that can be listened to whenever, wherever and as many times as the listener wants. The idea that a pod cast can be produced by just about anyone with access to the Internet has generated a lot of interest in educational circles. In ELT, the appeal is not only in providing additional listening input for students, but that students themselves can become involved in recording and producing the pod cast" (TE Editor: 2005). Portability is the outstanding feature of pod casts. Along with it, it gives learners the flexibility to control it in terms of speed and frequency. Pod casts are an excellent way of increasing learners' learning time. They can do it either on the computer of MP3. They download the material from the Internet and can listen to the exercise at any time. It is in line with the modern trend in ELT, which attaches great importance to learner autonomy. There are various types of pod casts available, which can be used with students like authentic pod casts, teacher pod casts, student pod casts, and educator pod casts. It can be used in various ways in teaching and learning. For example:

a) Record lectures
b) Include external presenters
c) Evaluation and feedback
d) Learner created reflections and interviews
e) Interviews with notable contributors to a particular field
f) News or course-related updates
g) Short introductions to new subject areas" (Siemens, George & Tittenberger, Peter: 2009).

Wikis

Wikis are well suited for collaborative work and brainstorming.

Alike pod casts, it can be used for teaching and learning in various ways. Wikis are an amazing tool, both for a teacher personally and for his or her class. The ability to share information and grow information with a wiki is truly wonderful. And since a wiki can be sorted by page topic Ñ rather than by date (as with a blog) Ñ it makes it a very powerful tool to use. "Wikis, like any tool for learning, are limited in use primarily by the creativity of the instructor or designer. Common uses include:

a) Course notes
b) Course syllabus
c) FAQ
d) Collaborative writing and group work
e) Brainstorming
f) Inviting experts (whose work may/may not be the focus of the wiki) to review completeness of learner wikis.
g) Content creation with educators from other universities/ schools (Siemens, George & Tittenberger, Peter: 2009)."

Interactive Practice Materials

CDs are an excellent source to practise 'crisp'areas of language areas where there is a very clear distinction between yes and no answers. They are very user friendly for one can use it according to one's time availability and can get instant feedback. Pete Sharma is of the view that "The increase in the number of interactive exercises on CD-ROM and the web has undoubtedly benefited the analytical learner. Students can practise 24/7 and receive instant feedback. However, many teachers and material writers would argue that this kind of practice is based on an outdated, stimulus-response methodology. These grammar exercises 'skew' the language, so on-line practice focuses on 'crisp' areas of language at the expense of 'fuzzy' areas. Here's a good example of this distinction:

Crisp: Is 'I went there': (a) Simple past? (b) Present perfect?

Fuzzy: What's the difference between (a) 'I did it' and (b) 'I've done it'? (Sharma, Peter: 2009).

Electronic Translators

"These provide many benefits, allowing students to cross-check between bi-lingual dictionaries and mono-lingual dictionaries, and encouraging them to review language. Yet, when used for production, they seem to encourage the selection of the wrong word in English, and teachers can quite easily spot an essay written with the help of one of these small machines. They also inhibit fluency if students take them out in discussion classes – which they frequently do" (Sharma, Peter: 2009).

Conclusion

For centuries technology has been used by language teachers. "Comenius created his picture and word lessons in the seventeenth century for the teaching of Latin. We know that the forerunner of the slide projector was used as early as the eighteenth century, and even a bonafide language course using phonograph records, text, and pictures was in use in Paris in the early 1099s" (Price, Karen, 1987: 155-159). When used appropriately, different ICTs are said to help expand access to education, strengthen the relevance of education to the increasingly digital workplace, and raise educational quality by, among others, helping make teaching and learning into an engaging, active process connected to real life. Teachers are key figures in the learning process. Their influence is fundamental to students' progress. To achieve the desired results in teaching English (i.e., guiding students to successful second language acquisition), teachers have to be aware of and adhere to certain essentials. They also need to take into account crucial factors such as classroom atmosphere, classroom management, tolerance, patience and passion. English language teachers need to be flexible because language learning and teaching are dynamic and subject to change, not to mention the fact that there is no single way to teach English. Maintaining a flexible teaching philosophy allows teachers to accommodate the various learning styles, greater diversity and numerous goals students bring with them to classroom.

Consequently, good English language teachers should embrace or at least recognize the constant change in the field of English language teaching. Additionally, they should always try different teaching methods, use a variety of classroom activities, and strive to seek out new ideas. The new ICT has broken down old barriers of time and space. It has made it possible to generate, store, transmit, retrieve and process information and knowledge at increased speeds and with increased efficiency and flexibility. In short, new ICT has opened up almost unlimited possibilities, for teachers and students in terms of information flow and human communication.

Works Cited

Brown, A. L. (1994). The Advancement of Learning. *Educational Researcher*, 23 (8), 4–12.

EnGauge. *North Central Regional Educational Laboratory*. Retrieved May 31, 2002 from http://www.ncrel.org/engauge/skills/21skills.htm

Haddad,Wadi D., & Jurich, Sonia. (2002). ICT for Education: Potential and Potency, in Haddad, W. & Drexler, A. (eds.), *Technologies for Education: Potentials, Parameters, and Prospects,* Washington DC: Academy for Educational Development and Paris: UNESCO, (pp.34-37.)

Majumdar. S. (Ed.) (2005). *Regional Guideline for Teacher Development for Pedagogy Technology Integration.* Thailand: UNESCO.

Thornbury, Scott. (2009). *On Interactive Whiteboards (again!)* Retrieved January 18, 2010 from http://www.teachingenglish.org.uk/blogs/scott-thornbury/ interactive-whiteboards-again.

Schacter, John. *The Impact of Educational Technology on Student Achievement. What the Most Current Research has to say.* (n.d.). Retrieved January 15, 2010 from www.mff.org/pubs/ME161.pdf

Sharma, Pete. (2009). *Controversies in Using Technology in Language Teaching.* Retrieved January 18, 2010 from http://www.teachingenglish.org.uk/think/ articles/controversies-usingtechnologylanguage-teaching 18-1-10

Siemens, George. & Tittenberger, Peter. (2009). *Handbook of Emerging Technologies for Learning* Retrieved January 18, 2010 from http://umanitoba.ca/learning_technologies/cetl/HETL.pdf

Smith, H. 2001 Smart Board Evaluation: Final Report. Retrieved from http://www.kented.org.uk/ngfl/ict/IWB/whiteboards/report.html#11

TE Editor. *Podcasting for ELT (2005*) retrieved January 18, 2010 from http://www.teachingenglish.org.uk/think/articles/podcasting-elt.

Wright, C. (Ed.). (2000). *Issues in Education and Technology: Policy Guidelines and Strategies,* London: Commonwealth Secretariat.

Price, Karen. (1987). The Use of Technology: Varying the Medium of Language Teaching. In Wilga M. Rivers (Ed.), *Interactive Language Teaching,* (pp.155- 169). Melbourne, OUP.

11

English Language Teaching through Cinema and Media: Innovative Design

— Dr. Ruchi Banger

English language training has always been of great importance which always imparted language efficiency but, nowadays, this training is going to be modified, simplified and exemplified day by day. New technology is introduced in it so that the training of English language may be implanted deeper and it should remain intact and stable in the minds of the students. The popularity and utility of English language are not hidden as this language is the most established language at the international level. From this point of view, its training is considered to be of great importance. So the new modes and aids by which training can be interesting as well as useful are to be developed as a result of the need of the hour.

Through books, English has been taught for a long time but with the change of time, new ideas regarding training have been developed. It has enriched the training style and made a better environment for the persons desiring to learn the language. In the modern age, TV, internet, radio and cinema are being used as tools for learning language by drawing attention and interest of the persons. Though internet, TV and radio, including newspapers, have been in our life for a long time yet these had not been introduced as aids in learning English language. This approach is rather new but quite effective in the sense that its impact on our mind is deeper.

Talking about cinema, it can be easily said that it provides an environment which is required for learning a language. It can be made clear with the help of the example that the person who watches a foreign movie in English language, would be more familiar with its culture and will learn the language more easily than a person who gets knowledge from other sources (or lectures). Undoubtedly, the person would go deep in the movie, would feel as if he himself were living among all the characters of the movie and would identify himself with others. Their way of speaking, culture, background and mind will give the learner a better understanding of society whose language he is trying to attain; it results in the increase of level of comprehension on the part of the learner. Arbind Chaudhuri's approach in his article 'Cinema for Learning Language' may be considered to illustrate and support this fact:

> "While watching a movie we try to identify ourselves in the characters. We relate the situations of the movie with our life. Movies work as a magic on us. Watching movies is important not only as entertainment but for education and awareness also.... Movies help a great deal in language learning. Language learning becomes easier when you are in an environment where the language is spoken you want to learn. Movies provide us that environment. Suppose you want to learn English, you can do so by living in England for some months. But it may not be feasible for everybody.

Movies in English language not only provide an atmosphere and cultural knowledge in which the language is spoken but also provide the skill of how to deal in various situations, the character's different pitches, tones and manner of speaking, imparting them minor details of speaking the correct language. Though in their first attempt they may not understand the exact situation for it they must watch a particular scene in which they have problems, more than one time, and observe the punctuation and pauses which are also equally important in order to convey the message to others. The non-verbal expressions can also help a lot while understanding the situation and character. Learners must observe the syntax of the sentences and statements by different characters and with the help of it, should create their own sentences also. The following excerpt from the movie "Good Fellas" (1990) may be discussed further regarding language and structure of sentences:

> "What do you mean, I'm funny?...You mean the way I talk? What?...Funny how? I mean, what's funny about it?..... But I'm funny how? I mean, funny like I am a clown? I amuse you? I make you laugh? I'm here to f.... kin' amuse you. What do you mean, funny? Funny how? How'm I funny?? How the f....k. am I funny? What the f...k is so funny about me? Tell me? Tell me what's funny..."

The above inquiry in the movie was made by Tommy who becomes furious with Henry's comment on Tommy as a jokester, one who makes everyone laugh. Thus, the comic scene is replaced by tension. Learners can understand the use of 'how' and ' what' here, including the structure of sentences which do not start from the question mark but convey to the listener through voice of tone that he is not stating that 'I make you laugh?', rather the tone refers that in real he is asking a question to his receiver. Learners may practise the very structure, the tone in which sentences are spoken by the writer in a group and become familiar with it.

Movies like 'One Day a Man Bought a House'; engaging animated and brilliantly narrated, 'The Sandman'; dark, scary and gothic and 'Rabbit'; deeply moral and very cleverly made, may help in learning English and we can cut our imaginative teeth through discussions on different characters and situations. We must consider, that watching movies is not enough, for it imparts vocabulary, accent and listening skill but cannot provide pupils speaking skill until they open their mouth to speak up and brush up and brew their tongue to make themselves familiar with the English language also. English language learning does not require a mind full of content, it demands constant practice through the tongue also. We also know that our mind gathers ideas and encodes ideas accordingly. For better results, one can record one's voice and compare the recent recording with that of the previous one to check one's progress in speaking skill. Widely acknowledged is the fact that teaching English through cinema can be effective. Geoff Barton is also of the view:

> "When I started teaching in 1985 there were two things we did which we grandly called Media Studies. One was to compare the front page of a tabloid and broadsheet newspaper. The other was to watch films. And I still do both with the classes I teach."

If the learners are not familiar with this language they may easily be baffled by the movie at once due to speed, fluency in which characters are talking to one another. So it is better to watch the movie by having certain pauses for analysis, intervals for discussion, and to reveal the problem regarding understanding the language or any dialogue and sort it out. The movie for three hours without interval will lead to monotony and reduce the interest of the learners. These types of threats to technology must be taken into consideration and such an environment should be created in which each and every learner can take part and have his/her own progress.

Our affection towards cinema is deeply rooted and is not new. This interest can be effectively used in learning language. It moves us one more step towards the culture, the language and the atmosphere which helps us in learning a language. English movies or movies dubbed from other languages into English are of great importance, whether it is love story, thriller, suspense, comedy or story of action. It provides the learners to learn new words from different fields. They can use it in similar situations and move forward on the way to learn English language. A particular way to teach English through cinema must be developed by the trainers. In this regard Vilma Tafani's (2009) words seem to be useful:

> "This can be done in a variety of ways as setting questions about the film, promoting discussions in small groups, asking the student to comment on various things, inviting criticism, etc."

Her advice is also equally relevant that the film can be stopped time to time to ask students what had happened till then and about future story also. Though teaching through cinema is not without deficiencies, we can overcome these drawbacks with a little planning. If this type of teaching is quite time-consuming, we can curtail many scenes and plan according to the need and taste of the students and their minds. The flood of electrical instruments has made the language instruments and other such devices cheaper today. It can be the most powerful and attractive aid in teaching of English if it is taken seriously and students are taught through it under proper guidance. As they take an interest in it, they can be taught easily, and less chances are there that they may lose their interest while teaching.

Larry M. Lynch's five reasons for English language teaching through movies are worth quoting here:

a) Movies in English are widely known.

b) Movies in English are easily available.

c) Different movie formats are available.

d) The length of viewing is controllable.

e) Use of sub-titles and close-captioning is controllable.

For English language teaching, cinema may compete with other sources of attainment of language for it reveals a variety of situations related to vocabulary including facial expression, way of speaking and tone. Dr. Manjulakshi's (2003) approach to it is quite appropriate when she says:

> "The language of cinema, on the whole, is more accessible to the average person than that of other media. The movies, in general, make use of colloquial style of speech....The cinema, being closer to informal popular speech, has two advantages: (1). It appeals to mass audience, and (2). It portrays everyday situations wherein popular language is more appropriate than the more formal variety."

Both electronic media and print media are easily feasible sources to teach English language. Any kind of difficulty, regarding training of English language through them, must be sorted out to open the window through which the fresh air of English language may enter into the student's mind. Seeing the news on TV may give information but it also imparts knowledge of correct pronunciation, accent and many other things would be beneficial for all the learners. They can repeat what they hear, can concentrate on the different movements made by mouth in order to produce a variety of sounds. It can help greatly in training. When learners discuss in a group, they may come to know whether they heard the news correctly or mistook it. After discussion, they can find out their deficiencies and can overcome them at a later stage.

Junetta Gillespie's (1987) approach to television regarding language teaching in 'The Role of Television as an Aid in Foreign Language Teaching' deserves to be quoted when he says that it provides:

> ".....opportunities for the use of television, including: as a motivator: in teaching grammar and composition; in listening comprehension practice; in conversation practice: in pronunciation practice; for teaching literature: and for teaching nonverbal elements of communication (context, kinesics, and culture)."

More than other technical instruments, television is available at every place. Even the people of lower strata of society have it. The learners who have potential of acquiring this language but unable to afford other things can be benefited equally by it. The combination of audio and visual signals and signs will rarely lead them to misconception, rather it will help in analyzing minor details of the language. For example, if learners listen to the news reader, any song or music, watch movies and even a cookery class in English language, it will impart to them sufficient vocabulary in each and every field, such as politics, society, sports, business and religion.

Every field has its certain vocabulary which should be acquired to talk about that field. So, it depends on us that in which manner we have to use the things we have. Media and cinema, though generally called sources of knowledge and entertainment, can be used in attaining the knowledge of language also as being the cheapest and having universal grip. The potential of TV as an effective 'educative device' can be conceived of seeing the variety shown in it. Illustrative of this view is Manjulakshi's opinion:

> "Television is the audio-visual media having the additional advantage of being able to use visual cues to reinforce the information being presented in spoken form. Thus even in this field language education plays a vital role, because additional cues compensate for dialectal difference between speakers and hearers."

For learning any language, four skills—reading, listening, writing and speaking—are recommended. Training through radio can also contribute in learning English. As being the cheapest among all media sources, it can improve listening skill. If the learners have difficulty in listening to news through the TV or learn the language through it as their mind may be diverted by observing audio and visual signals at the same time and they can lose their concentration over it, listening to the radio will help them a lot, for here they have only to listen and not to watch. Their constant exercises may impart to them better skills which they need. It enhances learners' creativity and allows them to use their own imagination and learn accordingly. Drawing scenes in the mind by listening to the radio may help in improving the listening skill. Adequate preparation is needed in order to give maximum benefit to the learners. For some persons, radio is considered a more effective and spontaneous medium for its particular potential. Dr. Manjulakshi mentioned mainly two reasons for it:

> "Firstly, it reaches even the remote corners of the country and has no physical impediments. Secondly, it imparts language education and provides entertainment and disseminates information to both literate and illiterate listeners."

BBC London 94.9 (Greatest London Voice Output for Greater London), Asian Gold Radio (Sky Digital, Asian Music), Saga 106.6 F.M. (East Midlands Easy Listening/Oldies/Speech), BBC

World Service and Voice of America can help the learners easily by giving them environment of the language they want to learn. But it must be kept in mind that only by listening alone one cannot acquire any language, rather he must also speak what he has listened. But there is an obvious difference to keep in mind between teaching through radio and television:

> "Nearly all that has been said so far applies to both radio and television. But there is, of course, an obvious difference between the two media. On the radio, you are totally dependent on your voice. No amount of facial expression, eye contact, gesture, or any other form of body language will help listeners to understand, enjoy, or agree with your ideas. You have to be as lucid and as verbally interesting and persuasive as you would be if you were talking on the phone or to a blind person."

Books, magazines, pamphlets and novels have been a constant source of knowledge and transmitting information from one person to another and from one generation to another. This print media can effectively be used in training of English language also. Reading of a novel gives us a training of how to express our thoughts and ideas to another. Different situations and scenes provide the learners a lot of knowledge regarding vocabulary, how to express views as well as the understanding of the society which is equally important in acquiring a language. These are beneficial even for slow learners. If they have difficulty with the speed of the language spoken in movies, on TV and on radio, it is then satisfactory for them for they can go back to the particular statement or portion again and again and take their own time and understand it. They can move ahead only after having an exact understanding regarding the language written there.

For kids or children, magazines like Champak and other comic stories may work, can stimulate their mind to engage themselves in reading and through interesting comic stories, related to animals' life, which is considered their favourite, they can understand the language also. A story related to the life of animals, funny incidents and morality shown at the end is good enough to raise their attention and impart knowledge of language which makes them speak up later. The stories should be planned out in such a format that it can easily be understood even if children have less knowledge of language. All these things improve and increase one's vocabulary and may prove a tool to make skills in language better.

"Billoo Tomcat was extremely fond of eating milk cream. He even used to steal to satisfy his taste buds. The animals of the jungle were also sick of him for his habit. Many a time a needle of suspicion pointed towards Billoo, but he always used to refuse point blank and never owned up his bad habit.

"He always had a stock answer, 'I swear by my mother, I have not stolen anything. If anybody proves it, I will get my moustaches shaven off.'"

"The best part of his luck was that he was never caught red-handed. Thus despite numerous complaints against him, King Sher Singh was unable to take any other stern action against him."

After reading such an interesting story they would themselves like to discuss it further. If they are asked to point out the meaning of words like 'extremely fond of', 'taste buds', 'needle of suspicion', 'stock answer', 'red-handed' and 'stern action' with the help of the background of the story, they can understand it themselves also and if they find any difficulty, can ask their trainer.

Before choosing the medium of learning English language, one must consider his taste to choose magazines and its contents so that one can meet one's needs. Women, if they like, can choose magazines like *Good Housekeeping* and *Femina*. The accurate and exact language used here can be as beneficial as other things:

> "Rakesh Mohan, liquor baron of the Mohan Meakins Groups, is a die-hard foodie, food columnist and author. He loves nothing better than rolling his sleaves up and innovating in the kitchen, turning out mouth-watering dishes, rich and yumm.... There is nothing better than cooking for people and have them appreciate it." (Padhke, Vikram, 2006: 118).

Newspapers are using nowadays Indian terms in English language which we call 'Indianization of English Language'. Learners should recognize such words also as they can use while using English language also. Such is the expression here:

> "You may think that politicians top the corruption charts in India, but ask the parliamentarians—they have their own take! A recent survey, involving 100 sitting MPs, carried out during the ongoing Budget session has thrown up some interesting views. According to them, the babus, the judiciary and media should rank much higher than politicians when it comes to indulging in graft. Only one MP shares the aam admi's view!" (*The Times of India*, 13 May 2010: 8)

Novels depict the scenes with minute details. Each and every action, movement and work of characters teach the learners exactly. They acquire accurate information regarding expressions and it is all that the learners have to do after learning language. Teaching through novels can make their expressions subtle. They learn or come to know, without any effort, the vocabulary they are not familiar with, but according to situation, they can understand the meaning of unfamiliar word also:

> "Minutes later, she was back in position, with her binoculars fixed to her eyes, watching the water with a closeness of attention that reminded Kanai of a textual scholar posing over a yet unde-ciphered manuscript: it was as though she was puzzling over a codex that had been authored by the earth itself" (Ghosh, Amitav, 2008: 268).

Here the word 'binoculars' may be understood easily by the learners even if they are not familiar with it. Novels enhance learners' descriptive ability also: how to describe a situation, characters' minute action and even how to depict a little movement. The minor details we find in novels is rare to find out elsewhere as the creative writer observes each and every action deeply and is free to express it. He is not bound regarding word limit as the writer of news or magazines is.

Novel gives ample space to learn language and effective expressions through it. Illustrative of this fact that how minor details are given and elaborated in novel, which is difficult to manage in magazines or newspapers.

> "Jaya took the old concubine's hands, averting her eyes from the scalp visible through the sparse white hair, Kuki Bai freed her hands impatiently and learned back against her tottered bolster cushion" (Mehta, Gita Raj, 1993: 255).

"The man was of fine figure, swarthy, and stern in aspect; and he showed in profile a facial angle so slightly inclined as to be almost perpendicular. He wore a short jacket of brown corduroy, newer than the remainder of his suit, which was a fustian waistcoat with white horn buttons, breeches of the same, tanned leggings, and a straw hat overlaid with black glazed canvas. At his back he carried by a looped strap a rush basket, from which protruded at one and the crutch of a hay-knife, a wimble for hay-bonds being also visible in the aperture. His measures, springless walk was the walk of skilled countryman as distinct from the desultory shamble of the general labourer: while in the turn and plant of each foot there was, further a dogged and cynical indifference personal to himself, showing its presence even in the regularly interchanging fustian folds, now in the left leg, now in the right, as he paced along." (Hardy, Thomas, *The Mayor of Caster bridge* 2008: 10-11).

The character's physical appearance, his dressing manner and movements are finely depicted; and allows learners to have vocabulary which can enrich their language and expressions through words like 'fustian waistcoat', 'horn buttons', 'straw hat', and 'hay-knife'. But as it is clear already that reading is not sufficient to acquire any language for 'practice makes man perfect'. They should take help of such vocabulary in their speaking and try their level best to follow the similar language.

Learners may have difficulty in describing or talking about such scenes themselves so like above sentences from novel will help them in such a situation where they have sufficient vocabulary and how this type of sentences can be constructed and communicated. English language can communicate each and every situation and action if we know how to choose words, how to form sentences which can convey such sense easily. Learners may exercise to describe such little actions in their own words and learn how to select vocabulary for their specific purposes.

The pictures included in magazines and newspapers speak a lot even before reading the text; thus, it gives better and clearer view in understanding the learner and with the help of it they, undoubtedly come across many more things.

The newspaper is considered the cheapest medium by all in general but its benefits are various as it may connect learners not only with the day-to-day affairs but also provide them various contents to read and analyse the language written in it. According to their taste, they are suggested to choose the news such as if a learner is interested in sports news he will hurriedly pick up the news to read it. This interest will force him spontaneously to read the newspaper and will also make familiar with so many words related to sports. But learners are suggested to go through news related to different fields so that no field should remain untouched regarding vocabulary as each and every field has some different terms and sets of vocabulary. It assumes great importance as it displays affairs of everyday life pertaining to different and various aspects of society and its system right from the personal to the international level:

> "At present Indian language newspapers show a tendency to use simple and colloquial forms of expression more frequently....Now-a-days newspaper reading habit is growing rapidly and widely. Thus there is the steady and expanding process of language education through newspapers. The educated families in south India a generation ago made it a point to read *The Hindu* daily newspaper as part of their daily English education." (Dr. L. Manjulakshi)

It is a well-known fact that language is ever-growing and ever-changing. Time and socio-cultural differences play vital role regarding changing language. English language also according to the need of Indian socio-culture, has been brewing for a long time. Reading newspaper will illustrate this fact appropriately. Similarly important are the words of Dr. L. Manjulakshi:

> "Some thirty years ago, most Indian languages newspapers made special effort to translate words and phrases into English language. Now they tend to simply transcribe foreign words in the native script. This tendency is supported by the spread of cable TV as well as by the globalization process."

His further awareness and doubt towards newspapers' responsibility also seem quite sound regarding various uses of newspapers as it is not limited only to sensational and exciting news only:

> "The language used should be of high standard, aiming at educating the public not only in terms of news content but also in terms of language use."

They can repeat what is difficult to them in newspaper, can underline and note down the unfamiliar vocabulary, learn it and use later while constructing sentences or communicating in English. It is easier but undoubtedly beneficial for it is easily available at even personal level; so is helpful even if learner does not go to a training centre to train himself. Monthly, weekly, fortnightly, biannual, annual magazines can also help in this respect as the newspapers do. More than newspapers, magazines can provide sufficient material on specific field. According to one's own interest, one must choose magazines such as children may choose comics, housewives can choose magazines like *Good Housekeeping* or *Femina*, if interested in fashion. Magazines like *Business World*, *Outlook*, *India Today*, *The Week*, *Outlook Traveller*, *Digit*, *MBA Today*, *MBA Science and Technology*, *Business Strategy*, *Journal of Information Systems* and *Soft Skills* are easily available in the market to read and learn the language through them.

It is found that many learners prefer such magazines rather buying newspaper daily to read. Thus, this depends on particular taste or individual differences. As newspapers and magazines are nearly the same in context, learners should be given choice to choose between both things. Vilma Tafani seems right in saying:

> "Magazines are also sources in language development in providing pictures to stimulate verbal or written stories.....topic may be under discussion in a language class."

Today's market is filled with such magazines that provide one enough material to read and go through them to learn the language. So many types of conversations get published from time to time which help the learners the reasonable command over answering the questions. One such conversation here is between Edward J. Ludwig, global Chairman and BW's Noimic Bisurba in the *Business World* would be worth quoting:

> Q. Is there a larger plan it make India a manufacturing hub?
>
> A. Not immediately, But over times we will continue to expand. So may be over a period of 10years, we will call India a hub for certain products.
>
> Q. What is your pricing strategy for India?
>
> A. The simple thing is that we do not determine our process. This is a very competitive place, and the market determines prices, we just have to make sure that our cost structure and value proposition is appropriate, so that we can get acceptable returns. (Noemie Bisserbe, 2010: 48-49).

But if learners are not interested in business news, it may become hectic when they analyse language through such news. So they can move towards social topics which also create interest:

> "When people from the villages flock to Mumbai trying to make a living, they set up little shanties or slum pockets at various parts in the city. Hundreds of families would travel together into Mumbai and setup shanties wherever possible, these shanties had neither electricity nor water

> supply and absolutely no sanitation facilities. As time passed, these same temporary shanties were reconstructed, built of bricks and cement... while everyone comments on the lack of sanitation facilities for slum dwellers and complains about hygiene issues why they ' do their business' on the roadside; here's an NGO that actually makes the efforts to change the situation." (Outlook, 26 April 2010: 52-53).

So many other sections of the magazine can equally give better understanding of the language when learners read it constantly, such as cover story, regional news, national and international, health and care, banking, security and reservations. Short notes are also given with pictures which simplify the notes and help the learners or readers to understand it. Learners may also be asked to write such notes over any particular topic to enhance and in sharpening their language skill:

> Are you happy now, Arundhati? Some 76 innocent lives lost, thanks to people like you who glorify Maoist Criminals.
>
> —*Ashwin, Chennai.*

The above note published in Out look may convey to reader the sense Ashwin wanted to say to all. It is written in satirical form and tells us Ashwin's dislike for Arundhati. There is not much difference between a magazine and a newspaper regarding the language used in them. Learners may have either of them to polish their language skills.

In addition to cinema, music can also be introduced as language teaching source for it consists of both language and melody. The flow of music and its spontaneity will arouse learners' interest while the language used in the music will undoubtedly enrich the learners' vocabulary, understanding of the syntax as well as intonation and accent so that they can improve their speaking skills and listening as well. It will also keep them away from exercises or practices which usually make them tired. Music is of general interest for all and the songs of foreign movies which are in English language may help in creating the same environment for learners living in India and thus can connect them with their environment and emotions. It is seen, people generally do not speak in English even if they know the reason behind it may be that they feel alienated with this language while they may be deeply attached with their own language. To sort out this problem, music may help a lot as it can form the dais where Indians can identify themselves with foreigners.

It can be beneficial in this respect that the learners will attach to this language even on emotional pedestal and they will not feel alienated while using this language. Once, with the help of it, learners are familiar with this language and consider this language as one of their own language rather than the foreign language, they can be expert in it in a short time. But their identification with that of foreigners is as essential in English training as class study for it. Information technology is spreading its web as fast as the working of the mind. Having a mobile or collection of such music is not at all difficult today rather it is in our hand as soon as we think to have it.

One more beneficial aspect of learning English through music is that it can be listened easily anywhere without any restriction. For clearer sound, we have earplugs which can help us to listen the music properly even in gardens, market place, while coming back or going to the workplace. It can save our time, for we need not learn through it while sitting in the class only. The most important thing to keep in mind is that it is better to provide a positive and healthy environment before training of English language, so the learners may grasp this language and love it as they love their own first language (L1) and feel intimacy with it. The same emotions and attachment must be felt by them with English also.

As music is melodious and spontaneous it helps the learner to learn the language which he is not familiar with. The song of Cathy Bollinger may attract every learner to listen English and get motivated to speak it well:

> What do we do with chocolate milk?
> Drink it with a straw

What do we chomp a carrot with?
Strong and healthy teeth
What kind of food can not be beat?
Strong and healthy teeth
What kind of food can't be beat?
A juicy Green leaf.

In the above song, learners may be prepared to answer questions starting with 'what'. Difficulty regarding words or sounds of words must be sorted out, and students must be encouraged to utter it again and again so that they can be master it and the tongue may be glib for such words and language. The melody will not make them disappointed. Rather it will make them laugh if they do not utter or sing the song in exact harmony, and this healthy atmosphere will encourage them listen to more and more songs and make fluent in their tongue. They must be taught the variations, pitch and tone in which the language is spoken. It will impart to them perfection in English language. It is the need of the hour to add music as a teaching aid for learners of all ages like it and will also love to teach through it. Learners may be asked to repeat the song until they sing it properly. They can jot down the summary of the song also and discuss it with others.

They should be aware of the fact that so many words in English have been taken from other languages. Hindi is also as much part of it.The growth of any language depends on the culture in which it is spoken. According to Indian culture, Indian words are involved in English language to enrich the English language according to Indian culture and ethos. The word 'lungi' in the following words is illustrative of this fact.

> "Kanai burst out laughing at the thought of Tokir walking down the aisle of a jet, in his lungi and vest" (*The Hungry* Tide: 268).

But even in the present age, if technique is used in various fields from teaching to production, it is sometimes also. When print the media is the most trustworthy aid in teaching, technology may deceive at the very moment we start an instrument to train ourselves for the English language. When a teacher starts his class through the technical language, the instruments may not work well or even start at that very exact time: So the class may be disturbed and the planning of the teacher also. Vilma Tafani's awareness about it seems quite sound:

> "Using various kinds of Media in the classroom has always been a challenge, and how to bring these media in the classroom is more than a challenge, Students and teachers should be able to use in their classrooms different media through different technologies."

The computer, for its perfect technical capacity, can be used as a powerful source in teaching English language. It helps in getting rid of the clutter of papers and hard copies used for English language learning. Just with a single click of mouse, we can exercise so many things related to grammar as well as speaking manner. In this respect, Majulakshi's comment is equally agreeable:

> "They express the correct use of language. They operate at high speed and provide opportunity for rectifying and correcting mistakes and errors. Thus computer, mainly having literary merits plays a very significant role in language education."

> "One comes to know about the language, culture and life style of the people of a particular place by watching movie on regular basis. It will allow you to learn the language of the movie. You can learn the usages of words appropriately from a movie" (Arbind Chaudhuri: *Cinema for Learning Language*).

India is a country of diversity not only in respect of culture and religion but also of language. Learners, who want to acquire English language, acquire it as L2 after their mother tongue, L1, which may be either Hindi, Bengali, Tamil or Gujarati. It is clear that all learners are not in such circumstances that they can go to a foreign country, involve themselves in their environment and learn English. The very situation forces language experts to draw out other sources which can provide the same atmosphere to learn English which is required and acquired in the countries where English language is spoken. Cinema and media have entered into the life of even the common man: literate and non-literate for long. These can prove beneficial sources in imparting language training to the learners in India. Novels, magazines, comics, movies and newspapers are considered on the same pedestal in language as training that of the Internet, computer, radio, television and music. Each source, here, is equally important to reach the destination of learners: to acquire English language.

This study aims at illustrating the fact that each and every medium, for teaching English language to learners, has its own special importance in its own respect. So, if used effectively, after understanding the need of learners and by acquiring suitable solutions regarding problems in teaching through these elements, learners may have a positive atmosphere and acquire the language in its broader aspect to meet their needs.

Works Cited

Barton, Geoff. *Ditching The Remote Control*. www.teachit.co.uk.

Cathy Bollinger: "What if" (song), http.// www.songsforteaching.net/blog/12.

Chaudhuri, Arbind, *Cinema for Learning Language*, http.// www.articlebase.com/language-article/cinema-for-learners-language.

Farog, Amitabh. Right Punishment. *Champak,* June (Second) 2006:10-11.

Ghosh, Amitav. (2008). *The Hungry Tide*. New Delhi: Harper Collins Publishers.

Gillespie, Junetta. (1987). "The role of Television as an aid in Foreign Language Teaching." *Language Laboratory,* University of Illinois, Urbana.

Goodfellas (1990), http.//filmsite.org.

Hardy, Thomas. (2008). *The Mayor of Casterbridge*. New Delhi: UBSPD Publishers' distributors Pvt. Ltd.

Kahn, John Ellinson, (1991). *Reader's Digest* "How to Write and Speak Better", London, New York, 516-517.

Lynch, Larry M., *Five Reasons to Use Popular Movies for English Language Teaching*, Cali, Columbia.

Manjulakshi, L. "Indian Mass Media and Language Education." *Strength for Today and Bright Hope for Tomorrow* (Ed.), M. S. Thiramalai, Volume 3, 4 April 2003.

Noemie Bisserbe. "Rivals Pose Opportunity". *Business World*. 12 April 2010: 48-49.

Padhke, Vikram. "Food". *Femina*, 8 Nov, 2006: 118.

"Providing Concrete Solutions." *The Weekly News Magazine: Outlook,* 26 April 2010: 52-53.

Tafani, Vilma. "Teaching English through Mass Media." *Acta Didactical Napocensia*, Vol. 2 No. 1, 2009.

The Times of India, 13 May 2010: 8.

12

Globalization of English Language Teaching through Information and Communication Technology

— Lt. (Dr.) Satendra Kumar

English Language Teaching in India has come a long way from year 1880 when only a few primary schools used English as the medium for teaching. Up to 1940, the grammar-translation method flourished, and the spread of English remained confined to education and office circles, yet again in a haphazard manner. By 1970, structural linguistics started making its presence felt in Indian classrooms in the shape of drills and exercises. The experimentation continued with bilingual method, direct method and finally the modern audio-lingual method. Around this time, all professional courses began to be taught in English, which had also become established as a library language and a subject for independent study. As compared to its establishment as an autonomous subject in other English-as first-language countries around 1940, ELT emerged as an autonomous subject in India as late as 1980 (Naik S. Avila, 2005).

With the advent of the new technology language is also changing its face, style and its expression. Language is maneuvering the mind of the people through media. It is the most powerful tool of media to reach the audience. Media circulate words, sounds and images that surround us. It tells us who is famous—from movie stars to scientists – and gives reasons. News reports tell us who these people are in 'real life'. Fictional presentations such as books, movies and TV dramas tell us what people do and are like. At the same time, mass media get us wondering how we fit in; they may also encourage feelings of connection with people whom we have never met. Newscasters, textbooks and even advertisements tell us that we are part of a society that extends far beyond what we can see. All this is possible because of the existence of language; without it media wouldn't have existed too. Language is the soul of media. Without it, media won't be able to survive and prosper.

With the advent of globalization of education, English Language has reached the height of its utility. Its communicative capacity has bestowed bliss as global English. English has been used all over the world not out of imposition but because of its progressive power. Today, English is accepted by almost all the universities in the world as an effective medium of education. It is dynamic and flexible. Besides, it is difficult to find out proper substitute for English in the universe. It has been taught and learnt as a second or third language by the speakers of other languages. However, its significance having communicative and educative value cannot be overlooked. India is a very fertile land where English has been nourishing for 150 years. It came to India through our oppressors and sought a suitable place in the hearts of Indians. Gradually, Indians became intimate with English studies and began to learn, speak and write English. It took a long period for Indians to honour English as a native identity.

Today, English has become the fundamental need of the younger generation of India. They have understood the significance of the language in almost all walks of life. Considering the importance of English, youngsters, especially in rural areas, are curious to acquire the knowledge of it. They want to learn, speak and write English like that of the native of the target language. But their economic, social, political, psychological background becomes a major obstacle in learning English. They are completing their undergraduation in colleges located in rural areas of India. These learners lack primary knowledge of English because of the lower standard of teaching at the primary level. Many, anyhow, memorize the materials in English and reproduce the answers without knowing the meaning. Many do not know even the very basic grammatical rules because they have never had an opportunity to use full and complete sentences in English.

Effective communication is the lifeblood of human relationship. It promotes the spirit of understanding and co-operation among all the aspects concerned with this relationship. Effective communication has certain conditions to fulfil like clarity of message, consistency in message, completeness and adequacy of message, information, systematic arrangement of message, suitability of message, feedback, conciseness, correctness, careful use of body language, etc. Communication through English is the most wanted asset of the modern time. Good communication is the backbone of the teaching and learning. Without proper communication, the teaching learning process is futile. Teaching learning is a two-way process. Therefore, teachers and learners both have to communicate for this purpose properly.

All communication skills, such as reading skill, listening skill, writing skill and verbal skill, are needed. These skills can be developed and acquired through the help of word-building, English vocabulary, and knowledge of English grammar, reading habits, listening habits, watching movies/English programmes, and writing habits. But during the teaching learning process, teachers face many difficulties. The difficulties are of various kinds. It can be because of the lack of proper exposure of the students or the lack of proper educational atmosphere. Most of the students are from the background which is devoid of education and knowledge. Sometimes, they do not know the ABC of English language even after the completion of their school-level study. They suffer greatly from the problems of spelling, pronunciation, reading, writing and communicating verbally. Those difficulties of the students create problems for the teachers also who have to cope with those problems.

Language is the means for understanding easily and communicating clearly. It is the outcome of society. English language is a connecting language. The use of English language is in vogue. The English language plays a pivotal role in the development of personality and for the growth of career. People need it very much in spite of its great necessity. It is also difficult to have command over the traditional standard of the language. The traditional English language has a prescriptive grammar. It is full of complexities. The traditional rules and methods are complicated and burdensome. They mar communications. They are like a speed-breaker or anti-motivator. They discourage students from learning and communicating freely. Hence, the motto of teaching should be to capture interest, boost confidence of learners, and apply modern tactics and methods for promoting and developing communication skills with the knowledge of English. Though the traditional methodology is considered useless, even then it is helpful for supporting the backbone of the language. It cannot be ignored totally. The soul can not be removed completely. The body without the soul cannot survive. It is true that learners/speakers need to learn and speak easy, simple functional English.

They need fast methods of learning. The time promotes computer English/mobile English, but for the proper knowledge of the language, conventional English is important and useful. New methods of learning and teaching should be used innovatively, and novel methods such as body language, audio-video aids, mimicry, group discussion, dialogue-construction, enactment of drama, would be very helpful in creating an atmosphere for learning language and boosting confidence of the learners. In this fast shrinking world, learners survive and non-learners perish. Technological change in the learning method and access to information redefine the process of knowledge acquisition as well as skill development. Comprehensive technology-enabled learning solutions that serve the needs of their users in innovative, intuitive and inspiring ways are needed. It is the new and useful gadgets and equipments which help us do this.

With the fast development of computer technology, language teaching in a setting other than the traditional classroom is a promising trend and digital language laboratory will definitely prove itself to be the most effective teach-ware of language. In this era of information and technology, the teacher of English must be competent in using audio-visual aids. As 'change is the law of nature', the teacher in twenty-first century should shed traditional concepts and techniques of classroom teaching, and should adopt the recent and innovative teaching techniques. An audio-visual aid is simply a tool that enhances teaching if used aptly. Teaching can be made innovative, interesting and effective by various techniques and strategies. Hence, so as to compete with the other countries, the Indian teacher has to adopt such techniques and skills to change the socio-economic scenario of the nation. In other words, it can be said that such innovative techniques will assist in the betterment of the student's language proficiency. In this way, audio-visual aid plays an indispensable and significant role in teaching English.

Technically, a language laboratory is an instructional technology tool consisting of a source unit that can disseminate audio materials to any number of students at individual seat or carrels. A language lab is a facility where a student or any aspirant can learn and familiarize with the language with the help and guidance of a teacher through a system, to improve his/her speaking and listening capacity. The language laboratory contains one teacher (master) console with different switches representing number of students and switches for different functions. This also has a microphone and a set of headphones. There are sound and light indications for the student asking a question or raising a query. The student units have one request switch, one head phone and one microphone. There is a set of amplifiers and speakers with built in audio recorder to broadcast pre-recorded tapes and record students' performance.

The development of information and computer technology (ICT) — electronic mail, internet, multimedia, language laboratory, possibility to use collaborating platforms—undoubtedly, influences the process of using them in everyday classroom teaching and learning. Actually it provides a new possibility of using ICT in the modernization of teaching-learning process, and with its help to increase the quality of education and meet the requirements set by the contemporary knowledge-based society. In order to be successful in one's professional career, today's school graduate alone with the key competencies needs also the computer literacy. ICT no longer serves to be a simple additional means but ICT is an indispensable part of the modern and contemporary learning environment. In order to achieve significant results in the implementation of ICT in education, there is a need of state level strategic projects, the goal of which is not to equip school with qualities and uptodate hardware but mainly the pre-service and in-service training of teachers for the pedagogical interaction of ICT in the teaching and learning process. Integration of ICT in foreign language learning provides a powerful learning environment to ensure project-based activity and cooperative learning, and different interactions: students-students, teacher-students and vice-versa.

India is a nation with rich diversity. It is a multi-lingual, multi-cultural, multi-religious abode for a heterogeneous mix of people. This indigenous plurality and diversity gives ample scope for the Indian media to spread its wings and match the varied tastes, sensibilities and ethnic identities of its multiple communities. The unprecedented advances in interactivity and multimedia capabilities together with a myriad of emerging technologies have enabled the creation of virtual learning environments that could be utilized to boost the development of English language skills among primary, secondary and higher level students. The quest for quality is still on. This is the age of information dominated by digital technology which has influenced all aspects of human life. Education is no exception. Now technology is in the process of change from Digital to Photon. Shortly Photonic Technology will be available for the use of the society. At present majority of devices are based on digital technology. One such device is the computer that is an electronic device which has the capacity to store, retrieve and process both qualitative and quantitative information fast and accurately. The computers were never developed for improving quality of teaching–learning process.

But researchers started using computers for teaching purpose. It gave birth to Computer Assisted Instruction (CAI), Computer Managed Instruction (CMI), Computer-Based Instruction (CBI), etc. People started developing CAI for teaching different subjects at school as well as higher education level.

Networking of computers gave birth to Information Technology (IT). UNESCO considered information technology as "Scientific, technological and engineering disciplines and management techniques used in information handling and processing, their application, computers and their interaction with men and machines, and associated social, economic and cultural matters". According to Smith & Cambell (1982), a mosaic of technologies, products and techniques have combined to provide new electronic dimensions to information management. This mosaic is known by the name of information technology. OECD (1987) treated information technology as "a term – used to cover technologies in the collection, processing and transmission of information. It includes microelectronic and info-electronic-based technologies incorporated in many products and production processes, and increasingly affecting the service sector. It covers *inter alia* computers, electronic office equipment, telecommunication, industrial robot and computer-controlled machine, electronic components and software products". The information technology leads to development of websites. Government, corporate sector, educational institutions, etc. started uploading the information on their websites. It provides facilities for chat, e-mail, surfing, etc. It opens up a new source of information which increased the limitation of access to information. Prior to IT, people were using only the print material for searching information. It limited the search. This limitation has been overcome by the IT.

IT was limited only to the textual mode of transmission of information with ease and speed. But the information, not only in textual form but in audio, video or any other media, is also to be transmitted to the users. Thus, the ICT = IT + Other media. It has opened new avenues, like, online learning, e-learning, virtual university, e-coaching, e-education, e-journal, etc. Third Generation Mobiles are also part of ICT. Mobile is being used in imparting information fast and cost effective. It provides e-mail facility also. One can access it anywhere. The ICT brings more richer materials in the classrooms and libraries for the teachers and students. It has provided an opportunity for the learner to get maximum information. It has broken the monotony and provided variety in the teaching–learning situation. The ICT being the latest, it can be used both at school and higher education levels in the following areas like Teaching, Diagnostic Testing, Remedial Teaching, Evaluation, Psychological Testing, Development of Virtual Laboratory, Online Tutoring, Development of Reasoning & Thinking, Instructional Material Development.

It is a well known fact that not a single teacher is capable of giving uptodate and complete information in his own subject. The ICT can fill this gap because it can provide access to different sources of information. It will provide correct information as comprehensive as possible in different formats with different examples. ICT provides online interaction facility. Students and teachers can exchange their ideas and views, and get clarification on any topic from different experts, practitioners, etc. It helps learners broaden the information. ICT provides variety in the presentation of content which helps learners in concentration, better understanding, and long retention of information which is not possible otherwise. The learners can get an opportunity to work on any live project with learners and experts from other countries. The super highway and cyber space also help in qualitative improvement of teaching–learning process.

ICT provides flexibility to learners which are denied by the traditional process and method. Flexibility is a must for mastery of learning and quality learning. On the Internet, many websites are available freely which may be utilized by teachers and students for understanding different concepts, improving vocabulary, developing reasoning and thinking, etc. ICT can help in preparing students for SAT, NET, GRE, TOEFL, etc. It helps pupils learn in English by enabling them to communicate, edit, annotate and arrange text quickly and flexibly. It can help pupils to access, select and interpret information; recognize patterns, relationships and behaviours; model, predict and hypothesize; test reliability and accuracy; review and modify their work to improve the quality; communicate with others and present information; evaluate their work; improve efficiency; be creative and take risks; gain confidence and independence, etc.

ICT can be used to integrate speaking, listening, reading and writing. It enhances interactive teaching and learning styles. It also extends pupils' ability to exercise choice, work independently and make connections between their work in English and in other subjects. For example, ICT can help pupils use a wide range of strategies to explore contrasts, comparisons and connections dynamically; annotate text in innovative ways; enrich or broaden the context of literary study; see texts in alternative versions; use a wide range of analytical and critical techniques; sort and process text and data quickly and efficiently; order and arrange text and data experimentally, using combinations of word, image, sound and hypertext; save, record, edit and adapt their work quickly and efficiently; retain evidence of the editing process so that it can be examined; change the organizational structure and qualities of texts to suit different audiences and purposes; compose multi-authored texts; select from a wider range of audiences, throughout the world; exercise choice of medium and design while composing.

The English language was first introduced to Americans by British colonization, beginning in the early seventeenth century. Similarly, the language spread to numerous other parts of the world as a result of British trade and colonization elsewhere and the spread of the former British Empire, which, by 1921, held sway over a population of about 470–570 million people: approximately a quarter of the world's population at that time. This divergence between American English and British English once caused George Bernard Shaw to say that the United States and United Kingdom are 'two countries divided by a common language'; a similar comment is ascribed to Winston Churchill. Likewise, Oscar Wilde wrote, "We have really everything in common with America nowadays, except, of course, the language" (*The Centerville Ghost*, 1888). Nevertheless, it remains the case that although spoken American and British English are generally mutually intelligible, there are enough differences to cause occasional misunderstandings or at times embarrassment – for example, some words that are quite innocent in one dialect may be considered vulgar in the other.

Language teaching practice often assumes that most of the difficulties that learners face in the study of English are a consequence of the degree to which their native language differs from English. A native speaker of Chinese, for example, may face many more difficulties than a native speaker of German, because German is closely related to English, whereas Chinese is not. This may be true for anyone of any mother tongue (also called first language, normally abbreviated (L1) setting out to learn any other language (called a target language, second language or (L2). Language learners often produce errors of syntax and pronunciation thought to result from the influence of their L1, such as mapping its grammatical patterns inappropriately onto the L2, pronouncing certain sounds incorrectly or with difficulty, and confusing items of vocabulary known as false friends. This is known as L1 transfer or 'language interference'. However, these transfer effects are typically stronger for beginners' language production, and SLA research has highlighted many errors which cannot be attributed to the L1, as they are attested in learners of many language backgrounds.

English spoken in India is no doubt different from the English spoken all over the world. There is a great deal of regional and educational differentiations which operate on various phonological, morphological, lexical and syntactic levels. We all know that English was introduced to Indians when the British started ruling India. They searched for Indian mediators who could help them administer India. They established missionary schools and universities in India with English as the medium of instruction. There was also a point of time when people felt that English would lose its influence and slowly die. There were many movements raised against the use of the language. Many English writers and poets gave up English and shifted to their regional languages to vent their thoughts through writings. But by then the language had already built up a strong base for its existence. Indians soon realized that giving away the language was not going to help them in anyway. They realized the fact that the language was going to help them in many ways as Kachru notes, "English now has national and international functions that are both distinct and complementary. English has thus acquired a new power base and a new elitism" (Kachru 1986, 12).

Though it originated from British English, Indian English has travelled a long distance and in its journey, it has been influenced by a number of factors that makes it a unique language of its kind. Many people believe that Indian English is closer to British English. But I håve my own opinion on this. There was a time when I too felt that Indian English is closer to British English. This could be because the education system in India is an extended version of the schools and educational institutes set up by British missionaries a long time ago. School curriculum strictly follows the rigid rules of the English language. I still remember that for long the most popular book for English Grammar in schools was one written by Wren and Martin. I also remember the elderly people at our home stressing more on correct usage of grammar and structures. This could be the outcome of the influence they had, being ruled by English people for so many years.

But with the change of time I have observed that Indians want to break up the rigidity of the language and accept it in a way which could be conveniently used by them and serve their purpose. Going through the recent trend of using English language, I feel it is equally influenced by American English and *desi* flavours as well. The way in which it has been modified in India is something very remarkable. Customizing the language and changing it according to our need is an ongoing process in India. And the good thing about the process is that this change is very positively accepted all over the world. English has lived in India for more than 200 years now. It has co-existed with many local languages reshaping and modifying itself as a tool to serve Indian patterns of life. It has adopted the linguistic and cultural ecologies and evolved beautifully in Indian socio-cultural contexts. The natural consequence of this process is normally termed as 'Indianisation of English' or 'A Foreign Language in *desi* Attire' as I termed it. I agree that this '*desi* attire' does not fit the language in any standard variety – British or American English—but it has created its own variety which is beautiful, attractive and capable enough of gaining the attention of the entire world. Indians find this English in '*desi* Attire' as very much their own as it is also known General Indian English (GIE) - a mixture of both-British as well as American.

The first language we learn to speak is called our native language. As a baby, we listened to our parents or other people speaking and then imitated the sounds we heard. Babies seem to be born with an ability to learn the language they hear. Native speakers learn as children to use the right words and arrange them in the right order without even thinking about it. If English is our native language, we will know that automatically. In all languages we speak with air exhaled from the lungs. We draw it into the lungs quickly and we release it slowly and then interfere with its passage in various ways and at various places.

The air released by the lungs comes up through the wind-pipe or trachea and arrives first at the *larynx or voice box.* The larynx contains two small bands of elastic tissue, which can be thought of as two flat strips of rubber, lying opposite each other across the air passage. These are *vocal cords.* The inner edge of the vocal cords can be moved towards each other so that they meet and completely cover the top of the windpipe, or they can be drawn apart so that there is gap between them known as the *glottis,* through which the air can pass freely: this is the usual position when we breathe quietly in and out.[3] When the air comes from the lung it passes through three ways: the first, through the mouth which is called oral, the second through the nose, that is called nasal, and finally through both that is called nasalized. When the air passes without friction then we a have voiceless sound. On the other hand, when there is friction or buzzing sound it is voiced sound. The complete system is known as pulmonic ingressive air stream mechanism (CTE Notes, CIEFL, Hyderabad).

Consonants: 24

1. p i ¼Q½ as in pen /pen/ Voiceless (1) /*Aspirated*
2. b c as in bad /b{d/
3. t V ¼B½ as in tea /ti:/ Voiceless (2) /*Aspirated*
4. d M+ as in dog /dQg/
5. k d ¼[k½ as in cat /c{t/ Voiceless (3) /*Aspirated*
6. g x+ as in god /gQd/
7. tS p as in chin /tSIn/ Voiceless (4)
8. X t as in June /Xu:n/
9. f Q as in fall /fO:l/ Voiceless (5)
10. v o as in voice /vOIs/
11. T Fk as in thin / TIn/ Voiceless (6)
12. ð n as in this /ðIs/
13. s l as in saw /sO:/ Voiceless (7)
14. z t+ as in zoo /zu:/
15. S Ó as in she /Si:/ Voiceless (8)
16. Z t+ as in vision /vIZn/
17. h gS as in home / h@Um/ Voiceless (9)
18. m e as in man / m{n/
19. n u as in name /neim/
20. N .k as in sing /sIN/
21. l y as in leg /leg/
22. r j as in red / red /
23. j ; as in yes / jes /
24. w o as in wet / wet /

Vowels: 20 (Pure 12 (05 Long, 07 Short) Diphthong 08) All Are Voiced:

1. A: vk as in arm /A:m/ LONG VOWEL
2. i: bZ as in seat /si:t/ LONG VOWEL

3. I b as in sit /sit/ SHORT VOWEL
4. e , as in set /set/ SHORT VOWEL
5. { ,s@vW as in sat /s{t/ SHORT VOWEL
6. vkWs as in sat /gQt/ SHORT VOWEL
7. vkSWW+++++++ as in all /O:l/ LONG VOWEL
8. U **m** as in full /fUl/ SHORT VOWEL
9. u: Å as in fool / fu:l/ LONG VOWEL
10. Ç: vWWW as in girl /gÇ:l/ LONG VOWEL
11. @ **v** as in ago /@g@U/ SHORT VOWEL
12. V **v** as in cut /kVt/ SHORT VOWEL
13. YU vks as in sew /sYU/ GLIDING TOWARDS U
14. aU vkm as in cow /kaU/ GLIDING TOWARDS U
15. eI , as in play /pleI/ GLIDING TOWARDS I
16. aI vkb as in my /maI/ GLIDING TOWARDS I
17. OI vWkb in boy /bOI / GLIDING TOWARDS I
18. IY bv as in near /nIY/ GLIDING TOWARDS Y
19. UY mv as in poor /pUY/ GLIDING TOWARDS Y
20. eY ,sv as in hair /heY/ GLIDING TOWARDS Y

Relationship between Sound and Spelling

English language system exploits its 26 Roman letters for 44 sounds. Being no one-to-one letter sound correspondence the speaker is left high and dry – speaks one thing, others understand another thing. Confused, befuddled and humiliated one uses, misuses and abuses the pronunciation of words as per one's own whim and fancy. The confusion that leads to verbal chaos is stated as under:

The same letters standing for different sounds

a) The letters *ch* stand for different sounds in the words *chain, machine, monarch.*
b) The letter *u* stands for different sounds (or combination of sounds) in *cut, put, rude, minute(n), bury, university*

The same sound represented by different letters (or combination of letters)

a) The k sound is represented by the letter k in *kit,* c in *cut,* q in *queen*, and the letters cc in *account,* ch in *chemistry,* ck in *rock*, and que in *cheque.* Furthermore, the same k sound is also found in the pronunciation of the letter **x** as in *fox.*

b) The vowel sound found in the word *eat* is represented variously by the letter i in *ski,* e in *even* and the letter ea in *beat*, ee in *keep*, ei in *receive,* ie in *relief,* uay in *quay,* eo in *people,* ey in *key*, oe in *foetus* (Sethi, J. and P.V. Dhameja, 1989).

Advice to Indian Learners

1) The correct patterns of English word accent, sentence stress and rhythm should be maintained.
2) The consonants /q/, /ð/, /v/ and /w/ should be acquired.
3) The voiceless plosives /p/, /t/ and /k/ should be aspirated, i.e. pronounced with a strong puff of breath after their release at the beginning of accented syllables.
4) The correct distribution of English consonants and vowels should be learnt by the constant use of a pronouncing dictionary.
5) The English vowels and diphthongs should be given correct length.
6) Unfamiliar proper names should be clearly pronounced.
7) In vocabulary and syntax the normal usage should be observed.
8) There should be no elision of syllables.
9) The reading of a set text should be done carefully with proper grouping of words and avoiding substitutions and omissions.
10) It is very important to maintain a qualitative difference between /i:/ and /i/. Even the use of a short /i/ for /i:/ may result in confusion between pairs of words like *bead* and *bid*.

11) If the diphthong /ei/ is to be acquired, sufficient length should be given to its first element, but it should be reduced before voiceless consonants.

12) Indian learners of English should carefully differentiate between GIE /e:/ and RP

13) /ei/ (as in *bale*), and also between GIE /å/ and RP /e/ and /ei/ as in *bed* and *bade*.

14) It is also essential to distinguish between **/å/** and /æ/. This leads to confusion between the minimal pairs like the following:

(RP /e/), GIE	**/å/** and /æ/
Bed	bad
Set	sat
Met	mat
Men	man

15) During the articulation of /Q:/ there should be no lip rounding, the retention of /r/ in all positions will help you maintain some of the contrasts like the following:

RP /A:/, GIE /	a: / /ë/
Card	cod
Part	pot

16) RP /V/ is often replaced by GIE /@/ in words like *bus, cup, sun, dust* which must be acquired by continuous rapt attention.

17) The distinction between /A:/ and /Q/ (GIE /a:/ and /ë/) in pairs like *last* and *lost* should be maintained.

18) In Indian English /ë: / does not exist. Most Indian speakers of English replace /ë:/ by GIE /a:/ in words like *all* and *ball*.

19) The distinction between /U/ and /u:/ should be maintained as in *look* and *loot*.

20) The distinction between /Ç:/ and /A:/ (GIE /Yr/ and /a:r/ should be maintained (Gimson, A.C., 1980).

RP /Ç:/	and /A:/
GIE /Yr/	and /a:r/
hurt	heart
curt	cart

21) The substitution of /s/ for /z/ in inflectional suffixes should be acquired to avoid the following confusion:

fans /fænz/	= fence /fens/
peas /pi:z/	= peace /pi:s/
knees /ni:z/	= niece /ni:s/
fears /fiYrz/	= fierce /fiYrs/
keys /ki:z/	= kiss /kis/

22) The substitution of /^h/ (or /^/) for English /q/ should be acquired to avoid the following confusion:

three /^h ri:/	= tree /tri:/
teeth /ti: ^h/	= teat /ti:t/
thought /^h ë:t /	= taught /të:t / (Bansal, R.K. and J.B. Harrison, 1983)

Each language has a different script and sound, and in foreign language learning, one tends to hear and speak on the basis of the sound system of one's own language. One has, therefore, to resist the pull of the mother tongue and again one's habits of listening and speech of foreign sound through ample exposure and practice. The present research paper, given its scope and depth, is limited and contained. Yet whatever little it explored is round and sound. GIE, the offshoot of RP, is gaining grounds and is emerging as a distinct study. What we Indians need is a little ear-training and to practise the spoken words, not in imitation but in association, repetition and its own distinction. The tips are not comprehensive and authoritative, rather tentative suggestions. Practitioners with their own observation and experience can marshal their own ideas and can extend the best that is known and thought: that is sound and sense in the English language. Whether it is picked up as a hobby or profession, its beauty lies in the fact that it is a way of lifelong learning and loving.

Indubitably, English language is one of the richest languages in the world, in respect of literature and culture. English literature contains some of the finest utterances of life and conduct. In it we have the 'Authorized Version of *Bible*', the perfection of the English language. It is the language with which Milton tried to assert eternal providence, 'to justify the ways of God to Men', the language through which Darwin expounded his 'Theory of Evolution', 'struggle for existence' and 'survival of the fittest'. The English language has given expression to great social ideas and great political ideas.

The first requirement for any author to produce any form of literature is to have an effective language. India is a multi-lingual country where English performs the function of a link language. English was used in India and elsewhere in colonies as 'a road to light', 'a tool of civilization', to cultivate a group, who identified themselves with the cultural and other norms of the political elite. After the colonial period ended, English gradually acquired the most dominant role and maintained its power socially and administratively over local languages. Ultimately the legal system, the national media, international administration and important professions were conducted in English. According to Allen, "English is the world's richest language with a rich literature."

Education never takes place in a vacuum but is deeply embedded in a socio-cultural milieu. Thus learning is a matter not only of cognitive development but also of shared social practices. The cognitive and the social go hand in hand in classroom learning. The primary process by which learning takes place is interaction, more specifically, an engagement between learners and teachers in joint activities that focus on matters of shared interest and that contain opportunities for learning. There are a number of ways in which teachers can help enhance the subject matter-knowledge and assist students in learning English as a second or a third language from an interactive and a socio-cultural perspective. According to B.O. Smith, "Teaching is a system of actions intended to induce learning", and we know that in India English is taught both as a second language and foreign language; so teachers of

English language should make a great effort to induce learning about English language. The English language teacher should teach English in such a way that the desired goal of learning is achieved. But in India, teachers of English language face some difficulties. Due to those difficulties the desired result is not achieved.

Works Cited

Ankney, B.R., The Use of Computer Aided Instruction with Educable Mentally Handicapped Students. Implications for Administrative Decision Making. *Dissertation Abstract International,* Vol. 49, No. 3, 1987.

Balasubramaniam, T. (1981). *A Textbook of English Phonetics for Indian Students.* Madras: Macmillan.

Bansal, R.K. and J.B. Harrison. (1983). *Spoken English for India.* Madras: Orient Longman.

Cosmos, G. J., A Comparison of Computer Based Individualized Instruction with the Traditional Group Learning Method on the Arithmetic Performance of 11th and 12th Grade Students. *Dissertation Abstract International,* Vol. 49, No.9, 1988.

Dash, Neena. *Teaching English as an Additional Language,* New Delhi: Atlantic Publication.

Dewal, O.S. (1974). *A Study of Difficulties in Teaching English and Effectiveness of Programmed Teaching.* Ph.D. (Edu.), M.S. University.

Ellis, Rad. *Understanding Second Language Acquisition.* Oxford University Press.

Gatenby. *English Language as a Foreign Language.* London Publication.

Gimson, A.C. *An Introduction to the Pronunciation of English.* Chapters 7 and 8, Edward Arnold, 3rd ed. 1980.

Naik S. Avila. (2005). *Communication Skills.* Nandu.

O'Connor, J.D. (1980). *Better Spoken English.* 3rd ed. Cambridge: Cambridge University Press.

R.N. Campbell & H.B. Allen, (1965). *Teaching English as a Second Language.* New York: Tata McGraw Hill.

Sansanwal, D. N. Information Technology and Higher Education. *University News,* Vol. 38, No. 46, 2000.

Sethi, J. and P.V. Dhameja. (1989). *A Handbook of Pronunciation of English Words.* New Delhi: Prentice Hall of India.

Sheorey, Ravi. *Learning and Teaching English in India,* New Delhi: Sage Publication.

Stern, H. H. *Fundamental Concept of Language Teaching*. Oxford University Press.

Stevick. W. Earl, *Teaching and Learning Language*. Cambridge Publication.

The Phonetic and Spoken English, CTE Notes, CIEFL, Hyderabad.

The Sound System of Indian English. CIEFL, Hyderabad. Monograph No.7, 1972, (rpt. 1976).

13

WebQuest for English Language Teaching

— Dr. Vikas Raval

In 1995, Dr. Bernie Dodge developed an instructional activity that he called a webquest. This paper briefly traces the history and increasing popularity of the webQuest instructional strategy. His original definition left much room for interpretation. As a result, there are many different ideas about what constitutes a webQuest. The paper examines the webQuest instructional strategy in the light of selected learning theories: Constructivism, Robert M. Gagné and his nine instructional events, cooperative learning, theory of scaffolding and constructivism. The paper has also informed research findings of the webQuest project carried out at the college level. The paper points out the need for research in this area of growing interest.

Introduction

The founder of webQuest, Professor Bernie Dodge of San Diego State University, defines it as an inquiry-oriented activity that uses resources on the World Wide Web. WebQuests pull together the most effective instructional practices into one integrated student activity. These web-based projects use World Wide Web sites to help students develop problem-solving and decision-making skills. WebQuests are interesting and motivating to teachers and students. An effective WebQuest develops critical thinking skills and often includes a cooperative learning component. Students learn as they search for information using the web, following a prescribed format that focuses on problem solving and authentic assessment. A well-written WebQuest requires students to go beyond simple fact finding. It asks them to analyze a variety of resources and use their creativity and critical-thinking skills to solve a problem.

Definitions of Webquest

a) An inquiry-oriented activity in which some or all of the information that learners interact with comes from resources on the Internet. (Bernie Dodge)

b) A "WebQuest", as implied by the name, is an inquiry-based, on-line learning activity. During this activity students work in groups, dividing assignments among each other, so that everyone participates in a group-assigned role. The objective of the activity is to promote "transformative" learning outcomes, accomplished through the reading, analysis, and synthesis of web-based information (en.wikipedia.org/wiki/WebQuest).

c) A WebQuest is an inquiry-oriented activity in which some or all of the information that learners interact with comes from resources on the internet, optionally supplemented with videoconferencing (http://webquest.sdsu.edu/about_webquests.html)

d) WebQuests are activities, using Internet resources, which encourage students to use higher order thinking skills to solve a real messy problem. WebQuests are a sub-set of Problem-Based Learning (PBL) (http://www.webquestdirect.com.au/whatis_awq.asp)

It can be defined in simpler terms. WebQuest involves:

i) Giving students a task.

ii) To complete the task, using online and offline resources.

iii) Gathering and transforming information.

iv) Producing some kind of output.

The above process can be represented visually through the following diagram:

The three-part WebQuest model

KINDS OF WEBQUESTS

There are at least two levels of WebQuests that should be distinguished from one another:

Short Term WebQuests

The instructional goal of a short term WebQuest is knowledge acquisition and integration. At the end of a short term WebQuest, a learner will have grappled with a significant amount of new information and made sense of it. A short-term WebQuest is designed to be completed in one to three class periods.

Longer Term WebQuest

The instructional goal of a longer term WebQuest is extending and refining knowledge. After completing a longer term WebQuest, a learner would have analyzed a body of knowledge deeply, transformed it in some way, and demonstrated an understanding of the material by creating something that others can respond to, online or offline. A longer term WebQuest will typically take between one week and a month in a classroom setting.

ATTRIBUTES OF WEBQUESTS

The attributes of a short term WebQuest are:

a) Knowledge acquisition and integration
b) Making sense of large amounts of information
c) Typically completed in one to three class periods.

The attributes of a long term WebQuest are:

a) Extending and refining knowledge
b) Analyzing a body of knowledge thoroughly and transforming it
c) Creating a product that others can respond to
d) Typically completed in one week to a month.

Attributes of WebQuests are different from "scavenger hunts," a much simpler approach that is as old as the web itself. In a typical scavenger hunt, students are given a list of items they must find (answers to questions, for example, or instances of data) and are set loose on the Web. WebQuests are much more structured and focus heavily on collaboration.

The Structure of WebQuest

So what is a WebQuest exactly? WebQuests which follow the original model developed by Bernie Dodge and his colleagues generally consist of six parts:

1) Introduction
2) Task/Instruction
3) Process.
4) Resources
5) Evaluation.
6) Conclusion.

The following is the brief outline of each of the above components of web quest:

> *Introduction:* A good webQuest will begin with an introduction, which motivates the students, introduces the topic, sets the stage for the whole activity and provides necessary background information, e.g., *Hold onto your hats! You are in for the ride of your life! You are about to embark on a journey into to the world of English grammar - the most feared place in school.* Using the links provided, you will discover the meaning behind and new uses for adjectives, adverbs, conjunctions, prepositions and more

Task/Instruction

According to Dr. Dodge, the task is the most important section of a WebQuest because it provides focus for the learners' activities. In 1999, Dodge identified and defined 12 common task formats:

1) Retelling,
2) Compilation,
3) Mystery,
4) Journalistic,
5) Design,
6) Creative product,
7) Consensus building,
8) Persuasion,
9) Self-knowledge,
10) Analytical,
11) Judgment, and
12) Scientific tasks (Dodge).

Tasks are often the creation of a product, such as an exhibit, artifact or presentation. Tasks may also be of a verbal form such as a debate, play or any other kind of performance.

The instructions, therefore, need to identify clearly the steps the students should go through. It should provide scaffolding for organizing the information gathered during the activity. Scaffolding is a term often used in relation to WebQuests, and is, as the metaphor suggests, a temporary structure designed to provide help at specific points in the learning process. It can provide guidance on how to gather, analyze and organize the information, and it should help learners act more skilled than they really are.

Within the WebQuest context three kinds of scaffolding are indentified. The following diagram represents it aptly:

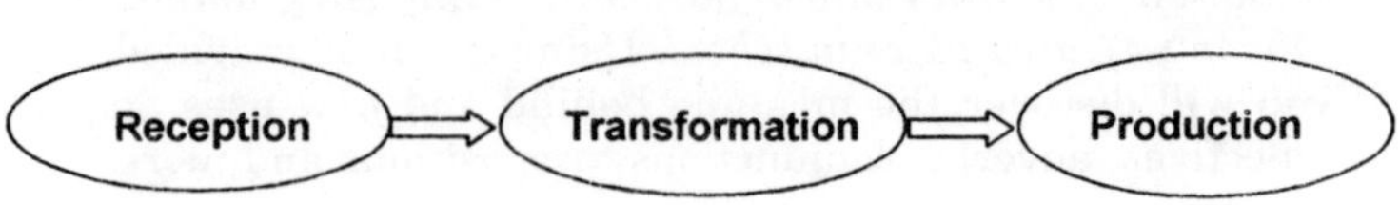

a) *Reception Scaffolding:* It helps students learn from a given resource and retain what was learned, e.g., giving students advice in using online dictionary.

b) *Transformation Scaffolding:* It helps students with transforming the information, finding patterns, brainstorming, or decision making, e.g., giving students a chart to complete with pros and cons for the different options they are considering.

c) *Production Scaffolding:* It helps students with the production aspects of the task providing them with template, models, writing guides etc., e.g., making judgements.

Naturally, these are all skills which the students can use in WebQuest.

Resources

The Resources section of a WebQuest provides a list of resources to assist learners in completing the task. Internet sites are pre-selected to allow learners to focus on the topic and avoid aimless surfing on the web. The practice of using preselected resources helps to maximize the use of instructional time and to minimize the likelihood of students inadvertently locating inappropriate content. Often resources are organized and divided by learner roles. Frequently, instructors identify a few Internet sites to provide background information for all learners. Additional websites are provided to specific learners to further educate them on their role or perspective. This practice helps to assure interdependence of the learners.

Conclusion

A final summary should set out what the students have accomplished by completing the WebQuest. This may also provide information on additional opportunities for extending the activity or doing further reading or research.

The Benefits

Here some of the advantages of using WebQuests with language students:

a) WebQuests are extremely motivational.

b) WebQuests are beneficial from a pedagogical point of view because they are challenging and they require students to be autonomous.

c) WebQuests involve exposure to a variety of forms of input.

d) WebQuests promote interdisciplinary work as the content may come from other areas of curriculum.

e) WebQuests are practical activities which provide students with situations in which real-life skills can be exploited.

f) WebQuests are a good use of time and resources, and encourage good organization and presentation of work.

g) WebQuests generally involve group work, which promotes team work and cooperation with others.

h) WebQuests can be used to teach reading strategies and to promote the development of reading comprehension. A webquest model developed by Maria Isabel Perez Torres finds a correlation between current approaches to teaching reading strategies and comprehension and WebQuests.

i) WebQuests enable students to engage with authentic material and meaningful content in the target language.

Designing Own WebQuests

Having read the above benefits of WebQuests it is better to discuss the way of designing own WebQuests. There are plenty of ready-made WebQuests available, which teachers of English can use. Simply type *Webquest* into any search engine and there will be a list of them. It can be saved to the hard drive by selecting, for example, File-Save in your web browser. It can then be opened in a text editor such as Notepad and edit the content. Moreover, the text can also be selected from the original web page and copy and paste into a word processor and can be given to students as a printed worksheet. However, many teachers prefer to design their own in order to make them relevant to their students' interests and abilities. There are several factors which need to be considered while producing own WebQuest:

a) The age, level, and linguistic ability of the students.
b) The teaching context into which the webquest is to fit.
c) The genre of the texts to be used
d) The content.
e) The linguistic and non-linguistic objectivities.
f) The available online and offline resources.

There are several sites that will help to prepare WebQuests with easy steps. Try:

a) *http://webquest.org/index,php*
b) *www.a-virtual.net/wq.*
c) *www.zunal.com*

At the same time, many web-based softwares are also available that help to prepare webquest instantly. One of the most famous web-based software for webquest is *zWebquest.* It is web-based software for creating WebQuests in a short time. *zWebquest* creates all the necessary files and puts them on the server automatically.

Before any teacher begins to use WebQuests, it is important to consider the following points:

a) Topic
b) The task
c) The process
d) The resources
e) The method of evaluation

WebQuest in the Light of Learning Theories

Robert M. Gagné and WebQuests

In *Conditions of Learning,* Robert Gagné summarizes five types of learning outcomes:

1) Intellectual skills,
2) Verbal information,
3) Cognitive strategies,
4) Motor skills, and
5) Attitudes.

He goes on to describe both the internal and external conditions necessary to achieve the various outcomes as well as offering suggestions on how to control the learning environment to facilitate desired learning outcomes.

Instructional designers using the WebQuest strategy may attempt to influence the learner's external environment to facilitate the desired learning outcome in much the way Gagné describes. Gagné recommends informing the learner of the learning objective, a common practice included in the Introduction section of a WebQuest. Gagné mentions the use of an advance organizer to aid in learning verbal information. Such advance organizers are often provided in the Process section of a WebQuest. Certain WebQuest design patterns and tasks may be more suitable to facilitate a desired learning outcome than others. For example, a self-knowledge WebQuest design may be used to assist learners in becoming aware of and even changing their individual attitudes.

Gagné offers a Theory of Instruction consisting of nine events. He correlates each instructional event with a specific internal process. The webquest format may be thought of in terms of Gagné's nine instructional events.

Cooperative Learning and WebQuest

Cooperative learning is a leading approach to classroom instruction. Individual students demonstrate increased academic success and increased social skills after completing cooperative learning group tasks (Stahl). The success of cooperative groups is documented in lower and middle elementary grades (Gillies & Ashman) as well as in college students (Soja & Huerta). In their nine-month investigation, Gillies and Ashman analyzed the group effect on individuals.

They found that structured tasks promote better retention and that higher-level cooperative tasks promote higher level thinking. They identified student interactions, task structure and type of task as important variables influencing higher performance in individuals. They concluded that cooperative learning was most effective at increasing individual comprehension, but interactive multimedia was most effective in increasing learner satisfaction. Traditional instruction was found to be less effective than either interactive multimedia or cooperative learning. The WebQuest instructional strategy combines desirable characteristics of both interactive multimedia and cooperative learning.

Lev S. Vygotsky, Scaffolding and WebQuest

Lev Vygotsky's theory emphasizes the importance of social interaction to learning. His "zone of proximal development" provides a conceptual basis for explaining the five basic tenets of cooperative learning: positive interdependence, face-to-face interaction, individual accountability, small-group and interpersonal skills, and group self-evaluation (Doolittle).

Vygotsky asserted that instruction should collaboratively engage students in whole and authentic activities within a meaningful and relevant cultural context. After encountering new learning in a social context, the learning can be internalized individually (Doolittle).

The tenets of cooperative learning and Vygotsky's zone of proximal development are embodied in the WebQuest instructional strategy. WebQuests foster positive interdependence with respect to learning goals, the learning task, assigned resources, interdependence of roles and the interdependence of the rewards. This interdependence enables students to develop based on their zone of proximal development when effective instructional designers provide stimulating activities and necessary resources for the student to develop (Doolittle).

Face-to-face interaction is embedded in the WebQuest strategy as students provide each other with assistance to complete the webquest task. To succeed, students must exchange resources and offer feedback. Individual accountability is essential as learners work to complete tasks. Each is accountable for completing individual tasks and mastering relevant material. Small-group and interpersonal skills are developed as students learn to work with others. Scaffolding instructions to develop skills such as brainstorming or consensus building assist in this development and encourage learners to examine issues from multiple perspectives. Finally, group self-evaluation allows group members, along with their teachers, to monitor progress and individual achievement. Scaffolding can take a variety of forms. Online scaffolding strategies identified by Bull et al. include visual cueing, separate pages offering instructions or describing useful processes, tutorials, help systems, advanced organizers, outlines, and flow charts (Bull et al). Each of these can be found in high-quality WebQuests.

Constructivist Theory and WebQuest

The founder of the theory of constructivism, Jean Piaget, suggested that through processes of *accommodation* and *assimilation*, individuals construct new knowledge from their experiences. When individuals assimilate, they incorporate the new experience into an already existing framework without changing that framework. The theory of constructivism suggests that learners construct knowledge out of their experiences. Constructivism is also associated with pedagogic approaches that promote active learning, or learning by doing. Webquest follows the following principles of the theory of constructivism:

Constructivist Learning Intervention

a) *The Nature of the Learner:* The learner as a unique individual.

b) *The Responsibility for Learning:* The learner being actively involved in the learning process, unlike previous educational viewpoints where the responsibility rested with the instructor to teach and where the learner played a passive, receptive role.

c) *The Motivation for Learning:* By experiencing the successful completion of challenging tasks, learners gain confidence and motivation to embark on more complex challenges.

d) *Instructors as Facilitators:* instructors have to adapt to the role of facilitators and not teachers, where a teacher gives a didactic lecture that covers the subject matter, a facilitator helps the learner to get to his or her own understanding of the content. In the former scenario the learner plays a passive role and in the latter scenario the learner plays an active role in the learning process.

The Nature of the Learning Process

a) *Learning is an Active, Social Process:* Constructivism strongly suggests that knowledge is first constructed in a social context and is then appropriated by individuals (Bruning et al.; M. Cole; Eggan & Kauchak). According to social constructivists, the process of sharing individual perspectives—called *collaborative elaboration* (Meter & Stevens)—results in learners constructing understanding together that wouldn't be possible alone (Greeno et al).

b) *Dynamic Interaction between Task, Instructor and Learner:* A further characteristic of the role of the facilitator in the constructivist viewpoint is that the instructor and the learners are equally involved in learning from each other as well (Holt and Willard-Holt). This means that the learning experience is both subjective and objective, and requires that the instructor's culture, values and background become an essential part of the interplay between learners and tasks in the shaping of meaning.

c) *Collaboration among Learners:* Learners with different skills and backgrounds should collaborate in tasks and discussions to arrive at a shared understanding of the truth in a specific field. Most constructivist models stress the need for collaboration among learners, in direct contradiction to traditional competitive approaches.

d) *Final Remarks:* A constructivist learning intervention is thus an intervention where contextualized activities (tasks) are used to provide learners with an opportunity to discover and collaboratively construct meaning as the intervention unfolds. Learners are respected as unique individuals, and instructors act as facilitators rather than as teachers.

Case Study – Improving English Grammar Through WebQuest

Regardless of the studies reported there is a particular area that has not been sufficiently explored which is the use of Web 2.0 tools and especially of WebQuest in teaching and learning English as a foreign language in higher education. The fact is that there is a lack of research into the implementation of a WebQuest as a language learning environment of collaboration. This study proposes the development of a language learning model which combines language learning activities with WebQuest projects that take place in face-to-face lessons and online in a WebQuest as a language learning platform.

Purpose of the Study

The purpose of this study was:

a) To test the applicability of WebQuest in teaching/ learning English language at the university level as an environment of collaborative learning that can increase motivation, participation, and collaboration among students.

b) To explore in what ways (to communicate, write in collaboration) and in what frequency the students used WebQuest.

c) To explore the potentials of a language learning model in second language course which combines WebQuest project. The results of the indepth study also aim to shed light.

d) On the impact of this language learning scenario (approaches and tools) on students' level of satisfaction compared with their prior learning experiences of traditional class teaching.

Research Questions

The research questions that guided this study were as follows:

a) Can the WebQuest be used successfully in teaching/learning English at the university level as an environment of collaborative learning that can increase motivation, participation, and collaboration among students?
b) In what ways and in what frequency the students used WebQuest during the *Improving English grammar* project?
c) Have the students faced any technical difficulties in using the Webquest as a learning tool and if yes how this affected the process of their language learning?
d) Can the WebQuest be used as an effective means of teaching/learning English language?

Theoretical and Technical Rationale Behind Webquest

"Learning is an active process of constructing rather than acquiring knowledge, and Instruction is a process of supporting that construction rather than communicating knowledge." (Duffy and Cunningham)

In this case study, using a constructivist approach to teaching, the emphasis is on a self-directed approach with the learner building knowledge through interactions with others in groups. Zunal.com (free WebQuest creator) has been chosen as a tool to support this learning language because it can be an ideal learning environment that fosters social constructive learning. Zunal.com affords the opportunity to offer collaborative, constructive learning more extensively in our educational environments. Constructivists believe that learning is a social meaning-making process, 'and that the interaction with other people is essential for individuals to learn new things. Regarding the WebQuests as the chosen type of web based projects, it seemed the perfect choice for the implementation of the Web 2.0 emerging technology in language learning. WebQuests are inquiry-oriented activities in which most or all of the information used by learners is drawn by the web. The researcher has chosen the following component parts of the WebQuest including an:

a) Introduction
b) A task
c) A process
d) Resources
e) Evaluation
f) Conclusion (Dodge et al., 1995).

In the Introduction, which is the most important part of the WebQuest project, the researcher has set the main goal to gain the attention of the students and introduce the activity, a real life situation. In the second step, the 'task', the students learn about the English tenses that will take on and what the result or product should actually be at the end of their WebQuest project. In the third part, the 'process', is where will be provided to the students the step-by-step instructions and guidance in order the task to be completed. The 'resource' part is the area where the students can find the hyperlinks that will explore for the task's completion. Finally, at the 'evaluation' part is where the researcher informs the students for the way that they will be evaluated. The researcher has taken the help of online rubric maker http://www.rubrics4teachers.com/ to finalized evaluation process.

Methodology

The case study was conducted at the Department of Mathematics and Humanities, Institute of Technology, Nirma University, Ahmadabad. It was part of a course named 'Introduction to Communication Skills'. The participants in this case study were vernacular medium students and basically students of science stream. All of them before attending the WebQuest project, had limited experience with technology.

Regarding their gender, most of them were girls (92%) and regarding their age, all of them were in their early twenties. Pre- and post-questionnaires, informal group interviews, teacher's observation lessons diaries, wiki's history pages were the instruments that were used to gather the data of this study. The course took place during the first semester of 2009–2010. The research was conducted over a four-week period during the last month of the semester. The course was divided in two parts. The first part included face-to-face discussion between the researcher and the students regarding WebQuest project and its educational use in the language teaching/learning.

The second part included the study discussed in this article: a series of English tense lessons. The researcher had divided students into different groups and different roles were assigned to them. Each member of the group had a concrete role to play separately in their project, and all the members together had to create and present a final work at the end based on the personal findings of each member. The tool that was used for the creation and publication of the webquests projects online is called *zunal.com.*

Results

Regarding the first research question, initial results indicated that there was observed a great collaboration attitude from the beginning of the study and a gradual increase of students' motivation and participation during the study. Referring to the second research question, the researcher noted that the students frequently used WebQuest to complete assigned works. They communicated with each other and their fellow students on their group work, for downloading tutors' notes or getting informed on the course's activities, more than asking guiding questions for problems occurred. As far as the third research question is concerned, students faced sometimes technical problems as using web 2.0 technologies. That affected them sometimes negatively on their procedure of learning because they lost time which caused them a little bit of stress. Despite all these problems, they enjoyed the experience, and they would like to experiment wiki tool in future classes too.

Referring to the fourth research question, it was found that satisfaction levels for the implemented blended learning scenario of the 88 per cent of the students were very high, despite the difficulties occurred in the use of WebQuest.

Drawbacks of WebQuests

The researcher and the participants observed the following drawbacks of WebQuest:

a) Access to Technology.
b) "Link rot", which, as the name suggests describes the phenomenon (where web links gradually become outdated).
c) To engage with authentic materials. (It is challenging to design a WebQuest for low level students as most published webquests are designed for native speakers of English).

Directions for Future Research

Research on the actual educational benefits of WebQuests is lacking. Although there seems to be an abundance of descriptive writing related to WebQuests, the literature is quite less when searching for research. Empirical studies needed to further explore the role that WebQuests play in building critical thinking skills and content. Are WebQuests more effective for teaching skills than content? With the growing interest in WebQuests, it is imperative that researchers explore ways to make it a more effective instructional tool. How can WebQuests be improved to better meet the needs of students and teachers?

References

Alm, A. (2006) 'CALL for autonomy, competence and relatedness: motivating language learning environments in Web 2.0', *The JALT CALL Journal*, Vol. 2, No. 3.

Dodge, B.J. (1995) *Some Thoughts About WebQuests*, available at http://edWeb.sdsu.edu/courses/edtec596/about_Webquests.html, (accessed on 22 July 2008).

Duffy, T.M. and Cunningham, D.J. (1996). 'Constructivism: Implications for the design and delivery of instruction', in Jonassen D.H. (Ed):

Handbook of Research for Educational Communications and Technology, New York: Simon and Shuster Macmillan.

March, T. (2004). *The Learning Power of WebQuests: Educational Leadership*, December, 2003, / January, 2004.

Dodge, D. (2001). FOCUS: Five rules for writing great WebQuests. *Learning and Leading With Technology, 28* (8), 6-9, 58.

Yang, S.C. and Chen, Y.J. (2007). 'Technology-enhanced language learning: a case study', *Computers in Human Behavior*, January, Vol. 23, No. 1, 860–879.

Clarke, J. H. (1990). *Patterns of Thinking: Integrating Learning Skills in Content Teaching.* Needham Heights MA: Allyn and Bacon.

Leinhardt, G. McCarthy Young, K. & Merriman, J. (1995). *Learning and Instruction*, Vol. 5, 401-408.

14

Information and Communication Technology as an Interface between Teachers and the Taught in ELT Class

— Dr. Sunil Kumar Jha & Dr. Rashmi Gupta

Introduction

The present paper pinpoints some of the interface areas between the teacher and the taught in English language teaching (ELT) class and further goes on to explain how Information and Communication Technologies (ICTs) have come forward to extend their supporting hands to bridge the gaps in between teachers and taught within the instructional system of the class. This paper also examines the unlimited potentials that remain mostly untapped in ICT that can better be optimally utilized in the process of planning, organizing, coordinating and controlling of ELT class.

English language teaching is basically set within an instructional system. There is a felt need to analyze this system incorporating ICT which is to enhance the productivity and utility of ELT class. This is a known fact that ELT depends by and large upon the formal as well as informal situations of the corporate system called 'a class'. Both teachers and the taught are part and parcel of it, and the holistic operation of this 'class' as a system is to give the quantitative, qualitative and also time-oriented output which is our 'knowledge product'. The optimal utilization of ICT keeps within its preview the understanding of the objective of the teacher as an individual and also the learning objective of the taught.

To have a better utilization of ICT we must gain perspectives on approaches, methods and techniques in ELT, and at the same time, we are to relate these approaches and techniques to our teaching situation. Where, on the one hand, behavioural objectives list the learning outcomes in terms of overt, observable behaviours, Expressive objectives talk more of learning by the taught in terms of cognitive processes which are less easily observable. The classroom being the first component of the teaching learning process the ICT needs to prove its validity in defining the interface between the other components called the teacher and the taught. To put it in another way, the classroom is the basic structure of the curriculum system and the 'players' or 'actors' or 'participants' of this milieu are the teachers and the taught. In fact, they are the grassroots in ELT hierarchies, the basic elements without which no consideration of teaching and learning can take place. The ICTs have to cope with the two basic perceptions in the classroom.

a) The perception which concentrates on the essential participants of the classroom, the teacher and the taught, their roles and their interaction with each other, and
b) The constructive ways of overcoming the limitations of a class 'room' through syllabus and methodological organization.

It is against this background that ICTs are facilitating the teacher and the taught in ELT class through a range of activities. ICTs have the potential to store, retrieve, manipulate, transmit or receive information in a digital form, thus helping both the teacher and the taught equally in sharing knowledge product which is standard English.

ICT to Meet the Dynamism of ELT Class

The classroom of ELT is to be considered as a place where dynamic action takes place, a place where both the teacher and the taught meet. Right it will be to say that it is the place where there is flux and change in activities and in learning. Traditionally learning in the curriculum has been organized in a classroom which is a room with desks and chairs for students and teachers and a blackboard as basic requirements. But with the intervention of the ICT tools encompassing digital and electronic devices it has added a very important dimension to it. It is under the impact of ICT that the basic essential value of the class in ELT has radically changed. The ICT is being exploited up to that extent so that a large, indigenous class rooms can be observed as valuable resources, and not as a constraint and handicap.

ICT tools in ELT class are helping the exposure to English in a systematic fashion, yet such hardware and software need be developed that may cope with the variables in the English classrooms. By variables we mean the different factors which teachers and taughts bring to their classrooms. These factors are:

a) Different language background and language skills,
b) Different age levels,
c) Different experiences,
d) Different thinking styles, etc.

Hence this need safely be mentioned here that the above-mentioned variables have dawned intricacies and complexities, thus making English language teaching a challenging task. ICT tools should have the realization of these complexities, and the methodology of ELT must change as per the need and requirement. It was in 1969 that Barnes gave a sample of the tools he had used for the analysis of classroom data. He was one of the first in the classroom research to point to the nature of teacher talk and student talk. Since then, the classroom interaction became the area of analysis. ICT tools keep within its purview this aspect of the classroom analysis which is known as classroom interaction. The IRF structure in the classroom is where the teacher makes all the initiating moves (I) to which students respond (R) and to which teacher gives feed back (F).

Here it is to be planned that if English language teachers make all the initiating moves of change of topic, of asking questions, of leading discussions, etc., taking the help of ICT tools and also giving feedback on the correctness of students responses via digital and electronic devices, then most of the interaction in the classroom will be teacher-centred. The use of the ICT tools in such a direction meets a great constraint. A question automatically comes: how much time do the students get for talk? If it is to cope with the English teaching practice then we think we have the least opportunities for the use of English available to the taught. ICT tools are to be helpful in increasing the taught's talk time, thus making ELT more effective.

ICT has taken so many innovative strides in the direction. Learner-focused practice materials and resources such as online dictionaries, information kits, etc., have opened a new avenue to them. ICT undertakes the responsibility to help the taught know how to use electronics, microprocessors and computers. Such coursewares are being prepared which are based upon different variables in the classroom.

In fact, the taught in the ELT class can get much effective treatment if it is understood that ICT is just a supplement and not a substitute. ICT is just a tool in the hands of the teacher to facilitate ELT. The personal touch of the quality English teacher has to play a decisive role. ICT tools have the potential to reshape ELT, thus ending the disjunction between teachers and the taught. By helping the critical thinking, team work and the role of the teacher have changed from being the storehouse of all knowledge to being guides or mentors and facilitators, who help students, navigate through the information made available by technology and interactive English communications.

The teachers have to help the taught gather and organize information, judge its value and decide how to present it to others. Moving from group to group and from student to student, they have to earn the acceptability of the students by giving personal touch to the ICT tools and their judicious operation in the classroom. To make the class room fertile and innovative, the ICT tools must help the systematic flow of information to be shared both by the teachers and the taught.

ICT Supports English Teacher in ELT Class

Effective and successful teaching in the classroom situations cannot be shaped as a thing of reality without a good teacher, and ELT class is not to be an exception to this rule. The attitude of the English teacher, his awareness of the various resources available to him, the drive in him to confront problems in the classroom are some of the prerequisites that must support the incorporation of ICT tools to enhance the effectiveness of ELT in the classroom. The attitude of the teacher to students, to what language learning is and then also his attitude towards the optimal and qualitative use of ICT tools are very important considerations. The quality of the teaching experience of the teacher is also an important factor that is instrumental. At the same time, the use of ICT tools must be made complementary and supplementary to the English teachers in understanding the problems of the taught, and solving them by following various strategies. The English teacher has to look positively at problems systematically. And, this means he is theorizing on the classroom. The thing is quite understandable here that the move that EL teacher takes towards theorizing is just the beginning of the development of researcher in him. Here it is that an English teacher is no longer a teacher alone, but a teacher consciously looking at his tools, his field, and so on and so forth, in a critical way.

The next very important point indicating the role that an English language teacher is playing in class is that of a resource find. ICT tools are the interfaces that can help the teacher form his perceptions on the learners in his class. His skill in adapting digital texts, his skill in using digital and electronic devices, his knowledge of grammar, etc., automatically add to his proficiency and efficiency.

ICT tools used by the English language teacher must encompass the three so important factors in the classroom situation, namely, the syllabus of English, the audio-visual texts designed in electronic mode for the taught, and also the examination system. How good an English teacher is in the use of the ICT tools encompassing the syllabus and text in the form of courseware depends on his craftsmanship. As an efficient crafts room, an English teacher should have the knowledge to design such computer software and handle them efficiently and optimally in the right place, at the right time, with the right pressure, etc. The matter is understandable here that to use the ITC tool well, it should be used judiciously. If ITC tool is used all the time it becomes quite boring for the teacher and the taught. In this case, the ELT becomes blunt and ineffective in the classroom.

Again, this may lead one to a paradoxical situation when it is said that too much dependency on ICT tools in handling the electronic text in the classroom decreases the level of the acceptability of the teacher. The taught find themselves in quite a monotonous situation. Therefore, the teacher should develop the ability in him to constantly measure the interest level of the taught. The software should be designed so that the activities and exercises are not adhering strictly to the English text alone. The taught must be given ample space for the deviation while making a search for the answers set against the background of the text. If the ICT tools are to increase the level of productivity in English language class there should be ample provision for the freedom from the hard constraints of the text.

The behavioural profile of the classroom consists of both the formal and informal mode of interactions in between the various components. The teacher and the taught are the two important human factors, in fact, the prime movers of all the components, including the ICT tools. The physical, emotional, social, intellectual and psychological make-up of both the teacher and the taughts need be harmoniously blended. To make a design from the mechanical go of life is the human tendency that cannot be neglected as a part of knowledge an English language teacher should share. True it is then to say that while handling the text aspect of ELT, the teacher should consider the limitation of the application of ICT tools as such.

The text designed in electronic mode gets the support of pictures and animation only to help the ELT free from monotony. The taught are given a chance in between to react to the text and here it is that the English teacher is not using it as a crutch but as a tool. As a good English teacher is known that various tools used by him in the class room are not to be his masters dictating their terms to him. Those tools in general and ICT tools in particular are to be used when they are needed. The texts of English in the electronic mode should not be displayed at the cost of the interest of the taught.

The other most important aspect of the teacher that holds our attention is the examination system. The ICT incorporates varied softwares which have the potentials in them to make the examination system far more productive. There is an ample scope for designing such software programmes which may cater to the pedagogic purposes of ELT in the classroom. The cognitive intellectual understanding is to be the heart of the matter. The examinations are geared to check out the actual learning taking place in terms of English language skills. ICT needs to be handled by the teacher so that more open, flexible questions focusing on English language skills of the taught may be tested and not merely on the component of the English syllabus.

In short, it can be said that the ICT tools and resources can be used efficiently by a teacher in the English class if they are honed, refined and shaped by him before they are ready to be put to use. This shaping of ICT is not just the shaping of the ICT tools, but of an English teacher too, as a master craftsman. The knowledge of the basics of ICT tools is quite mandatory on the part of the teacher in ELT.

ICT Extension to Support the Taught

The use of the ICT tools in the classroom initiates from teacher fronted classroom and extends to the taught making him the point at which the learning is made possible. This is no denying the fact that teaching is meaningless without learning, and ELT is no exception to this rule. In the classroom situation the taught is a very important component. It has been the general observation that the teachers in the classroom have their own emotional drive in them to make things happen in the classroom this way or that way even at the cost of the interest of the taught. Willy-or-nilly, they are working under the constraints of the syllabus, the course material, the limitation of time and space in the classroom and various other types of pressures working on them. They are found to be in such a hurry that the teaching becomes almost teasing to the taught. English language teaching takes within the purview of its consideration of this interface area with utmost care. Such ICT tools are being designed so that the interest of the taught may not get eclipsed.

In modern ELT perspective, the taught get prime consideration right from the point of course designing, lesson planning to the final implementation of English teaching in the classroom situation. ICT tools have come in handy to solve such a grave area of LT. The inclination of the course material is inclined mostly towards the taught. The focus is on learning. All the teaching activity is geared by ICT tools towards helping learners to stand on their own feet.

When we are to talk about the taught-centred ELT, our emphasis is on decision making. Educationists have come up with solutions. Breen and Candlin have formulated the opinion of autonomy in the classroom. The choice of the taught on what to study, when to study and how to study, is to get prime consideration. The taught are allowed freedom till they are themselves making decisions regarding the best. ICT tools are being designed to make things like that happen in the classroom. Thanks to ICT tools we have such an electronic system of networking where the taughts are the most active participants in the classroom activity.

The evolution of digital laboratory and other ICT computing and communications facilities have supported variously teaching, learning and a range of activities in ELT. The taught are helped to improve the IT capability of understanding of how information structured in a database. They are updated in using software, e.g., word processing or e-mail to communicate effectively. ICT in their varied forms are made accessible to them. The language lab which has a teacher track and a student track helps in effective implementation of communication. Standard functions of ICT tools such as intercom and grouping / conferencing / monitoring are built in to cover up the interface area of ELT. The English teachers are now made to hold a position to listen into a student's audio signal at any moment, without subjecting them to any pressure by standing over them.

In fact, the interface area in between the teacher and the taught can better be exploited in the ELT class if Class Digital Language Lab System is made with three main components: Teacher terminal, Taught terminal and the software for teacher PC, with all the terminals interconnected. The development in the field of ICT has made it quite easy to install such software for English teacher capable of providing all the features required in the classroom context.

ICT has gone up to that extent of making available to the taught in the classroom workstations for independent study. The files in the computers are present to them digitally so that they may work through their exercises at their own pace, independently of the teacher. ICT tools are today in a position to enhance learning rather than on teaching strategies. Still there is the felt need of ICT tools hunting for the resources to stretch the taught's capabilities, and to measure their success in rising to the challenges posed by the English curriculum. Much of the success of ICT depends on ICT training programmes that may improve teachers' as well as the taughts' ICT skills. The ongoing ICT initiatives have got a very challenging task ahead so far as practising ELT in the classroom situation is concerned.

Limitations of ICT Tools

Language learning in general, and English language learning in particular, focuses on actual learning processes that take place in the minds of individuals. The theories of psychology and linguistics help a lot in understanding the individuals and their cognitive, intellectual and linguistic posers. The English language teacher should have the understanding of the major schools of thought pertaining to the psychology of learning so that they may extrapolate and apply what is relevant for practical purposes. The major schools of psychology are:

a) Behaviourism,
b) Cognitivism,
c) Development psychology,
d) Affective psychologists, etc.

Psychological Perspective

The behaviour of both the teacher and taught can be interpreted in terms of stimulus and response. A particular stimulus may a give similar response of an individual. This is called conditioning. The law of exercise suggests that repetition reinforces the stimulus-response bond. The law of readiness established the necessity of attention and motivation for learning. ICT tools can help the teacher use different methods to motivate the taught to learn English language against the background of learning set so that they may give an explosive start. Asking a question, cracking a joke, etc., are some methods to achieve this set. Here the purpose of the English teacher is to capture the attention of the taught and to set the stage for the leaning process. To make optimal exploitation of the use of ICT tools in ELT, the teacher has to get the taught to a stage where they are impatient to find out what comes next. No doubt, at the same time the content of teaching itself and the manner in which this content is presented to the learner are also very important aspects of the motivation of the taught.

Cognitivist Approaches

The cognitivist approaches to English language learning have helped ELT in more creative and flexible way. The behaviourist principle that language learning is a matter of conditioning does not hold true in all the cases. The cognitivists have their different say regarding it. To them the learner of a language process has some kind of mechanism. The input to the learner is not just a number of utterances to be memorized and imitated but they are like processing data which allow him to produce other sentences. The cognitive theories of language learning stress the rule of insight, hypothesis formation and learning through discovery. To them, the amount of exposure is rather less important as they believe that very limited exposure to language data may be enough to provide effective learning. To them, the taught possess some processing mechanism which enables the handling of data effectively. It can be against the background of the knowledge of cognitivist that such software and courseware should be designed so that ICT may improvise the contest of ELT. The networking of the ICT tools must facilitate such cognitive approach in the ELT class so that it may prompt the taught to be creative in the processor language operation. So far as we know, the cognitivist regards all learning as discovery, or problem solving. The taught master the language by discovering all the correct rules for the use of language. The ICT tools have to work in such a contest. In fact, this is the interface area where ICT tools need to be adjusted to increase the rate of the productivity of the learning process.

Sociological Perspective

The ELT class can better be made operative as well as productive through ICT if some socio-linguistic factors exhibit in the classrooms. Such factors are mainly concerned with the taught. Linguists from Saussure to Chomsky have mainly a focused on the study of language and competence where the pure and abstract forms of language are studied. This is known as the linguistic competence. Quite different than that the sociological perspective of the ELT class is mostly inclined towards the communicative competence. The ICT tools must cope with the following factors relevant in the ELT class:

a) The learner must acquire communicative competence side by side with linguistic competence.

b) The learner of English language must not be inhibited by his/ her error. The ICT tools should be designed so that the learner may try to master fluency in English. Here the teacher's attitude towards errors committed by the taught for English language operation must change.

c) The taught must be aware about the complexity of life in a multilingual society.

There is no denying the fact that English language as the means of communication is not used in a vacuum. Knowing the grammatical rules but also knowing when to use, what to use and whom to use, that is knowledge of how the system is put to use in the performing of social actions of different kinds. ICT tools have come forward in this regard. Such computer programmes and software have come to limelight which help the English language teacher as well as the taught explore not only grammar of forms but also grammar of functions. English grammar of forms makes them familiar with the grammatical rules and structure to show how the system and subsystem of English language work. But the grammar of English language function puts together (i) the grammatical structure of English language and (ii) how these can be used in the broader social context. Because those who study and use English language are mainly concerned with how they can do things with the language, how they can make meanings, get attention to their problem and interact, influence their friends and colleagues. Such electronic texts need to be prepared so that ELT may exploit maximum benefit in a class contest. Such software programmers which are mostly against the background of the social aspects may be related to these problems:

a) Giving invitations
b) Making applications
c) Giving directions
d) Agreeing/disagreeing politely/impolitely
e) Accepting offers/jobs and so on

In fact, the software programmes must inculcate such items and material that may enhance the communicative competence. The knowledge of the grammar and vocabulary of English language, rules of speaking, how to use and respond to different types of language appropriately can help the linguistic competence of the taught.

Conclusion

Many changes have taken place in practising and using ICT for English language learning and teaching. Gone are those early days of the microcomputer when both the teacher and the taught did not have a great deal of choice in the range of software. Earlier such programmes were not available sufficient to catch up with the interface area of ELT in the classroom situations. The texts of the software were found dry and not too capable of exploiting the English teaching resources in the class. Only multiple–choice and gap-filling exercises were there to trap the attention and zeal of the taught in the English class. Audio and video were not available. The network system was also very poor.

But the twenty-first century has already welcomed such ICT tools that may cover up the maximum of the time space and activities in the classroom. We have already made available for us excellent whiteboards and associated software. Ranges of so-called web tools have appeared that are useful for the production of language. But the major recommendations are (a) both the teachers and the taught in ELT classes should have access to ICT tools (b) the English teachers should update themselves with the latest innovations taking place in methods and materials, and also practise English teaching areas (c) the ICT tools must bring to them innovations catering to the needs and requirement of the classroom. Maximum accessibility to ICT and appropriate use of interactivity in English Language class using standard ICT tools is the demand of the time.

Works Cited

Anderson, Anne and Tony Lynch. (1988). *Listening*. Oxford University Press.

Anderson, J.R. (1985). *Cognitive Psychology and its Implications* (2nd Ed.). New York: W.H. Freem and Co.

Britton, James. (1975). *Teaching Writing in Davies, A Problems of Language and Learning*. London: Heinemann.

Geddes, Marion. (1988). *How to Listen*. London: BBC.

Ghosh, R.N. and B.K. Das. (1973). "Teaching the Skills of Reading" in *The Methods of Teaching English*. Hyderabad: CIEFL.

http://www.unescobkk.org/filea domin/user upload/let/e.

http://www.ictrdf.org.pk/fp-aeltt.htm

http://www.callandthelearner.info/

http://europe.univ-lyon2.fr/teacher-education-in-CALL/topic1/index.html

http://www.bbc.co.uk/schools/gcsebitesize/business/production/methodsofproductionrev1.shtml

http://ec.europa.eu/education/policies/lang/doc/ict.pdf

http://ec.europa.eu/education/policies/lang/doc/ict.pdf

http://www.slideshare.net/teacher_sofia/icts-advantages-and-disadvantages-in-elt

http://netla.khi.is/greinar/2004/009/index.htm

http://oswaldoipc.wordpress.com/

http://www.academypublisher.com/ojs/index.php/jltr/article/viewFile/0103211214/1799

http://www.crulp.org/research/Project-Details/Aelt.htm

http://www.mcgrawhill.com.sg/elt/catalog/ELTAsia2010/ELT_Asia_2010_classroom_prof_resources_(158-169)bind.pdf

Mc Arthur, T. (1983). *A Foundation Course for language Teachers*, Cambridge: Cambridge University Press.

Richards, J. C. (1990). *The Language Teaching Matrix.* Cambridge: Cambridge University Press.

Srivastava, R.N. (1980). "Societal bilingualism and language Teaching in India", *Indian Journal of Applied Linguistics.*

Sterr, H.H. (1983). *Fundamental Concepts of Language Teaching.* OUP.

15

Envisaging the Pedagogical Implications for the Oral Presentations in EFL Classrooms

— Vikrant Sehgal

Introduction

This paper outlines a study that explores what factors EFL learners consider to be important when making presentations. Three hundred and four undergraduate students were surveyed at a large private university in India. A 30-item questionnaire was used to discover what components are considered to be important to learners in doing effective English presentations. Descriptive statistics and principal component analysis were used to analyze the results of the data. The results indicate that the participants consider the following three factors as the major criteria for effective English oral presentations: clarity of speech and voice quality; correctness of language; and interaction with the audience. Based on the outcome of the study, this paper further delineates the pedagogical implications for oral presentations in EFL.

As an alternative form of assessment, peer assessment has been utilized in oral presentation activities in various educational contexts (Boud, Cohen & Sampson, 1999; Patri, 2002). Echoing the concept of a student-centred approach to instruction, students can take an active role in their own language learning through the use of peer assessment activities. Opposed to teacher-only assessment, oral performances can also be evaluated from the views of learners' peers. Obtaining feedback from peers is vital to communicative language learning situations like oral presentations because of the notion of interaction between learners (Earl, 1986; Rust, Price & O'Donovan, 2003). Furthermore, students can achieve a higher level of learning through interaction with their peers and instructors (Earl, 1986; Rust et al., 2003).

Thus, peer assessment is considered an important activity to develop students' learning, and to facilitate autonomy among learners. In most classrooms, however, the assessment criteria are already established by the classroom teacher, with students' ideas not incorporated into these pre-existing rubrics. This lack of student input might lead to a low reliability of peer assessment. Because students are not well aware of the description of each evaluation criterion, some students might not be able to assess their peers' performances properly. As a result, their views might be different from those of their instructor. Additionally, pre-existing criteria might deprive students of the afore-mentioned benefit of increased autonomy from peer assessment activities because they are not involved with establishing the criteria.

Therefore, it is useful to explore students' views of which aspects of oral presentations are most effective which, as a result, will become the criteria of peer assessment activities. In doing so, instructors will find out what aspects of oral presentation students consider important. Defining and creating the evaluation rubric together with their instructor, learners will gain more responsibility for their learning as well as to improve the reliability of the peer assessment activities themselves.

The present study explores exactly which aspects of oral presentations Indian university students view to be most effective. Incorporating students' ideas while establishing the criteria for presentations is an important factor when considering a learner-centred approach in EFL classes. Therefore, this paper will suggest specific ideas as to how to carry out oral presentation activities using student-established evaluation criteria. A description of Indian university students' views on effective presentations will yield valuable data both for oral presentation activities and their assessment. A secondary aim of the research is to suggest a set of specific recommendations to improve peer assessment activities for oral presentations in ES/FL classrooms.

To summarize the above, the primary focus of this research is as follows: to make learners more cognizant of the importance of presentation skills in English; to get learners more involved in the evaluation process; to urge learners to think about the criteria that form an effective presentation; to have learners involved in the formulation of the evaluation criteria; and have learners receive evaluation from their peers as well as reflect critically on this method of measurement and how it effects their own oral presentations. It should be noted that this paper should not be considered exclusive to the Indian context. In fact, the fundamental concepts and results of this paper can be applied to most Asian contexts and beyond.

Review of the Literature

There has been a marked increase in the popularity of peer-evaluation activities in EFL classes (Cheng & Warren, 2005; Finch, 2003; Hadley, 2001; Johnson & Johnson, 1999; King, 2002) due to the increasing number of teachers emphasizing the importance of communication skills in the classroom (Hadley, 2001; King, 2002; Nunan, 2002; Richards & Rodgers, 2001). Thus, teachers need to become more cognizant of the principles and methods of peer evaluation. EFL students, especially in business fields, are well aware of the impact of competent presentation skills in English. In fact, students who are preparing for the working world tend to take presentation classes as a part of their regular degree programmes (Nakamura, 2002). However, to date, most of the work in peer evaluation has been done in ESL and EFL writing classes (see Duke & Sanchez, 1994; Hedgcock & Leftkowitz, 1992; Pica, 1984; Lalande, 1982; Zamel, 1985), so a more thorough look at peer assessment for EFL oral presentations is warranted. Advocates of peer assessment highlight learner autonomy as one of the benefits of conducting this type of evaluation (Cheng & Warren, 2005; Johnson & Johnson, 1999), as each student takes responsibility for his or her own active learning (Cheng & Warren, 2005; Patri, 2002).

Thus, learners can become more cognizant of exactly what they are learning through peer assessment activities. In addition, there is a general consensus that involving students in their own correction is helpful in developing skills useful in academic life (Cheng & Warren, 2005) and enhancing interpersonal relationships among learners (Earl, 1986). A combination of teacher-, peer-, and self-evaluation seems to yield the most successful results (Bachman & Palmer, 1989; Hadley, 2001; Hedgcock & Lefkowitz, 1982; Lalande, 1982). However, in spite of the usefulness and reliability of peer evaluation (Freeman, 1995; Hughes & Large, 1993; Patri, 2002), it remains an area of EFL that has not been well researched, as seen in the dearth of theoretical and empirical studies published in this emerging field of study (Patri, 2002).

Zamel (1985) maintains that teachers' feedback on ESL compositions is at times inconsistent. Cohen (1985) suggests that teachers' comments on student work are confusing and vague, while Truscott (1996) came up with similar results stating that teachers should abandon correcting student errors altogether. Hedgcock and Leftkowitz (1982) state that more attention is paid to content and organization in peer-evaluated work, two very important elements in the evaluation of oral work. Indeed, it seems teachers tend to focus on form and accuracy when marking, so getting learners to conduct peer-evaluation has the potential of circumventing this problem. The problems of traditional feedback methods found by these researchers clearly have implications for the classroom, and points to the need for a more useful evaluation method. Peer evaluation offers a remedy for these problems.

Although teachers will always feel the need to correct their learners' work, a balance needs to be found between teacher-assessed work and work that is peer-evaluated. In a traditional teacher-centred classroom, students tend to adopt a passive attitude toward the assessment of their oral performances because they are being rated by a single person: the teacher. Further, the evaluation criteria are usually set by the teacher, so learners have no input into the grades they receive. One method around this is to have learners involved in the creation of the assessment rubrics to be used in class (Patri, 2002).

This evidence points to the fact that it is the type of feedback given to learners that is of ultimate importance. Peer-evaluation gives the benefit of learners learning from their peers, while being actively involved in their classmates' work (Birdsong & Sharplin, 1986; Cheng & Warren, 2005). Indeed, peer-evaluation tends to have a double-pronged effect: it helps the evaluator notice errors, and also assists the presenter in learning where he or she can improve.

Another related factor is the possibility that students not trained in the art of peer evaluation may demonstrate problems that have been outlined in literature. For example, previous studies have indicated that certain biases – such as friendship bias – may exist when learners evaluate their peers (Dochy, Segers & Sluijsmans, 1999; Falchikov, 1995; Morahan-Martin, 1996). If learners are explicitly taught the form and practice of peer evaluations, this problem can be remedied quite easily (Finch, 2003; Jacobs, 1987; Newkirk, 1984). Therefore, giving our learners the correct tools to undertake peer-evaluation activities has the potential to greatly enhance the reliability and usefulness of such activities.

Oral presentation assessment criteria consist of multi-faceted factors: language, content, delivery, and visual aids. It is incumbent among teachers to clearly delineate these factors to their learners before undertaking any peer assessment activities in class. In a classroom setting, the criteria for assessment are usually established by the teacher, who also has the responsibility of judging students' presentation performances. However, this single rater practice raises reliability issues (Bachman & Palmer, 1989). As such, there is a good possibility that an instructor's assessment is not objective or consistent enough to meet the needs of his or her learners. The consensus among researchers is that if learners are explicitly aware of the criteria used to assess them they will be better able to apply the method of evaluation to their own learning styles, and thereby to their own benefit as learners (Rust et al., 2003).

Further, students are able to comprehend and critically assess marking criteria that they have a hand in making, and have more difficulty comprehending marking criteria that are imposed on them by teachers (Orsmond, Merry & Reiling, 2000). The development of the criteria is just as important as the assessment itself, so great care must be taken by learners when considering just how to mark their peers (Erwin & Knight, 1995). However, the criteria must be presented in an operational manner that is understandable to students; a process the students themselves can have a hand in creating (Dochy et al., 1999).

Lastly, it has been found that learners demonstrate extremely positive attitudes towards peer-evaluation activities (Birdsong & Sharplin, 1986; Cheng & Warren, 2005; Duke & Sanchez, 1994), and that such activities can foster intrinsic motivation and confidence in the language learner (Finch, 2003). Accordingly, learners actually enjoy evaluating each other's work, and have much to gain from performing this activity. Indeed, Topping (1998) maintains that learners evaluate their peers in a comparable manner to their teachers, which suggests it is worthwhile for teachers to seriously consider using peer-evaluation activities in class. However, learners must be given the correct tools to do so, and need to be trained accordingly before undertaking any serious peer-evaluation activities (Cheng & Warren, 2005).

Participants

This study was conducted in the Autumn of 2009 at a large private university in India. Some 304 undergraduate students voluntarily participated in the study. The students were studying in the Economics, Business Administration, and Science and Engineering faculties. All students were taking an oral presentation class, which was a required subject in their English course as indicated by the questionnaire.

Research Methods

The aim of the study is to explore what kinds of oral presentations Indian university students consider to be effective. In order to answer the research question, an attitude survey was conducted. Descriptive statistics and principal components analysis using SPSS13.0 were employed to interpret the results. The questionnaire was developed based on the literature review and informal conversations with university students and EFL specialists who have taught oral presentations in both EFL and ESL contexts. The questionnaire consisted of thirty items across the following evaluation criteria of oral presentations: eye-contact; voice; English; originality of content; clarity; PowerPoint; body language; and time management (see the evaluation rubrics in Appendix 1). The criteria and the description of the rubrics were modified for this study by identifying common rubrics from related studies (e.g., Cheng & Warren, 2005; King, 2002; Nakamura, 2002; Patri, 2002).

In order to spread the responses from the participants out (Likert, 1932), item statements were categorized into positively and negatively phrased statements. Each item was measured using a 5-point Likert-type scale (for positive statements, from 1= strongly disagree to 5= strongly agree; and for negative statements the coding was reversed). Chronbach's alpha was checked to establish the reliability of the instrument developed for gathering the data for the study. This figure was determined to be .843, and thus reliable.

Results of the Principal Components Analysis

In order to ascertain what kinds of oral presentations the participants consider to be effective, a principal component analysis with a varimax rotation was carried out using SPSS13.0. Regarding the salient value for a component loading, we examined Tabachnick and Fidell (1996) who proposed a rule of thumb that loadings of .30 (absolute) or above be used to specify variables that load on each component, and Steven's (1996) recommendation that using loadings which are approximately .40 (absolute) or higher for identifying variables that load on a particular principal component. Also, in a sample of 300 (Stevens, 1996), factor loading of .298 (.149 X 2) at alpha =.01 and above are required for practical significance. In a practical sense, selecting factor loadings of .40 meets the criteria. We decided to choose the value of .40 in order to select the components. As a result, three components were retained and interpreted as follows:

1) Factor 1 has the largest number of loadings from 9 variables (items 3, 8, 9, 17, 21, 23, 26, 27, and 30), accounting for 22.8 per cent of the total variance. Items 3, 8, 9, 17, 21, and 22 dealt with comprehension of speech. Items 23, 26, 27, and 30 are all related to the speaker's voice quality. Therefore, Factor 1 was labeled as *Clarity of Speech and Voice Quality*.
2) Next, the variance of Factor 2 drops sharply on the scree plot, and accounts for 6.84 per cent of the total. It received loadings from 4 variables (items 10, 15, 28, and 29). All of these items are concerned with the English language itself, so this group was labeled *Correctness of Language*.
3) Factor 3 received loadings from three variables (items 11, 20, and 24). These items dealt with the speaker's attention to the audience. Therefore, it was labeled *Interaction with the Audience*.

Discussion

From the results of the present study, three components were identified to influence Indian university students' views on effective oral presentations: Clarity of Speech and Voice Quality; Correctness of Language; and Interaction with the Audience.

Regarding Factor 1, Clarity of Speech and Voice Quality, it was noted that participants judge an effective presentation on the combination of clarity of the presenter's presentation and his or her voice. Thus, in the process of making evaluation rubrics, teachers should pay attention to this factor by incorporating examples of good presentations and by demonstrating a clear and understandable voice. It is suspected that some students, especially those in the lower levels of proficiency, may confuse the clarity of speech component with that of a person who simply just speaks with a loud voice. Therefore, teachers must explain the component items of Factor 1, and how clarity of speech and voice quality can positively impact an oral presentation. This will serve to act as guidance for learners striving to become more effective presenters.

With respect to Factor 2, Correctness of Language, from the results of the descriptive statistics, participants in this study tended to be tolerant of grammatical errors during oral presentations. Although the students might not put serious emphasis on the correctness of language, the fact that it is included as a component here carries some weight. Component items of this factor involve the accuracy of speech and pronunciation. This factor is considered important for the preparation stages of oral presentations, and can be dealt with by teachers in class by clearly explaining the implications of these criteria to their learners, so they can factor this into their evaluations. Further, when preparing to assess their peers, learners should be made aware of the significance of the correctness of language criteria. Thus, learners can prepare transcripts of their presentations, which can then be checked by their peers. The presenter's peers can then focus on grammatical accuracy and vocabulary use. This will ensure that a complete understanding is obtained by both presenters and their peers.

Factor 3, or Interaction with the Audience, refers to the physical attention the presenter gives to the audience. This physical attention involves eye contact, body language and paying attention to the audience's response to the presentation. It can be a difficult task to judge exactly how much eye contact and body language are sufficient in oral presentations in the Indian EFL context. This is partly due to these factors not being strongly rooted in Indian culture (Lusting & Koester, 2003). However, with practice, teachers can assist learners in overcoming potential problems in these areas by reiterating that in real world situations presenters are expected to pay attention to the audience because the presentation should be aimed at the target audience (Lucas, 1997). Teachers can demonstrate and stress the importance of presenter-audience interaction, and learners can prepare for evaluating their peers' interaction with the audience with adequate training. This can be done by teachers and students in class: by giving both good and bad examples of presenter-audience interaction.

CONCLUSION AND PEDAGOGICAL IMPLICATIONS

Based on the results of this study, we can draw some conclusions about recommendations on how to best prepare our learners for oral presentations. As teachers, we can prepare our learners to be aware of the above criteria and the effect they have on the efficacy of oral presentations in EFL classrooms.

In the light of the work done on peer assessment in writing classes and elsewhere, a more open approach to our learners' evaluation is needed (Rust et al., 2003). One suggestion is to use an integrated method of feedback: one in which learners write an outline for their presentations first, evaluate each other's work, and then make their presentations based on the corrections given by their peers.

Learners then do their presentations in class while the teacher and the other students evaluate that presentation using rubrics they have had a hand in creating (Cheng & Warren 2005; Orsmond, Merry & Reiling, 2000). Consequently, learners from the present study stated that these methods were exceptionally useful in assisting them in becoming more proficient at making oral presentations. Specifically, comments from learners suggested that if teachers take time to demonstrate how and when to use eye contact, how to organize a presentation, connect with an audience, use body language and manage time, and how to construct an effective PowerPoint presentation, the learners can build upon their existing knowledge to use in future presentations. Methods that seem commonplace to most teachers are not so to learners in our classes, thus we must ensure we expend the correct amount of time and energy into giving our learners the tools they need to become effective presenters in the target language. Students wanting to improve their competence in this area of language study will surely benefit from such training.

Along these lines, the first step is for teachers and learners to establish marking criteria. Involving learners in this process will be of great benefit to them in preparing for their own presentations (Orsmond, Merry & Reiling, 2000). Secondly, learners must clearly understand the criteria set out for evaluating presentations. Teachers can carry out practice sessions with their learners by having them watch and evaluate past presentations on video. Teachers need to monitor that learners are using the criteria correctly and applying the tenets of the rubric in an accurate manner. Third, after the appropriate training has been completed (which may take two to three class periods), students prepare their presentations (individually or in groups) with the criteria they helped create firmly in mind. Next, learners evaluate their peer's presentations with the rubric they helped create. Finally, after the presentations are completed, learners receive their evaluation from their peers and reflect on their performance and how to improve on it. All of this can serve to be extremely useful not only to the learners in our classes, but also to teachers using these techniques in EFL presentation classes.

The question remains as to exactly what constitutes good spoken performance in the EFL classroom? For the purposes of EFL classes and in general, the authors deem it vital for learners to be able to communicate their message to the audience in a convincing manner. Thus, grammatical correctness is not of the utmost importance. What are most important are the objectives, organization and presentation of the speech, as well as the communication of both the message and of the presenter with his or her audience. These are factors which can literally make or break an oral presentation in the EFL classroom. As teachers, we must inform our learners of their importance, practise them repeatedly, and then reiterate exactly how they can affect the overall message in a presentation.

Peer evaluation can be a valuable method in assisting EFL learners in how to properly structure English oral presentations. By taking part in peer-evaluation activities, learners gain a firm knowledge of the form and process of what makes an effective oral presentation. By involving them in the process of actually creating the rubrics to be used in evaluating their peers, we are giving our learners opportunity gain independence while learning more about exactly what makes a successful presentation.

Future research should focus on surveys that target instructors' ideas of what constitutes a good oral presentation, since there is bound to be some differences in attitude between students and instructors over what constitutes a good oral presentation. For instance, native instructors of English might have different criteria from those of their students due to cultural differences. Discovering the differences between the two groups will become a stepping stone that will lead to more effective instruction in EFL oral presentation classes. In accordance with the notion of a student-centered approach, both teachers and students should negotiate with each other over their views on oral presentations.

As argued earlier in this paper, performing an oral presentation is a complicated task that involves multi-faced language characteristics. To enhance the reliability of oral presentation activities, they should be evaluated by both teachers and learners. They are useful to both groups interested in utilizing classroom peer evaluation activities as a method of improving learners' knowledge of exactly what makes an effective oral presentation in English. Therefore, interaction with both sides is necessary so that peer evaluation can be considered a useful and effective communicative activity in EFL language learning contexts.

References

Bachman, L.F., & Palmer, A.S. (1989). The construct validation of self ratings of communicative language ability. *Language Testing, 6*, 14-29.

Birdsong, T., & Sharplin, W. (1986). Peer evaluation enhances students' critical judgment. *Highway One, 9*, 23-28.

Boud, D., Cohen, R., & Sampson, J. (1999). Peer learning and assessment. *Assessment and Evaluation in Higher Education, 24*(4), 413-26.

Cheng, W. & Warren. (2005). Peer assessment of language proficiency. *Language Testing, 22*(1), 93-119

Cohen, A. (1987). Student processing of feedback of their compositions. In A. Wenden and J. Rubin (Eds.), *Learner Strategies in Language Learning*. Englewood Cliffs, N.J.: Prentice Hall.

Dochy, F., Segers, M., & Sluijsmans, D. (1999). The use of self-, peer-, and co-assessment in higher education: A review. *Studies in Higher Education, 24*(3), 331-35.

Duke, C., & Sanchez, R. (1994). Giving students control over writing assessment. *English Journal, 83*, 47-53.

Earl, S.E. (1986). Staff and peer assessment: measuring an individual's contribution group performance. *Assessment and Evaluation in Higher Education, 11*, 60-69.

Erwin, T.D. & Knight, P. (1995). A transatlantic view of assessment and quality in higher education. *Quality in Higher Education, 1*(2), 179-188.

Falchikov, N. (1995). Peer feedback marking: developing peer assessment. *Innovations in Higher Education, 11*(2), 146-65.

Finch, A. (2003). Reflective instruments for self-assessment in Korean EFL classrooms. *The Korea TESOL Journal, 6*(1), 63-86.

Freeman, M. (1995). Peer assessment by groups of group work. *Assessment and Evaluation in Higher Education, 20*, 289-300.

Hadley, A. O. (2001). *Teaching Language in Context* (3rd ed.). Boston, MA: Heinle & Heinle.

Hedgcock, J., & Leftkowitz, N. (1992). Collaborative oral/oral revision in FL writing instruction. *Journal of Second Language Writing, 1*(3), 255-76.

Hughes, I.E., & Large, B.J. (1993). Staff and peer-group assessment of oral communication skills. *Studies in Higher Education, 18*(3), 379-85.

Jacobs, G. (1987). First experiences with peer feedback on compositions: student and teacher reactions. *System, 15*, 325-33.

Johnson, D., & Johnson, R. (1999). Cooperative learning and assessment. *JALT Applied Materials Cooperative Learning*, 164-178

King, J. (2002) Preparing EFL learners for oral presentations. *The Internet TESOL Journal, 8*(3). Retrieved November 1, 2007 from http://iteslj.org/Lessons/King-PublicSpeaking.html

Lalande, J. (1982). Reducing composition errors: An experiment. *The Modern Language Journal, 66*, 140-49.

Likert, R.A. (1932). A technique for the measurement of attitudes. *Archives of Psychology, 140, 5-53.*

Lucas, S.E. (1997). *The art of public speaking* (6th ed.). New York: McGraw Hill. Lusting, M.W. & Koester, J. (2003). *Intercultural Competence Interpersonal Communication across Cultures* (4th ed.). Boston, MA: Allyn & Bacon.

Morahan-Martin, J. (1996). Should peers' evaluations be used in class project?: Questions regarding reliability, leniency, and acceptance. *Psychological Reports, 78*, 1243-50.

Nakamura, Y. (2002). Teacher assessment and peer assessment in practice. *Education Studies, 44*, 203-215

Newkirk, T. (1984). Direction and misdirection in peer response. *College Composition and Communication, 35*, 301-11.

Nunan, D. (2002). Listening in language learning. In J.C. Richards & W.A. Renandya (Eds.), *Methodology in Language Teaching* (pp. 238-241). Cambridge: Cambridge University Press.

Orsmond, P., Merry, S., & Reiling, K. (2000). The use of student derived marking criteria in peer and self-assessment. *Assessment and Evaluation in Higher Education, 25*(1), 23-38.

Patri, M. (2002). The influence of peer feedback on self-and peer assessment of oral skills. *Language Testing, 19*(2), 109-31

Pica, T. (1984). Second language acquisition theory in the teaching of writing. *TESOL Newsletter, 18*(2), 5-6.

Richards, J. C., & Rodgers, T. (2001). *Approaches and Methods in Language Teaching*. Cambridge: Cambridge University Press.

Rust, C., Price, M., & O'Donovan, B. (2003). Improving students' learning by developing their understanding of assessment criteria and processes. *Assessment and Evaluation in Higher Education, 28*(2), 147-164.

Stevens, J. (1996). *Applied Multivariate Statistics for the Social Sciences* (3rd ed.). Mahwah, NJ: Lawrence Erlbaum Associates.

Tabachnick, B.G. & Fidell, L.S. (1996). *Using Multivariate Statistics* (3rd ed.). New York: Harper Collins College Publishers.

Topping, K. (1998). Peer assessment between students in colleges and universities. *Review of Educational Research, 68*, 249-76.

Truscott, J. (1996). Review article: The case against grammar correction in L2 writing classes. *Language Learning, 46*(2), 327-69.

Zamel, V. (1985). Responding to student writing. *TESOL Quarterly, 19*, 79-101.

Appendix 1: The Rubric for Judging Speech Quality

Eye contact	Rapport with, and sense of the audience
Voice	Show confidence; appropriateness of pace; volume; and articulation
English	Clear pronunciation; appropriate use of vocabulary good structures/register; conciseness; and clarity of expressions
Originality of Content	Good choice of topic; clear objective/ purpose statement; and unique ideas about the chosen topic

Clarity	Good connection of ideas; appropriate use of signal words; well structured; clear conclusions
PowerPoint	Attractive; appropriate use of paragraphing, headings, numbering, spacing, and illustrations.
Body Language	Appropriate gestures to keep audience's attention
Time Management	Management of the allocated time of oral presentation

16

Association of Technology in English Teacher Education

— Suruchi Dubey

We live during a time when the challenge of change is taking place in the form of literacy and meaning—as digital and multimedia resources across the threshold of our world. Literacy and language learning are being redefined by the digital communication and multimedia technologies that are quickly becoming part of the routine in our everyday lives.

As we look at the technologies found in the modern age, it is important to consider the challenges and new avenues that encircle language teaching, as we guide students and teachers learning within technologically information environment. We have entered an era in which educators can no longer choose to ignore the responsibility of teaching with and about technological tools. Teaching students about the computer and other technological tools as a part of the normal curricula together within the aim of developing their abilities to use these tools to complete language activities, will prepare them in using the technology. Hence, in the present, literacy does not simply mean the ability to read and write a particular language—it also involves abilities and practices related to the particular media through which texts are transmitted.

The role of language literacy in today's educational system delineates that to be literate in any society, a person must be able to use written and oral languages for a wide range of purposes. Literate people have a set of skills, knowledge, values, understandings and relationships that allow them to use language for reading and writing on the job, at home, in school, travelling purpose and so forth. According to Topping (1997), technological literacy refers to language activities (reading, writing, spelling) which are delivered supported, accessed or assessed through computers or other electronic means:

a) New ways of reading and writing text.
b) New ways of communicating with others.
c) New attitudes to communication.
d) Skills of analysis and problem solving.
e) Skills of information processing and computing.

Teachers can use multimedia technology to give more colourful, stimulating lectures, how computers can be used to stimulate and develop writing skills, collaborate with peers in foreign countries, and do authentic kind of research that is valuable to the adult work. The use of technology in education has certain objectives:

a) Allows learners to explore a variety of activities related to many areas.
b) Learners can develop problem-solving strategies and work habits that will be useful in any career or occupation.
c) Learners should develop a greater appreciation for the work of art.
d) Effort to develop "soft skills" within the learners as well as an opportunity for the learners to see how the system works together.
e) Academic class instruction to work in an applied way.

Throughout the twentieth century the uses of the term have increased to the point where it now encompasses a number of "classes" of technology:

1. *Technology as Objects*: tools, machines, instruments, weapons, appliances—the physical devices of technical performance.

2. *Technology as Knowledge*: The know-how behind technological innovation.
3. *Technology as Activities*: What people do—their skills, methods, procedures, routines.
4. *Technology as Process*: Begins with a need and ends with a solution
5. *Technology as a Socio-technical System*: The manifestation and use of objects involving people and others in combination.

Technology's Distinct Characteristics

1. *It is Related to Science:* Although there is certainly a relationship between science and technology, there is exception in certain high technology industries, very little technology that can be classified as applied sciences. Technology is marked by different purposes; different processes, a different relationship to established knowledge and a particular relationship to specific contexts of activity. A change in the material environment is the explicit purpose of technology and not as in the case with science, the understanding of nature; accordingly its solution are not right or wrong, verifiable or falsifiable, but more or less effective from different points of view.
2. *It Involves Design*: At the centre of technology lies design. That "design is the very core of engineering" is affirmed by the requirement that all degree engineering courses should embody it. The design process in technology is a sequential process which begins with the perception of a need, continues with the formulation of a specification, the generation of ideas and a final solution, and ends with an evaluation of the solution.
3. *It Involves Making*: The motivating factor behind all technological activity is the desire to fulfil a need. For this reason all designs should be made or realized whether they be through prototype, batch or mass production or some form of three-dimensional or

computer model—if the need is to be truly fulfilled, the design is to be legitimately evaluated, and the design activity is to have been purposeful and worthwhile.

4. *It is Multidimensional*: Not only can design and production involve cooperation between different specificatism (between, for example, designer, production engineer and materials scientists), but may involve the "technologist" in performing a multitude of functions, such as working with others, operating within budgets, persuading decision makers, communicating to clients and working to deadlines.
5. *It is Concerned with Values*: Technology is informed by values at every point. Value decisions may be called for not only in relation to the specific design criteria (i.e. aesthetic, ergonomic and economic judgements, suitability for purpose and ease of manufacture) but also in relation to the rightness or wrongness of a particular solution in ethical terms.
6. *It is Socially Shaped/ Shaping*: Technologically enterprises are determined not by advances in knowledge or simply by the identification of needs, but by social interest. Of the new potential technologies available at any one time only a few are developed and become widely implemented. In this way technology is shaped by society, by consumer's choice. Yet it can also be argued that technology shapes society—the technology of the motor car, for example, has shaped our environment and our whole way of life.

Although the changes are taking place slowly, most teachers have a wide variety of technological resources at their fingertips that they can use to make their lectures beneficial to the students. The study of language and literature can encompasses a wide variety of topics ranging from the historical to the psychological. Computers can put all this information at our fingertips instantly and so they are extremely beneficial to the discipline multimedia classrooms. They provide a combination of visual as well as audio stimulation that greatly enhance the learning experience.

In English, technology includes cameras, audio equipments, computers technology, scanners, printers, CD equipments—almost any device that can access, present, manipulate and communicate words, sounds and images to enable us to create meaning.

The World Wide Web is another resource that teachers can turn to: dictionaries, virtual libraries and electronic books can all be polled on the screen in a multimedia classroom. Furthermore, for teachers wanting to find information on the web, innovation in education has a wide representation including sites such as multimedia learning materials and schools online. English teachers have always used some technology but the explosion in digital technologies has opened up new and exciting possibilities.

Why use Computer Technology in English?

There are two kinds of reasons for using computer technology in English. First, there are the benefits to teachers and students in any learning areas:

For students, technology can

a) Be very motivational,

b) Be the source of a significant amount of reading material,

c) Be fun, and when it's fun you learn! and

d) Help students to produce excellent published work

For teachers technology can

a) Allow for the easy production, storage and retrieval of prepared materials Such as certificates and work required sheets.

b) Free up communication with other teachers

c) Help teachers to find information easily

d) Assist good teaching but not replace it!

Secondly, there are the challenges and opportunities presented by computer technology that make it an increasingly important part of English in particular. These include:

Examples of How Emerging Technologies can be Used in English

Word processing/ desk top publishing	**Making letters, Making words Making signs, Writing own, Illustrated books**	**Publishing—stories, poems,letters, brochures, reports, essays, signs, articles, reviews, recounts, biographies, diaries, journals, signs, information, arguments, illustrations books**	**Publishing—stories, poems, resumes, scripts, research log**
Internet for information	Information relating to themes Getting suitable images to illustrate work	Information about writers Search for song/lyric Search for any topic	Author information topic search
Discussiongroups		Discussion groups	Engaging in discussion about particular reading
Web page Design	Personal web page On school sites	Personal C web page Personal websites	Producing construction Onlinemagazine production
CD-ROM Information	Researching topics	CDROM interactive educational games	Researching topics Researching writers
Interactive bookreading	Shared reading of interactive books for pleasure		A critical literacy approach to interactive books
Drawing	Drawing letters of the alphabet	Making book cover	Constructing cartoons Illustrated writing for effect

	Band-A	Band-B	Band C and D
Digital image manipulation	Cutting, pasting and manipulating digital pictures to illustrate own writing	Placing appropriate photographs into document to promote ideas	Altering structuresand features for effect, i.e., making a colour photo into a grey one to illustrate a sad poem
Sound recording	Recording spokenstories works	Adding sound to published from a novel	Interviewingcharacters
Graphic organizing	The lifecycle of an insect	Using a graphic organizer to show student's own family	
Games	Word building and spelling games	Using spellingprograms for drill and practice to broaden studies	A study of the gender/ violence aspects of games
Talking Books	Sharing talking books		Producing own talking books Using power point type software
Chat lines	Probably best accessed on intra-net	Open interview possibilities	
e-mail		e-mail to friends e-mail for information	e-mail dialoguebetween teacherand students email authors

a) The emergence of new kinds of texts and the consequent need to teach students to create and use these texts effectively;

b) Changing need to teach students how to make judgements about appropriate use of different avenues of communication;

c) The pervasiveness and power of texts created through computer technology and the consequent need to teach students to be critical readers and viewers of the texts.

Each of these is discussed briefly below.

Creating and Using New Kinds of Texts

Such as hypertexts, web page, e-mail communication and multimedia texts.

Many of these texts blend the written, spoken and visual, so students can express ideas in exciting and powerful ways. The choices available to the creators and users of texts are expanding rapidly, so English needs to start helping students to make informed choices.

Multimedia texts challenge readers and viewers to integrate information and ideas in new ways. Making meaning from the interplay of words, sounds and vision involves a sophisticated set of skills, that have not necessarily been highly valued in the past:

"..... for hundreds of years western culture has privileged the verbal (print and oral) as the pre-eminent mode of conveying meaning and producing knowledge. However, with the arrival of the new communication and information technologies, the reign of the verbal has been at least interrupted, if not overthrown." (Synder, 1998)

Hypertext heralds a different way of accessing texts since, even more than with traditional print or screen texts, the reader or viewer actively creates an individual text through choices made. We can choose to jump from link to link in different ways, creating many possible texts from one set of material. Adults often comment ironically on the almost irresistible lure of hypertext links that invite us to flit from site to site, searching for the better, brighter site that surely waits just one screen away. We need to explore the same issue with students to ask what effect this has on our understanding and how we judge when it is better to resist or go with the lure.

Judging the Appropriate use of New Kinds of Texts

When we use computer technology to make and access texts, we operate in changing social contexts. E-mail, discussion groups and chats rooms create qualitatively different contexts for communication. Teachers often comment that the kinds of relationships they and their students establish through these kinds of channels are unlike others they are familiar with.

For example, with no status cues, such as paper quality, handwriting or letterhead, e-mail is potentially a great leveller. While this has possible advantages, we also need to establish new ways of judging authenticity and credibility. As there is a clamour for better suggestions, there is a need for everyone to make judgments about the appropriate use of new texts. Students need to weigh up the relative advantages of e-mail, letter, fax or phone call in any particular situation as all will become increasingly available.

Other questions arise, such as:

a) What is appropriate information to include on a personal home page?
b) What are the pros and cons of computer chat?
c) If e-mailing someone we don't know, what is an appropriate tone to use?
d) Does layout matter?
e) What are the social and personal implications of not having access to computer technology to communication?

Critically Reading and Viewing Computer-based Texts

While teachers have been busy learning to use computer

technology, the emphasis has understandably been on practical applications rather than on critical analysis. Now that critical literacy is recognized as a significant part of English teachers are starting to develop a critical approach to computer technology. The same kinds that we are asked:

a) Who is privileged in this text?

b) Who might this text exclude or marginalize?

c) What attitudes and values are implied in this text?

Just as students increase their personal power when they improve their traditional literacy skills, they also gain significant social power through competent, critically-aware use of new communication technology. English teachers are in a powerful position to help students develop this new dimension of literacy.

Issues Involved in Using Computer Technology in Classrooms

a) Developing a whole-school approach. This involves considering how students will be taught basic skills; what kinds of priority will be given to students in accessing computers; security and privacy implications of the use of computer technology; intranet development and use.

b) The teaching strategies needed to accommodate the computers. As students' access to information improves so that they can go beyond what the teacher or school provide and can locate information much closer to its source, the relationship between the teacher and the students inevitably changes.

Technology and Assessment

Technology can be used in all areas of English. Activities are limited by the imagination of the teacher and cross all languages modes and strands. There are very few of the English outcomes that exclude the use of technology.

Examples of English Profile that can be Accessed through Technology

Writing:

	Level 1	*Level 2*	*Level 3*
Texts	Produces written symbols with the intention of conveying an idea or message.	Uses writing to develop familiar ideas, events andinformation.	Writes sustained texts characterized by complexity of purpose and subject matter and a need for formality in language and construction.
Contextual understanding	Recognise that written language is used by people to convey meaning to others.	Adjust writing to take account of aspects of contexts, purpose and audience.	Selects text type, subject matter and language to suit a specific audience and purpose.
Linguistic structures and features	Demonstrates emerging awareness of how to use conventional written symbols for expressing ideas and information.	Controls most distinguishing linguistic structures and features of basic text types such as stories, procedures reports and arguments.	Controls spellings, syntax and text structures to meet the demands of most expository and imaginative writing.
Strategies	Experiments and practices ways of representation ideas and information using written symbols.	When prompted, uses a range of strategies for planning, reviewing and proofreading own writing. Uses a multi-strategy approach to spelling.	Critically evaluates others written texts and uses this knowledge to reflect on and improve own.

Speaking and Listening

	Level 1	*Level 2*	*Level 3*
Texts	Interacts informally with teachers, peers and known adults in structured classroom activities dealing briefly with familiar topics.	Interacts confidently with others in a variety of situations to develop and present.	Works effectively with others in situations characterized by complexity of purpose, procedure and subject matter, and a need for formality in speech and attitude.
Contextual understanding	Shows emerging awareness of school purposes and expectations for using spoken language.	Considers aspects of contexts, purpose and audience when speaking and listening in familiar situations.	Considers the inter-relationships between texts, contexts, speakers and listeners in a situation.
Linguistic structures and features	Draws on implicit knowledge of the linguistic structures and features of own variety of English when expressing ideas and information and interpreting spoken texts.	Controls most linguist structures and features and features of spoken language of interpreting meaning and developing and presenting ideas and information in familiar situation.	Uses awareness of differences between spoken and written language to construct own sentences in structured, formal situations.
Strategies	Monitors communication of self and others.	Assist and monitors the communication patterns of self and others.	Uses a range of strategies to present spoken texts in formal situations.

Reading and Viewing

	Level 1	*Level 2*	*Level 3*
Texts	Role plays being a competent reader and consistently interprets some familiar written symbols. Constructs meanings from visuals texts with familiar content, particularly texts designed to be viewed in segments.	Justifies own interpretations of ideas, information and events in texts containing some unfamiliar concepts and topics which introduce relatively complex linguistic structures and features	Constructs meanings from a range of texts, including those characterized by complexity of construction and subject matter.
Contextual understanding	Makes connection between own knowledge and experience, and the ideas, events and information in texts viewed and heard read aloud.	Explains possible reasons for people's varying interpretations of texts.	Considers a variety of interrelationships between texts, contexts, readers or viewers and makers of texts.
Linguistic structures and features	Demonstrates emerging awareness and use of symbols and conventions when making meaning from texts.	With teachers guidance, identifies and discusses how linguistic structures and features work to shape readers' and viewers' understanding of texts.	Identifies and comments on the impact of techniques intended to shape readers' and viewers' interpretation and reactions to texts.
Strategies	Recognizes and uses cues to predict meaning in visual and printed texts.	Recognizes and uses cues to predict meaning in visual and printed texts.	Uses reading and viewing strategies that enable detailed critical evaluation of texts.

The Effect of Technology on English Language Technology

Technological innovations are developing at the same time with the growth of English, and are changing the way in which we communicate. The Internet has facilitated the growth of the English Language Learning. Most drill exercises are used to motivate the language learning skills. The writing process is another area where computers have added a great deal of value. (Warschauer, 1998). Most word-processors now come with spell-checks, giving weak spellers some help in finding their errors and recognizing the correct spelling from a list of options. Dictionaries can run in the background and be accessed with a keystroke. Many dictionaries incorporate some grammar help, and some have sound and video clips to help learners recognize a word when it is spoken and put into context.

Hypermedia provides numbers of advantages for language learning. First of all, a more authentic learning environment is created just like in the real world because listening is combined with seeing. Secondly, skills are easily integrated because of varieties of media make it natural to combine reading, writing, speaking and listening in a single activity. Third, teachers as well as students have a great control over their learning since they can not only go at their pace but even on their own individual path. They also can go forward and backward to different parts of the programme in on particular aspects and skip other aspects altogether.

Pronunciation which is worked in particular has been benefited from multimedia. Many of the English pronunciation programmes have video clips and animations of the mouth making specific sounds. Some vocabulary programmes use speech recognition technology to help students see how close they have come to the target pronunciation. Interactive video research gave some of the first results about multimedia effectiveness in language teaching.

Works Cited

Brown, H.D. (2000). *Principles of Language Learning and Teaching*, Fourth Edition, 161 2

Chen, J.F. (1997). *Computer generated error feedback and writing process,* A link TESL- EJ, 2 (3) [electronic document] Available at http://violet.berkeley.edu/cwp/TESL-EJ/ej07/al.html.

Graddol, D. (2000). *The future of English? A guide to forecasting the popularity of the English Language in the twentieth century* (2nd edition). The British Council.

Taylor, M.B., and Perez (1989). *Something to do on Monday,* La Jolla, CA.

Wang, Y.M. (1993). *E-mail dialogue journaling in an ESL reading and writing classroom.* Unpublished dissertation, University of Oregon at Eugene.

Warschauer, M.(1997). Comparing Face-to-Face and Electronic Discussion in the Second Language Classroom, *CALICO Journal*, 13 (2and3), 7-25. Retreived on 28, Nov., 2009 from http://www.gse.uciedu/markw/comparing.html

Bibliography

Alptekin, C. (1993). Target-language Culture in FFL Materials. *ELT Journal, 47* (2), 112-142.

Al Seghayer K (2001) 'The Effect of Multimedia Annotation Modes on L2 Vocabulary Acquisition: A Comparative Study' *Language Learning and Technology* 5/1: 202232

Anderson, G.; Herr, K.; Nihlen, A. (1994). *Studying Your Own School: An Educator's Guide to Qualitative Practitioner Research.* Corwin Press Inc.: CA.

Anderson, P. S., & Lapp, D. (1988). *Language Skills in Elementary Education.* New York: MacMillan.

Annamalai, E. (2001). *Managing Multilingualism in India.* Sage Publications: New Delhi.

Arroyo C (1992) 'What is the Effect of Extensive Use of Computers on the Teaching Achievement Scores of Seventh Grade Students?' (ERIC Document Reproduction Services No. ED 353544)

Arsham, H. (2005). *Impact of the Internet on Learning and Teaching.* http:/ / home.ubalt.edu/ntsbarsh/interactive.htm

Ashok Kumar. (2010). *Swiftly Shifting Paradigms of English Language Teaching (ELT) in India.* New Delhi: AuthorsPress.

______________ ; (2010). *English Language Teaching (ELT): New Perspective.* New Delhi: Atlantic Pub.

Athlemoolan, L. (2006). 'The Role of Drama-in – Education in the English Second Language Classroom', *The Journal of English Language Teaching (India),* Vol. 44/1.

Atkinson, D. (1990). "TESOL and Culture". *TESOL Quarterly,* 33/4:625-654.

Atkinson, T. & Davies, G. (2005). Computer Aided Assessment (CAA) and Language Learning, Module 4.1. *Information and Communications Technology for Language Teachers.*

Bachman, L. F. and A.S. Palmer. (1996). *Language Testing in Practice: Designing and Developing Useful Language Tests.* Oxford: Oxford University Press.

Bachman, L. and A. Cohen. (1998). *Interfaces Between Second Language and Language Testing Research.* Cambridge: Cambridge University Press.

Bailey, Kathleen M., and Lance Savage. Eds. (1994). *New Ways in Teaching Speaking.* Alexandria, Virginia: Teachers of English to Speakers of Other Languages, Inc.

Baker, Ann, and Sharon Goldstein. (1990). *Pronunciation Pairs: Teacher's Manual.* Cambridge, England: Cambridge University Press.

Baldridge, Jason. (1996). *Reconciling Linguistic Diversity: The History and the Future of Language Policy in India,* http://www.ling.upenn.edu/jason2/papers/ natlang.htm [9 August 1998].

Bationo, B.D. (1992). 'The Effects of Three Feedback forms on Learning through a Computer Based Tutorial', *CALICO 10/1:* 4552

Bayley, R. (1991). "Variation Theory and Second Language Learning: Linguistic and Social Constraints on Interlanguage Tense Marking". Doctoral dissertation, Stanford University, Stanford., CA. In Bachman, L. and A. Cohen. 1998. *Interfaces Between Second Language and Language Testing Research.* Cambridge: Cambridge University Press.

_______________ ;(1994). Interlanguage Variation and the Quantitative Paradigm: Past Tense Marking in Chinese-English. In E. E. Tarone, S. M. Gass, and A. D. Cohen (eds.), *Research Methodology in Second-Language.* Hillsdale, NJ: Lawrence Erlbaum.

Bayer, Jennifer. (1990). *Language and Social Identity, Multilingualism in India.* Clevedon: Multilingual Matters Ltd: 101-111.

Benson, P. (2001). *Teaching and Researching Autonomy in Language Learning.* Essex: Pearson Education Limited.

Benson Phil & Voller Peter, (eds.), (1997) *Autonomy and Independence in Language Learning.* London: Longman

Berge, Z. and Collins, M. (1995). *Computer-mediated Communication and The Online Classroom.*, New Jersey: Hampton Press.

Berko-Gleason, J. (1993). *The Development of Language.* New York: MacMillan Publishing Co.

Bernstein, B. (1970). A Socio-linguistic Approach to Socialization. In Gumperz and Hymes. (eds.) 1972. *Directions in Sociolinguistics.* New York: Holt, Rinehart & Winston.

Bilaystok, (1990). *Communication Strategies.* Oxford: Basil Blackwell.

Birdsong, D. (1989). *Meta-linguistic Performance and Interlanguage Competence.* New York: Springer.

Bonvillain, Nancy. (1993). *Language, Culture and Communication: The Meaning of Messages.* New Jersey: Prentice Hall.

Borg, S. (2007). Research Engagement in English Language Teaching. *Teaching and Teacher Education, 23* (5), 731-747.

Bowen, C. P. (1999). Technology Helps Students Learn Grammar. *Communication: Journalism Education Today*, *32* (4), 17-18.

Bowen, J. Donald. (1979). Contextualizing Pronunciation Practice in the ESOL Classroom. In *Teaching English as a Second or Foreign Language*. Marianne Celce-Murcia and Lois McIntosh. Eds. Rawley, MA: Newbury House Publishers, Inc.

______________ ; Harold Madsen, and Ann Hilferty. (1985). *TESOL Techniques and Procedures*. Boston: Heinle & Heinle.

Bowen T. & Marks J. (1994). *Inside Teaching. Options for English Language Teachers*. Oxford: Heinemann.

Brandl K (1995). 'Strong and Weak Students' Preferences for Error Feedback Options and Responses' *The Modern Language Journal* 79/2: 194211

Braverman, Judi. (1994). Total Physical Response Vocabulary Practice. In *New Ways in Teaching Vocabulary*. Ed. Paul Nation. Alexandria, Virginia: Teachers of English to Speakers of Other Languages, Inc.

Brett, P. (1995). 'Multimedia for Listening Comprehension: The Design of a Multi-media Based Resource for Developing Listening Skills', *System* 23/1: 7785

______________ ; (1997). 'A Comparative Study of the Effects of the Use of Multimedia on Listening Comprehension', *System* 25/1: 3953

______________ ; (1998). 'An Intuitive, Theoretical and Empirical Perspective on The Effectiveness Question for Multimedia', http://perswww.wlv.ac.uk/~le1969/index.htm (last accessed, 14/4/04)

______________ ;(2000). *'The Design, Implementation and Evaluation of a Multimedia Application for Second Language Listening Comprehension'*. http://perswww.wlv.ac.uk/~le1969/PhDthesis.html

______________ ; & Motteram G. (Eds.) (2000). *A Special Interest in Computers*, Kent: IATEFL

Brooks, N. (1960). *Language and Language Learning*. New York: Harcourt Brace and World.

Brown, H. D. (1994). *Teaching by Principles. An Interactive Approach to Language Pedagogy*. Prentice-Hall.

______________ ;(1994). *Principles of Language Learning and Teaching* (3rd Ed.). Englewood Cliffs, NJ: Prentice Hall.

Brown, J. D. (1995). *The Elements of Language Curriculum: A Systematic Approach to Curriculum Development*. Boston: Heinle and Heinle.

Brown, Steven. (1993). Ten Things to Do Before Reading, in *New Ways in Teaching Reading*. Ed. Richard R. Day. Alexandria, Virginia: Teachers of English to Speakers of Other Languages, Inc.

Brumfit, C. J., & Johnson, K. (Eds.). (1979). *The Communicative Approach to Language Teaching*. Oxford: Oxford University Press.

______________ ; C (Ed) (1985). *Computers in English Language Teaching*, Oxford: Pergamon Press

Busbee, E. (2001a). The Computer and the Internet: Are They Really Destined to Play a Major Role in English Teaching? *English Teaching*, 56(1), 201-225.

Carr, P. (1993). *Phonology*. London: Macmillan.

Cartwright, L. (1977). The Teacher as Communicator. In M. Gill and W. J. Crocker (Eds.), *English in Teacher Education* (41-67). New England: University of New England.

Cassady, J. K. (1998). Wordless Books: No-risk Tools for Inclusive Middle-grade Classrooms. *Journal of Adolescent and Adult Literacy. 41*, 428-432.

Catchcart, R. (1986). "Situational Differences and the Sampling of Young Children's School Language. In R. Day (Ed.), *Talking to Learn: Conversation in Second Language Acquisition* (pp. 118-140). Rowley: Ma: Newbury House.

Catford, J. C. (1977). *Fundamental Problems in Phonetics*. Edinburgh University Press.

Cazden, C. (2001). *Classroom Discourse: The Language of Teaching and Learning.* Portsmouth, NH: Heinemann.

Celce-Murcia, M., & Hawkins, B. (1985). Contrastive Analysis, Error Analysis, and Inter-language Analysis. In M. Celce-Murcia (Ed.), *Beyond Basics: Issues and Research in TESOL* (pp. 6-77). Rowley, MA: Newbury House.

_______________ ; (1987). Teaching Pronunciation as Communication. In J. Morley (Ed.), *Current Perspectives on Pronunciation* (pp. 1-12). Washington, DC: TESOL

_______________ ; (1991). *Teaching English as a Second or Foreign Language.* Rowley, MA: Newbury House.

_______________ ; Marianne, and Janet M. Goodwin. (1991). Teaching Pronunciation. In *Teaching English as a Second or Foreign Language.* Ed. Marianne Celce-Murcia. Boston: Heinle & Heinle.

_______________ ; Brinton, D., & Goodwin, J. (1996). *Teaching Pronunciation: A Reference for Teachers of English to Speakers of Other Languages.* Cambridge: Cambridge University Press.

Chapelle, C. (1998). 'Multimedia Call: Lessons to Be Learned from Research on Instructed SLA', *Language Learning and Technology,* Vol. 2, No. 1, 2234 http://polyglot.cal.msu.edu/llt/vol2num1/article1/index.html

_______________ ; (2001). *Computer Applications in Second Language Acquisition: Foundations for Teaching, Testing and Research.* Cambridge: CUP

Chatel, R. G. (2002). New Technology, New Literacy: Creating a Bridge for English Language Learners. *The New England Reading Association Journal, 38* (3), 45-49.

Chatterjee, K. K. (1976). *English Education in India: Issues and Opinions.* New Delhi: Macmillan.

________________ ; (2006). *English Language Teaching in India, in Indian Book Chronicle,* ed. P. C. Mathur, Jaipur, October 2006.

Chaturvedi, M. G. (1974). *Language Teaching and Learning in India.* New Delhi: NCERT

Chen, C. Y., & Huang, H.Y. (2003). L2 Acquisition of Subject-Prominence by EFL Students in Taiwan. *English Teaching & Learning, 27*(4), 99-122.

Chen, H. J. (1999). 'Creating a virtual language lab: an EFL experience at National Taiwan Ocean University', *ReCALL Online* 11/2: 2030 http://www.hull.ac.uk/cti/eurocall/ recall/rvol11no2.pdf

Cheshire, Jenny. (1991). *English around the World: Sociolinguistic Perspectives.* Cambridge: CUP.

________________ ; (1991). Introduction: Sociolinguistics and English Around the World. In *Cheshire*: 1-12.

Chew, P. (2005). The Rise and Fall of Communicative Language Teaching. In *Asian EFL Journal*, May 2005, *Conference Proceedings of The Future of English Education in Asia: 'Making Connections'.* Pusan: The Asian EFL Journal Press.

Cho, K.S., & Krashen, S. (1994). Acquisition of Vocabulary from the Sweet Valley Kids Series. *Journal of Reading 37*, 662-667.

Chomsky, N. (1959). "Review of Verbal Behavior" by B.F. Skinner. *Language* 35:26-58.

________________ ; (1965). *Aspects of the Theory of Syntax.* Cambridge, Mass: MIT Press.

________________ ; (1968). *Language and Mind.* New York: Harcourt Brace &World.

________________ ; (1979). *Language and Responsibility.* Brighton, East Sussex: Harvester Press.

Chun, D. & J. Plass, (1996). 'Facilitating Reading Comprehension with Multimedia', *System* 24/4: 503519

Clarke, M. (1988). *'The Short Circuit Hypothesis of ESL Reading or When Language Competence Interferes with Reading Performance'* in Carrell, P., Devine J. & Eskey D. (eds.).

Clark, R. E. (1994). Media will Never Influence Learning. *Educational Technology Research and Development, 42* (2), 21-9.

Clashen, H. Eisenbeiss, S. and Vainikka, A. (1994). "The Seeds of Structure: A Syntactic Analysis of The Acquisition of Case Marking". In T. Hoekscra and B. Schwartz (eds.). *Language Acquisition Studies in Generative Grammar,* pp. 85-118. Amsterdam: John Benjamins. In Archibald, J. (ed.) *Second Language Acquisition.* Oxford: Blackwell.

Clément, R., Gardner, R. and Smythe, P.C. (1977), Motivational Variables in Second language Acquisition: A Study of Francophone Learning English, *Canadian Journal of Behavioural Science*, 9, 123-33.

Cobb, T. (1997). Cognitive Efficiency: Towards a Revised Theory of Media. *Educational Technology Research and Development, 45* (4), 21-35.

Cohen, A. and E. Aphek. (1981). "Easifying Second Language Learning", *Studies in Second Language Acquisition* 3:221-36.

Collentine, J. (2000). Insights into the Construction of Grammatical Knowledge Provided by User-Behavior Tracking Technologies. *Language Learning & Technology. 3* (2), 44-57.

Collerson, J. (1977). Language in Teacher Education. In M. Gill and W. J. Crocker (Eds.), *English in Teacher Education* (98-134). New England: University of New England.

Cook, V. J. (1991). *Second Language Learning and Language Teaching.* London: Edward Arnold.

______________ ; (1992). *Evidence for Multi-Competence Language Learning*, *42*, 557-591.

Corson, D. (1998). *Changing Education for Diversity.* Open University Press.

Cotterall, S. (2000). Promoting Learner Autonomy Through Curriculum: Principles for Designing Language Courses. *ELT Journal 54* (2), 109-117.

______________ ; (1999). *Key Variables in Language Learning: What do Learners Believe about Them? System, 27*, 493-513.

Crawford, J. (1990). How Authentic is the Language in Our Classrooms? *Prospect, 6* (1), 47-54.

Cronnell, Bruce. (1979). Spelling English as a Second Language. In *Teaching English as a Second or Foreign Language*. Eds. Marianne Celce-Murcia and Lois McIntosh. Rowley, MA: Newbury House Publishers, Inc.

Crystal, David. (1988). *The English Language*. London: Penguin Books. Ltd.

______________ ; (1995). *The Cambridge Encyclopedia of the English Language*. Cambridge: CUP.

Cunningsworth, A. (1995). *Choosing Your Course Book.* Oxford: Macmillan Heinemann.

Cummins, J. and Swain, M. (1986). *Bilingualism in Education: Aspects of Theory, Research and Practice.* London: Longman.

Dalton, C. & Seidlhofer, B. (1994). *Pronunciation.* Oxford: Oxford University Press.

Dalton, D. (1997). Some Techniques for Teaching Pronunciation. *The Internet TESOL Journal*, 3 (1), January.

D'Angelo, K. (1979). Wordless Picture Books: Also for the Writer. *Journal of Language Arts. 56* (7), 813-814.

Dang, A. (2004). Reasons for Poor Teaching Quality. *Improving English Teaching*, Hanoi: Vietnam National University.

Das Gupta, J. (1970). *Language Conflict and National Development: Group Politics and Language Policy in India.* University of California

Davies, M. & Crowther, D. (1996). 'The Benefits of Using Multimedia in Higher Education: Myths and Realities', *Active Learning* 3, http://www.ilt.ac.uk/public/cti/Active Learning/issue3/crowther/ index.html

Davis, K. (1995). "Qualitative Theory and Methods in Applied Linguistics Research". *TESOL Quarterly 29,427-453.*

Day, R. & Conklin, G. (1992), March). *The Knowledge Base in ESL/EFL Teacher Education.* Paper Presented at the 1992 TESOL Conference, Vancouver, Canada.

Day, R. (1993). Models and the Knowledge Base of Second Language Teacher Education. *University of Hawai'i Working Papers in ESL, 11* (2), 1-13.

Day, Richard R. (1993). Ed. *New Ways in Teaching Reading.* Alexandria, Virginia: Teachers of English to Speakers of Other Languages, Inc.

Degler, L. S. (1979). Putting Words into Wordless Picture Book. *The Reading Teacher*, 32 (4), 399-402.

Dickinson, L. (1978). Autonomy, Self-Directed Learning and Individualization. In *Individualization and Autonomy in Language Learning* (pp.7-28). London: Modern English Publications and the British Council.

_______________ ; (1987). *Self-Instruction in Language Learning.* Cambridge: Cambridge University Press.

_______________ ; (1988). Learner Training. In A. Brookes & P. Grundy (Eds.) *Individualization and Autonomy in Language Learning* (pp. 45-53). London: Modern English Publications and the British Council.

_______________ ; (1992). *Learner Autonomy 2: Learner Training for Language Learning.* Dublin: Authentic.

_______________ ; (1993). Talking Shop: Aspects of Autonomous Learning. *ELT Journal 47* (4), 330-336.

Dickinson, L. & Carver, D. J. (1980). Learning How to Learn: Steps Towards Self-Direction in Foreign Language Learning in Schools. *English Language Teaching Journal, 35*, 1-7.

_______________ ; & Wenden, A. (1995). Autonomy, Self-Direction and Self-Access in Language Teaching and Learning. Special issue of *System, 23* (2).

Dittmar, Norbert. (1976). *Socio-linguistics.* London: Edward Arnold Publishers.

Doff, Adrian.(1988). *Teach English—A Training Course for Teachers.* Cambridge, England: Cambridge University Press.

Donaldson, R. P., & Kotter, M. (1999). Language learning in Cyber Space: Teleporting the Classroom into the Target Culture, *CALICO Journal, 16* (4), 531-557.

Dörnyei, Z. (2001). *Teaching and Researching Motivation*. Essex: Longman.

_____________ ; (2001). *Motivational Strategies in the Language Classroom.* Cambridge: Cambridge University Press.

Douglas, D. (1986). "Communicative Competence and Tests of Oral Skills". In Bachman, L. and A. Cohen. (1998). *Interfaces between Second Language and Language Testing Research.* Cambridge: Cambridge University Press.

Dubin F, Eskey D. & Grabe, W. (eds.), (1986). *Teaching Second Language Reading for Academic Purposes,* Reading Massachusetts: Addison Wesley

Durkin, K. (1986). *Language Development in the School Years.* Brookline Books, Cambridge, MA.

Eckman, F. (1991). "The Structural Conformity Hypothesis and the Acquisition of Consonant Clusters in the Interlanguage of ESL Learners". *Studies in Second Language Acquisition* 13:23-41.

Edge, J. (1994). Toward Communication in and about Second Language Teacher Education. *TESOL Quarterly, 28* (2), 395-400.

Edmondson, J. (1985). "Biological Foundations of Language Universals". In Ellis, R. 1994. *The Study of Second Language Acquisition. (Seventh Impression).* Hong Kong: Oxford University Press.

Educational Testing Service. (1996). *TOEFL Test of Written English Guide.* Princeton, NJ: ETS.

Edwards, John R. (1982). "Language Attitudes and Their Implications." In Ryan & Giles: 20-33.

Egbert, J. (May 2002). A Project for Everyone: English Language Learners and Technology in Content-area Classrooms. *Learning and Leading with Technology, 29*(8), 36-41.

Ellis, Greg. (1996). How Culturally Appropriate is the Communicative Approach? *ELT Journal, 50* (3), 213-18.

Ellis, G. & Sinclair, B. (1989). *Learning to Learn English: A Course in Learner Training.* Cambridge: Cambridge University Press.

Ellis, R. (1985). *Understanding Second Language Acquisition.* 7th Impression, 2000. Oxford: Oxford University Press.

_____________ ;(1986). Activities and Procedures for Teacher Training. *ELT Journal, 40* (2), 91-99.

_____________ ;(1990). Activities and Procedures in Teacher Education. In J. Richards and D. Nunan. (Eds.) *Second Language Teacher Education.* Cambridge: Cambridge University Press.

_____________ ;(1990). *Instructed Second Language Acquisition.* Cambridge, MA: Basil Blackwell.

_____________ ; (1991). *Understanding Second Language Acquisition.* Oxford: OUP.

_____________ ;(1994). *The Study of Second Language Acquisition. (7th impression).* Hong Kong: Oxford University Press.

______________ ;(1997). *The Study of Second Language Acquisition*, Oxford: Oxford University Press.

______________ ;(1997). *SLA Research and Language Teaching*. Oxford: Oxford University Press.

______________ ;(2003). *Task Based Language Learning and Teaching*. Oxford: Oxford University Press.

______________ ;(2005). Principles of Instructed Language Learning. *Asian EFL Journal*, 7(3).

______________ ; & Barkhuizen, G. (2005). *Analyzing Learner Language*. New York: Oxford University Press.

EnGauge. North Central Regional Educational Laboratory. Retrieved May 31, 2002 from http://www.ncrel.org/engauge/skills/21skills.htm

Epstein, S., Flynn, S. and Martohardjono, G. (1998). "The Strong Continuity Hypothesis in Adult L2 Acquisition of Functional Categories". In S. Flynn, G. Martohardjono and W. O'Neil (eds.). *The Generative Study of Second Language Acquisition*, pp. 61-77. Hillsdale, NJ: Erlbaum. In Archibald, J. (ed.) *Second Language Acquisition*. Oxford: Blackwell.

Ersöz, A. (2004). Key to Effective Teaching: Intrinsic Motivation. In G.Durmuþoðlu-Köse (Ed.), *Proceedings of the 5th International Inged-Anadolu ELT Conference* (pp. 51-54). Eski°ehir, Turkey.

Esch, E. M. (1997). Learner Training for Autonomous Language Learning. In P. Benson and P. Voller (Eds.), *Autonomy and Independence in Language Learning* (pp.164-175). London: Longman.

Eskey, D. (1973). 'A Model Program for Teaching Advanced Reading to Students of English as a Second Language' *Language Learning* 23/2: 169184

______________ ; (1988). 'Holding in the Bottom: An Interactive Approach to The Language Problems of Second Language Readers' in Carrell P., Devine J. & Eskey D. (Eds).

______________ ; & Grabe, W. (1988). 'Interactive Models for Second Language Reading: Perspectives on Instruction' in Carrell P., Devine J. & Eskey D. (Eds).

Finch, A.E. (1998). Designing and Using a Learner Journal for False Beginners: Self- Assessment and Organization of Learning. *Self-Access Language Learning Newsletter*, Retrieved June 25, 2006 from http://lc.ust.hk/HASALD.

Fishman, J. A. (1972). "The Relationship between Micro-and Macro-sociolinguistics in the Study of Who Speaks What Language to Whom and When." In Pride, J. B. & Holmes, Janet (Eds). *Socio-linguistics*. Harmondsworth: Penguin Books Ltd: 15-32.

______________ ; (1989). *Language and Ethnicity in Minority Sociolinguistic Perspective*. Clevedon: Multilingual Matters.

Flynn, S. (1996). "A Parameter-setting Approach to Second Language Acquisition" in W. Ritchie and T. Bhatia (eds.). *Handbook of Second Language Acquisition,* pp. 121- 58. San Diego: Academic Press. In Archibald, J. (ed.) *Second Language Acquisition.* Oxford: Blackwell.

Freeman, D. (1989). Teacher Training, Development and Decision Making: A Model of Teaching and Related Strategies for Teacher Education. *TESOL Quarterly, 23* (1), 27-45.

_____________ ; & Richards, J. (Eds.). (1996). *Teacher Learning in Language Teaching.* Cambridge: Cambridge University Press.

_____________ ; (2002). Second Language Teacher Education. In R. Carter & D. Nunan (Eds.), *The Cambridge Guide to Teaching English to Speakers of Other Languages* (pp. 72-79). Cambridge: Cambridge University Press.

Fry, Edward Bernard. (1963). *Teaching Faster Reading: A Manual.* Cambridge, MA: The University Press.

Gardner, R.C. (1983). "Learning Another Language: A True Social Psychological Experiment". *Journal of Language and Social Psychology.* Vol. 2, 219-240.

_____________ ; (1985). *Social Psychology and Second Language Learning: The Role of Attitudes and Motivation.* London: Edward Arnold.

_____________ ; (1988). The Socio-Educational Model of Second Language Learning: Assumptions, Findings, and Issues. *Language Learning*, 38, 101-126.

_____________ ; (1996), Motivation and Second Language Acquisition: Perspectives, *Journal of the CAAL*, 18 (2): 19-42.

Gardner, R.C., Lalonde, R.N. and Moorcroft, R. (1985), The Role of Attitudes and Motivation in Second Language Learning: Co-relational and Experimental Considerations, *Language Learning: A Journal of Applied Linguistics*, 35/2: 207-227.

_____________ ; and Lambert, E. (1972), *Attitudes and Motivation in Second Language Learning*, Rowley, MA: Newbury House.

Gardner, R., Smythe, P., Clement, L. & Glicksman L. (1976). Second Language Learning: A Social Psychological Perspective. *Canadian Modern Language Review, 32*, 198-213.

Garinger, D. (2001). Textbook Evaluation. *TEFL Web Journal, 1.*

_____________ ; (2002). *Textbook Selection for the ESL Classroom.*

Ghosn, I. (2002). Four Good Reasons to Use Literature in Primary School ELT. *ELT Journal, 56* (2), 172-179.

Gibbons, P. (2006). *Bridging Discourses in the ESL Classroom: Students, Teachers and Researchers.* London; New York: Continuum.

Gimson, A.C. (1989). *An Introduction to the Pronunciation of English.* London: Edward Arnold.

Gleason, H. A. (1955). *An Introduction to Descriptive Linguistics*. New York: Holt, Rinehart & Winston.

Goodman, K. (1967). 'Reading: A Psycho-linguistic Guessing Game' *Journal of the Reading Specialist* 6: 126135.

Goodwin-Jones, B. (2004). Emerging Technologies, Language in Action: From Web Quests to Virtual Realities. *Language Learning & Technology, 8* (3), 9-14.

Gonzalez-Bueno, M., & Perez, L.C. (2000). Electronic Mail in Foreign Language Writing: A Study of Grammatical and Lexical Accuracy, and Quantity of Language. *Foreign Language Annals, 33* (2), 189-198.

Gorlach, M. (1991). *Studies in Varieties of English Around the World*. 1984-1988. Amsterdam/Philadelphia: John Benjamin's Publishing Company.

_______________ ; (1995). *More Englishes: New Studies in Varieties of English 1988-1994*. Amsterdam: John Benjamin's.

Gower, R., Phillips, D. & Walters, S. (1995). *Teaching Practice Handbook*. Oxford: Heinemann.

Graddol, David. "Thoughts from Kolkatta on English in India." *English Today 100,* Vol. 25, No. 4 (December 2009). United Kingdom: Cambridge University Press.

Granger, S. (1994). The Learner Corpus: A Revolution in Applied Linguistics. *English Today. 10* (3), 25-29.

Graves, D. H. (1983). *Writing: Teachers and Children at Work*. New Hampshire: Heinemann Educational Books.

Green, J. L. (1983). Exploring Classroom Discourse: Linguistic Perspectives on Teaching-Learning Processes. *Educational Psychologist, 18*, 180-99.

_______________ ; & Wallat, C. (1981). Mapping instructional conversations: A socio-linguistic Ethnography. In J. L. Green, & C. Wallat (Eds.), *Ethnography and Language in Educational Settings*. Norwood: Ablex.

Green, S. (ed.), (2000). *New Perspectives on Teaching and Learning Modern Languages. Clevedon: Multilingual Matters*. Review by D. Ayoun

Gruba, G. (2004). Computer Assisted Language Learning (CALL). In A. Davies & C. Elder (eds.), *Handbook of Applied Linguistics*. Oxford: Blackwell.

Gutierrez, K. D. (1994). How Talk, Context, and Script Shape Contexts for Learning: A Cross-Case Comparison of Journal Sharing. *Linguistics and Education, 5*, 335-65.

Gupta, Anthea Fraser, (1996). "Reading A: English and Empire: Teaching English in Nineteenth Century India." In Mercer, Neil & Swann, Joan. *Learning English: Development and Diversity*. London: Routledge: 188-194.

Haddad,Wadi D., & Jurich, Sonia. (2002). ICT For Education: Potential and Potency, in Haddad, W. & Drexler, A. (eds), *Technologies for Education: Potentials, Parameters, and Prospects,* Washington DC: Academy for Educational Development and Paris: UNESCO.

Halliday, M. A. K. 1970. Language Structure and Language Function. In John Lyon (ed.), *New Horizons in Linguistics.* New York: Penguin Books. 140-165.

_____________ ; (1973). *Explorations in the Functions of Language.* London: Edward Arnold.

Hall, R. A. (Jr.), (1969). *Introductory Linguistics.* Delhi: Motilal Banarasidas.

Halsall, Paul. "Thomas Babington Macaulay on Indian Education". 17 Oct. 2007 <http://www.fordham.edu/halsall/mod/1833macaulay-india.html>

Hamers, Josiane F. & Blanc, Michel H. A. (1989). *Bilinguality and Bilingualism.* Cambridge: CUP.

Hammond, R. M. (1995). Foreign Accent and Phonetic Interference: The Application of Linguistic Research to the Teaching of Second Language Pronunciation. In P. Eckman (Ed.), *Second Language Acquisition: Theory and Pedagogy.* New Jersey: Lawrence Erlbaum Associates.

Hampel, R., & Baber, E. (2003). Using Internet-Based Audio-Graphic and Video Conferencing for Language Learning. In U. Felix (Ed.), *Language learning on-line: Towards best practice.* Lisse, The Netherlands: Swets & Zeitlinger.

Hampel, R., & Hauck, M. (2004). Towards an Effective Use of Audio Conferencing in Distance Language Courses. *Language Learning & Technology, 8* (1), 66-82.

Handscombe, J. (1994). Putting it All Together. In F. Genesee (Ed.), *Educating Second Language Children: The Whole Child, The Whole Curriculum, The Whole Community.* New York: Cambridge University Press.

Harris, D. P. (1986). *Testing English as a Second Language.* New York: McGraw Hill.

Harklau, L. (2005). Ethnography and Ethnographic Research on Second Language Teaching and Learning. In E. Hinkel (Ed.), *Handbook of Research in Second Language Learning and Teaching.* Mahwah, NJ: Lawrence Erlbaum

Harmer, J. (1991). *The Practice of English Language Teaching* (Rev. Ed.). Longman.

_____________ ; (2000). *How to Teach English.* Beijing: Pearson Education Limited.

Harsch, Kenny. (1994). Vocabulary Enrichment Through Word Association. In *New Ways in Teaching Vocabulary.* Ed. Paul Nation. Alexandria,

Virginia: Teachers of English to Speakers of Other Languages, Inc. 128-129.

Harwood, N. (2005). What do We Want EAP Teaching Materials for? *Journal of English for Academic Purposes, 4* (2), 149-161.

Hatch, E. & Wagner-Gough, J. (1976). Explaining Sequence and Variation in SLA. *Language Learning, Special Issue, 4,* 39-47.

Heaton, J.B. (1990). *Writing English Language Tests* (3rd Ed.). New York: Longman.

Hedge, T. (1993). Key Concepts in ELT. *ELT Journal, 47* (2), 92.

_______________ ; (2000). *Teaching and Learning in the Language Classroom.* Oxford: Oxford University Press.

Hertel, T.J. (2003). Using an E-mail Exchange to Promote Cultural Learning. *Foreign Language Annals, 36* (3), 386-396.

Higgins, A. & Postle, G. (1993). Changing Paradigms: From Correspondence Schools to open Learning. *Towards 2000: Schooling Through Distance Education,* SPERA Proceedings of the First National DE Conference, Toowoomba, Australia.

Hoch, F. S. (1985). Computer Literacy and the Foreign Language Teacher. *CALICO Journal, 3* (1), 17-18, 32.

Hoven, D. (1999), 'A Model for Listening and Viewing Comprehension in Multimedia Environments', *Language Learning and Technology* 3/ 1: 88103

Hsieh, L. T. (2001). Business English: How and What to Teach. *The Bulletin of National Ping Tung Institute of Commerce, 3,* 59-70.

Huang, S. J. & Liu, H.F. (2000). Communicative Language Teaching in a Multimedia Language Lab. *The Internet TESL Journal, 6* (2). Retrieved May 23, 2005, from http://iteslj.org/Articles/Lee-CALLbarriers.html

Huntoon, Diane. (1994). Verb Pass for Fluency Development. In *New Ways in Teaching Speaking.* Alexandria, Virginia: Teachers of English to Speakers of Other Languages, Inc.

Hutchby, I. (2001). *Conversation and Technology: From the telephone to the Internet.* Malden, MA: Blackwell.

Hyman, L. (1975). *Phonology: Theory and Practice.* New York: Holt.

Isbell, K. (1999). Intercultural Awareness Through Drama. *English Teaching Forum Online, 37*(1). Retrieved December 13, 2006 from http://exchanges.state.gov/forum/vols/vol37/no1/p10.htm

Jain, R.K. (1985). *Essentials of English Teaching.* Agra: Vinod Pustak Mandir.

Jan, L.C. (2000). An Experimental Computer and Internet Based English Writing Course in CCIT. *Journal of C.C.I.T., 19,* 229-261.

_______________ ; (2002). Interactive Online Discussion in an Internet Assisted English Writing Course. *Journal of C.C.I.T., 31* (1), 39-58.

Jayshree Mohanraj, *Spoken Conversational English*, CIEFL, Hyderabad.

Jenkins, J. (2003). *World Englishes: A Resource Book for Students*. London: Routledge.

Jespersen, O. (1922). *Language: Its Nature, Development and Origin*. New York: W. W. Norton & Company Inc.

Jordan, R.R. (1997). *English for Academic Purposes: A Guide and Resource Book for Teachers*. Cambridge: Cambridge University Press.

Kachru, Braj, B. (1982). "English in South Asia." In Bailey & Görlach. *World Englishes*. 353-383.

_______________ ; (1983). *The Indianization of English. The English Language in India*. Oxford: OUP.

_______________ ; (1986a). *The Alchemy of English. The Spread, Functions and Models of Non-Native Englishes*. Oxford: Pergamon Press Ltd.

_______________ ; (1986b). "English Education in India: A Socio-linguistic Profile of Indian English." Nagoya Gakuin Daikagu Gaikokugo Kyoiku Kiyo, No. 15:11-30.

_______________ ; (1986c). "The Power and Politics of English." In *World Englishes*, Vol. 5, No. 2/3: 121-140.

_______________ ; (1986). *The Alchemy of English: The Spread, Function and Models of Non-native Englishes*. New York: Pergamon Press Inc., p.12.

_______________ ; (1987). "The Spread of English and Sacred Linguistic Cows." In Gurt. *Language Spread and Language Policy Issues, Implications and Case Studies*. Washington DC: Georgetown University Press: 207-228.

_______________ ; (1994). "English in South Asia". In Robert Burchfield (ed.). *The Cambridge History of the English Language*. Vol. V: *English in Britain and Overseas. Origins and Development*. Cambridge: CUP: 497-626.

_______________ ; (1996). "Opening Borders with World Englishes: Theory in the Classroom." In: On *JALT 96: Crossing Borders. The Proceedings of the 23rd Annual JALT International Conference on Language Teaching/Learning*. Hiroshima, Japan: 10-20.

_______________ ;1997. "World Englishes and English-using Communities." In *Annual Review of Applied Linguistics* 17: 66-87.

Kannan, J. & Macknish C. (2000). Issues Affecting On-line ESL Learning: A Singapore Case Study. *The Internet TESL Journal, 6* (11).

Kandiah, Triru. (1991). "Variation in Society—The Background and Its Impact." In *Cheshire*: 271-287.

Kao, C.C. (1999). An Investigation into Lexical, Grammatical, and Semantic Errors in English Compositions of College Students in Taiwan. *Fu Hsing Kang Journal, 67*, 1-32.

Kavitha, V. *Attitudinal Factor in Second Language Acquisition An Illustrative Example from a Class in University*. Language in India, Volume 9: 5 May 2009, http://www.languageinindia.com/may2009/kavithaattitudinal.html, 12 March, 2010.

Kavanagh, F. J. & Mattingly, G. (eds.), (1972). *Language by Ear and by Eye*, Cambridge, MA: MIT Press

Kelly, G. (2000). *How to Teach Pronunciation*. Essex: Longman

Kenworthy, J. (1987). *Teaching English Pronunciation*. London: Longman.

Kern, R. & Warschauer, M. (2000). Introduction: Theory and Practice of Networked-based Language Teaching. In M. Warschauer & R. Kern (Eds.), *Network-based Language Teaching: Concepts and Practice*. New York: Cambridge University Press.

Kitade, K. (2000). L2 Learners' Discourse and SLA Theories in CMC: Collaborative Interaction in Internet Chat. *Computer Assisted Language Learning, 13* (2), 143-166.

Kitao, S. Kathleen, (1993). Teaching Transitions. In *New Ways in Teaching Reading*. Ed. Richard R. Day. Alexandria, Virginia: Teachers of English to Speakers of Other Languages, Inc.

Kodchedkar, S. (2002). *Readings in English Language Teaching in India*. Chennai: Orient Longman.

Kohonen, V. (1987). *Towards Experiential Learning of Elementary English 1. A Theoretical Outline of an English and Finnish Teaching Experiment in Elementary Learning*. Tampere: University of Tampere.

_______________ ; (1989). *Experiential Language Learning Towards Second Language Learning as LearnerEducation*. Bilingual Research Group Working Papers. Santa Cruz, CA.: University of California.

_______________ ; (1992a). Experiential Language Learning: Second Language Learning as Cooperative Learner Education. In D. Nunan (Ed.), (1992a) *Collaborative language learning and teaching* (pp. 37-56). Cambridge: Cambridge University Press.

Kramsch, C. (1985). Literary Texts in the Classroom: A Discourse Perspective. *The Modern Language Journal 69* (4), 356-366.

_______________ ; & Andersen, R.W. (1999, January). Teaching Text and Context through Multimedia. *Language Learning & Technology, 2* (2), 31-42. Retrieved June 7, 2004, from http://llt.msu.edu/vol2num2/article1/

Kreutzer, M., & Neunzig, W. (1997). Computer Assisted Learning, Teacher Training and An Evaluation of a Seminar for Language Teachers. *CALICO Journal, 14* (2-4), 65-79.

Ladefoged, P. (1982). *A Course in Phonetics*. New York: Harcourt Brace.

Lambert, W.E. (1963b), Psychological Approaches to the Study of Language Part II: On the Second Language Learning and Bilingualism. *Modern Language Journal* 14, 114-121.

_______________ ; (1974). *Culture and Language as Factors in Learning and Education*. In F. F. Aboud & R. D. Meade (Eds.), *Cultural Factors in Learning and Education*. Bellingham: Western Washington State University.

Lantolf, J. (2000). *Socio-cultural Theory and Second Language Learning*. New York: Oxford University Press.

Lazar, G. (1993). *Literature and Language Teaching: A Guide for Teachers and Trainers*. Cambridge, England: Cambridge University Press.

_______________ ; (1993). *Literature and Language Teaching*. Cambridge: Cambridge University Press.

_______________ ; (1994). Using literature at lower levels. *ELT Journal, 48* (2), 115-124.

Lee, K. (2000). English Teachers' Barriers to the Use of Computer-Assisted Language Learning. *The Internet TESL Journal, 6* (12).

Lee, S. (2000). Teaching Writing Using a Bulletin Board on the Internet: A Preliminary Study. *English Teaching, 55* (3), 171-191.

_______________ ; & Krashen, S. (2002). Predictors of Success in Writing English as a Foreign Language: Reading, Revision Behavior, Apprehension, and Writing. *College Student Journal, 36*, 532-543.

Lee, W.R. (1994). *Language Teaching Games*. Oxford: Oxford University Press.

Lennon, P. (1989). Introspection and Intentionality in Advanced SLA. *Language Learning, 39*, 375-395.

Leech, G. (1998). Preface. In S. Granger (Eds.), *Learner English on Computer*. London and New York: Addison Wesley Longman.

Lemke, J. L. (1990). *Talking Science: Language, Learning, and Values*. Norwood, NJ: Ablex.

Levy, M. (1997). *Computer-Assisted Language Learning: Context and Conceptualization*. London: Clarendon Press.

Lewis, M. & Hill, J. (1992) *Practical Techniques for Language Teaching*. Hove: Language Teaching Publications.

Liaw, M. L. (2001). Exploring Literary Responses in an EFL Classroom. *Foreign Language Annals, 34*, 35-45.

Lightbown, P. (1985). Great Expectations: Second Language Acquisition Research and Classroom Teaching. *Applied Linguistics, 6* (2), 173-189.

_______________ ; & Spada, N. (1993). *How Languages are Learned*. Oxford: Oxford University Press.

Lindauer, S. K. (1988). Wordless Books: An Approach to Visual Literacy. *Children's Literature in Education, 19* (3), 136-142.

Lin,Yen-Chi A. (2004). *An Assessment of the International Students' Attitudes Toward Technology-Based Learning: English as a Second Language (ESL) Implication*. Mississippi State University. DAI. A 65/02, 478.

Liou, H. C., & Yeh, H. Y. (2000). *A Study of Using Web Articles to Support College English Students' Ideas in Writing.* Paper presented in Learning Societies in the New Millennium: Creativity, Caring & Commitments. International Conference on Computers in Education / International Conference on Computer-Assisted Instruction, Taipei, Taiwan.

Littlewood, W. (1990). *Communicative Language Teaching.* Cambridge: Cambridge University Press.

_______________ ; (2000). Do Asian Students Really Want to Listen and Obey? *ELT Journal, 54* (1), 31-35.

Llosa, L. (2007). Validating a Standards-based Classroom Assessment of English Proficiency: A Multi-trait-Multi-method approach. *Language Testing, 24* (4), 489–515.

Logan, S. & Moore, N. (2004). Implementing Learner Training from a Teacher's Perspective. In H. Reinders (et al) (Eds.), *Supporting Independent Learning in the 21st Century: Proceedings of the Independent Learning Association Conference*, the University of Melbourne, Australia.

Mahapatra, B.P. (1990). "A Demographic Appraisal of Multi-lingualism in India." In Pattanayak: 1-14.

Majumdar. S. (Ed.), (2005). *Regional Guideline for Teacher Development for Pedagogy Technology Integration*, Thailand: UNESCO.

MacCarthy, P. (1978). *The Teaching of Pronunciation.* Cambridge: Cambridge University Press.

Matas, C.P. & Birch, G. (2000). Web-based Second Language Grammar Development: Researching the Options. *CALL-EJ Online, 1* (3).

McCarthy, C.P. (1998). Learner Training for Learner Autonomy on Summer Language Courses. *The Internet TESL Journal 3* (7).

McCrum, Robert, Cran, Willian, McNeil, Robert. (1988). *The Story of English.* London: Faber& Faber Ltd. & BBC Books.

McEnery, T. & Others (1995). A Statistical Analysis of Corpus Based Computer vs. Traditional Human Teaching Methods of Part of Speech Analysis. *Computer-Assisted Language Learning, 8* (2-3), 259-74.

McGrath, I. (1995). *Feeding, Leading, Showing, and Throwing: Process Choices in Teacher Training and Trainer Training, in Learning to Train: Perspectives on the Development of Language Teacher Trainers.* Prentice Hall Europe, in association with the British Council.

McGregor, L., Tate M. and Robinson, K. (1977). *Learning through Drama: Report of the School Council Drama Teaching Project* (10-16).

McNamara, J. (1973). Nurseries, Streets and Classrooms: Some Comparisons and Deductions. *Modern Language Journal, 57*, 250-255.

Meganathan, Rama. *English Language Education in Rural Schools of India: The Situation, the Policy and the Curriculum.30 .10. 2009.* http://www.teachingenglish.org.

Mehan, H. (1979). *Learning Lessons: Social Organization in the Classroom.* Cambridge MA: Harvard University Press.

Mehrotra, R.R. English in *India*: The Current Scene *ELT* Journal 1977 XXXI (2): 163-170. London: OUP, 1977

Meunier, L. E. (1994). Computer-assisted Language Instruction and Co-operative Learning. *Applied Language Learning 5* (2), 31-56.

Milton, J. & Garbi, A. (2000). VIRLAN: Collaborative Foreign Language Learning on the Internet for Primary Age Children: Problems and a Solution. *Educational Technology & Society, 3* (3).

Mo, L. (1999). On the Participants of English Listening Course and Their Functions. *Journal of PLA University of Foreign Languages, 109*(4), 75-78.

Morley, J. (1987). *Current Perspectives on Pronunciation.* Washington, DC: YESOL.

______________; *(1991). The Pronunciation Component in Teaching English to Speakers of Other Languages.* TESOL Quarterly, 25 *(1), 51-74.*

______________; *(1991). Listening Comprehension in Second/Foreign Language Instruction. In* Teaching English as a Second or Foreign Language. *Ed. Marianne Celce-Murcia. Boston: Heinle & Heinle.*

Mullins, P. (1992). *Successful English Language Learning Strategies of Students Enrolled in the Faculty of Arts, Chulalonkorn University, Bangkok Thailand.* United States International University, San Diego, CA.

NCERT. (2005). *National Curriculum Framework.* New Delhi: NCERT.

Nunan, D. (1989) *Designing Tasks for the Communicative Classroom.* Cambridge: Cambridge University Press.

______________; *(2002). Learner Strategy Training in the Classroom: An Action Research Study. In J.C. Richards & W. A. Renandya (Eds.),* Methodology in Language Teaching. *Cambridge: Cambridge University Press.*

______________; *and Lindsay Miller. (Eds). 1995.* New Ways in Teaching Listening. *Alexandria, Virginia: Teachers of English to Speakers of Other Languages, Inc.*

Nunn, R. (2005). Competence and Teaching English as an International Language. *Asian EFL Journal.* 7 (3). Retrieved Mar. 5, 2007 from http://www.asian-efljournal.com/September_05_ rn.php

Nutta, Joyce (1998). Is Computer-based Grammar Instruction as Effective as Teacher-Directed Grammar Instruction for Teaching L2 Structures? *CALICO Journal, 16* (1), 49-62.

Nystrand, M. (1997). *Opening Dialogue: Understanding the Dynamics of Language and Learning in the English Classroom.* New York: Teachers College Press (with A. Gamoran, R. Kachur, & C. Prendergast).

O'Brien, T. (1981). The E-R-O-T-I Model: A Stimulating Guide for Teacher Training. *In British Council ELT Documents, 110*, 54 - 61.

Oberprieler, G. (1999). Outcome-based Learning and The Role of CALL in South Africa. In R. Debski & M. Levy (Eds.), *WorldCALL: Global Perspectives on Computer-assisted Language Learning.* Swets & Zeitlinger.

O'Grady, William, Michael Dabrovolsky, and Mark Aronoff. (1993). *Contemporary Linguistics: An Introduction.* New York: St. Martin's Press.

Oxford, R. (1990). *Language Learning Strategies: What Every Teacher Should Know.* Rowley, Mass.: Newbury House.

Oxford, R. L. (2006). Task-based Language Teaching and Learning: An Overview. *Asian EFL Journal, 8* (3).

Palmer, H.E. (1917). *The Scientific Study and Teaching of Languages.* London: Harrap.

Parkinson, B., & Thomas H.R. (2000). *Teaching Literature in a Second Language.* Edinburgh: Edinburgh University Press.

Parrott, M. (1993). *Tasks for Language Teachers.* Cambridge: Cambridge University Press.

Patrikis, P.C. (1997). The Evolution of Computer Technology in Foreign Language Teaching and Learning. In R. Debski, J. Gassin & M. Smith (Eds.), *Language Learning Through Social Computing* (p.176). ALAA& The Horwood Language Centre.

Pennington, M.C. (1990). A Professional Development Focus for the Language Teaching Practicum. In J. Richards and D. Nunan, (Eds), *Second Language Teacher Education* (pp. 132 - 151). Cambridge: Cambridge University Press.

Philips, M. (1987). Potential Paradigms and Possible Problems for CALL. *System, 15*(3), 275-287.

Pfaff, C. W. (1987). *First and Second Language Acquisition.* MA: Newbury House publications. Cambridge.

Pathak, R. S. (1999). *Teaching English in India.* New Delhi: Creative Books.

Pattanayak, D. P. (1990). *Multilingualism in India* (Ed.). Clevedon: Multilingual Matters Ltd.

_______________ *; (2005).* India: A Multilingual Perspective. *A Report. New Delhi: NCERT.*

Pennycook, Alastair. (1994). *The Cultural Politics of English as an International Language.* Harlow: Longman Group Ltd.

Plaister, Ted. (1994). My Friends Call Me Ted. In *New Ways in Teaching Speaking*. Alexandria, Virginia: Teachers of English to Speakers of Other Languages, Inc.

Plaister, Ted. (1994). Using a Box of Raisins to Promote Speech. In *New Ways in Teaching Speaking*. Alexandria, Virginia: Teachers of English to Speakers of Other Languages, Inc

Platt, J., Weber, H., Ho, M.L. (1984). *The New Englishes*. London: Routledge & Kegan Paul.

Poplack, Shana. (2001). 'Code Switching: Linguistic' in *International Encyclopedia of the Social & Behavioral Sciences*, Elsevier Science Ltd.

Price, Karen. (1987). The Use of Technology: Varying the Medium of Language Teaching. In Wilga M. Rivers (ed.), *Interactive Language Teaching*, (pp.155- 169). Melbourne, OUP.

Raimes, Ann. (1983). *Techniques in Teaching Writing*. New York: Oxford University Press.

Ramanathan, H. (2008). Testing of English in India: A Developing Concept. *Language Testing, 25* (1), 111-126.

Richard C. Jack (2006), *Intro: New Interchange. English for International Communication*. Cambridge: CUP.

Richards, J.C. and Rodgers, T.S. 2002. *Approaches and Methods in Language Teaching*. Delhi, Cambridge University Press.

Richards, J. & Nunan, D. (Eds.). (1990). *Second Language Teacher Education*. Cambridge: Cambridge University Press.

R.N. Ghosh, *Indian Bi-lingualism and the Teaching of English*, CIEFL, Hyderabad.

Roach, P. (2000). *English Phonetics and Phonology*. Cambridge: Cambridge University Press.

Robinett, B.W. (1978). *Teaching English to Speakers of other Languages: Substance and Technique*. Minneapolis: University of Minnesota Press.

Robinson, P. (2001). *Cognition and Second Language Instruction*. Cambridge: Oxford University Press.

_______________ *; (2002). The Pervading Influence of Neo-Confucianism on the Korean Education System.* Asian EFL Journal, 4 *(2).*

_______________ *; (2003). Teaching English Pronunciation Skills to the Asian Learner. A Cultural Complexity or Subsumed Piece of Cake?* Asian EFL Journal, *June.*

Romaine, Suzanne. (1995). *Bilingualism* (2nd ed.). Oxford: Blackwell Publishers.

Rost, M. (1990). *Listening in Language Learning*. London: Longman.

_______________ *; (2001). Listening. In R. Carter & D. Nunan (Eds.),* The Cambridge Guide to Teaching English to Speakers of other Languages *(pp. 7-13). Cambridge: Cambridge University Press.*

Ryan, Ellen Bouchard & Giles, Howard. (1982). *Attitudes Towards Language Variation*. London: Edward Arnold. 1982

Saghal, Anju. (1991). "Patterns of Language Use in a Bi-lingual Setting in India". In Cheshire: 299-307.

Salem, N. M. (2006). *The Role of Motivation, Gender and Language Learning Strategies in EFL Proficiency*. Lebanon: American University of Beirut.

Salmien, J. (1998). *Using Wordless Books in Your ESL Class.* Paper presented at the Annual Meeting of the Teachers of English to Speakers of Other Language. PP. 17-21.

Sankoff, D. (1998). 'A Formal Production-based Explanation of the Facts of Code Switching'. *Bi-lingualism: Language and Cognition* I (1): 39-50.

Sanyal, S.C. (1987). *English Language in India & Indo-Anglian Prose Style*. London: TEFL.

Sapir, E. (1919). *Selected Writings in Language, Culture and Personality.* Berkeley and Los Angeles: University of California Press.

_______________; *(1921).* Language: An Introduction to the Study of Speech. *New York: Harcourt, Brace & World.*

Saussure, Ferdinand de. (1983). *Course in General Linguistics.* Eds. Charles Bally and Albert Sechehaye. Trans. Roy Harris. La Salle, Illinois: Open Court.

Schacter, John. *The Impact of Educational Technology on Student Achievement. What the Most Current Research has to say.*

Schegloff, E., Jefferson, G., & Sacks, H. (1977). The Preference for Self-correction in the Organization of Repair in Conversation, *Language, 53* (2), 361-382.

_______________; *(1979). The Relevance of Repair to Syntax-for-Conversation. In T. Givon (Ed.),* Syntax and Semantics , Volume 12, Discourse and Syntax. *(pp. 261-286). New York, Academic Press.*

Schinitzer, E. (1995). English as an International Language: Implications for the Inter-culturalists and Language Educators. *International Journal of Intercultural Relations, 19* (2), 227-236.

Schnackenberg, H.L. (1997). *Learning English Electronically: Formative Evaluation in ESL Software.* ERIC Document Reproduction Service No. ED403877.

Scovel, T. (1969) Foreign Accent: Language Acquisition and Cerebral Dominance. *Language Learning, 19,* 245-254.

Scott, Baldauf. (November 23, 2004). "A Hindi-English Jumble, Spoken by 350 Million". *Christian Science Monitor*. http://www.csmonitor.com/2004/1123/p01s03-wosc.html.

Scrimshaw, P. (Ed.), (1993), *Language, Classrooms, and Computers,* Routledge: London

Scrivener, J. (1994). *Learning Teaching: A Guidebook for English Language Teachers*. Oxford: Heinemann.

Sebastian, Richard J. (1982). "An Integrative Perspective for the Study of Attitudes Towards Language Variation." In Ryan & Giles: 1-19.

Seelye, H. (1984). *Teaching Culture: Strategies for Inter-cultural Communication*. Rev. edition. Lincolnwood, IL: National Textbook Company.

Shanahan, D. (1997). Articulating the Relationship between Language, Literature, and Culture: Toward a New Agenda for Foreign Language Teaching and Research. *The Modern Language Journal, 81*, 164-74.

Sharkova, Krassimira D. (1996). *A Reflective Model of Language Teacher Education: An Integration of Theoretical with Competency based Training in an Awareness Raising Context.* Paper presented at the 1996 IALS Symposium for Language Teacher Educators.

Sharma, Pete. (2009). *Controversies in Using Technology in Language Teaching*. Retrieved January 18, 2010 from http://www.teachingenglish.org.uk/think/articles/controversiesusingtechnologylanguageteaching 18-1-10

Sheerin, S. (1997). An Exploration of the Relationship between Self-access and Independent Learning. In P. Benson & P. Voller (Eds.), *Autonomy and Independence in Language Learning* (pp. 54-65). London: Longman.

Sheorey L Ravi (2006), *Learning and Teaching English in India*. New Delhi: Sage Publications India Pvt. Ltd.

Siemens, George. & Tittenberger, Peter. (2009) *Handbook of Emerging Technologies for Learning*. Retrieved January 18, 2010, from http://umanitoba.ca/learning_technologies /cetl/HETL.pdf

Singleton, D. (1989). *Language Acquisition: The Age Factor*. London: Multilingual Matters. Skiba, Richard. (1997). 'Code Switching as a Countenance of Language Interference', *TESL Journal, Vol. III, No. 10, October 1997*, http://iteslj.org/, accessed on 15 Jan 2010.

Skidmore, D. (2000). From Pedagogical Dialogue to Dialogical Pedagogy. *Language and Education, 14* (4), 283-296.

Slimani, A. (1989). The Role of Topicalization in Classroom Language Learning. *System, 17*, 223–234.

Smith, H. (2001). Smart Board Evaluation: Final Report. Retrieved from http://www.kented.org.uk/ngfl/ict/IWB/whiteboards/report.html#11

Sook, K.H. (2003). The Types of Speaking Assessment Tasks used by Korean Junior Secondary School English Teachers. *Asian EFL Journal,* Retrieved 23 March 2008 from www.asian-efl-journal/dec_03_sub.gl.htm

Somaratne, W. (1957). *Aids and Tests in the Teaching of English.* Oxford: Oxford University Press.

Spolsky, R. (1978). *Educational Linguistics: An Introduction*. Rowley, Mass: Newbury House.

Srivastava, A.K. (1990). "Multilingualism and School Education in India: special features, problems and prospects." In Pattanayak: 37-53.

Stockwell, G., & Harrington, M. (2003). The Incidental Development of L2 Proficiency in NS-NNS Email Interaction. *CALICO Journal, 20* (2), pp. 337-360.

Strevens, P. (1974). Some Basic Principles of Teacher Training. *ELT Journal*, 29 (1), 19-27.

______________; *(1977)*. New Orientations in the Teaching of English. *Oxford: Oxford University Press.*

Swain, M. (1985). *Communicative Competence: Some Roles of Comprehensible input and Comprehensive output in its Development.* Massachusetts: Gass and Madden.

Swan, M. & Smith, B. (Eds.). (1987). *Learner English: A Teacher's Guide to Interference and other Problems.* Cambridge: Cambridge University Press.

Sweet, H. (1899). *The Practical Study of Languages: A Guide for Teachers and Learners.* London: JM Dent.

Sweet, Henry. (1964). *The Practical Study of Languages*. London: OUP.

Tarone, E. (1987). Some Influences on the Syllable Structure of Interlanguage Phonology. In S. Weinberger (Ed.), *Interlanguage Phonology: The Acquisition of a Second Language Sound System.* Cambridge, New bury House Publishers.

______________; *(1988)*. Variation in Interlanguage. *London: Edward Arnold.*

______________; *E., Swain, M. and Fathman, A. (1976). "Some Limitations to the Classroom Applications of Current Second Language Acquisition Research".* TESOL Quarterly *10:19-31*.

Taylor, R.P. (ed.), (1980). *The Computer in the School: Tutor, Tool, and Tutee*. New York: Teachers College Press.

TE Editor. *Podcasting for ELT (2005) retrieved January 18, 2010 from* http://www.teachingenglish.org.uk/think/articles/podcasting-elt.

The Beginnings of English Literary Study in British India. *Oxford Literary Review*, IX. London: OUP, 1987

The Hindu on India server, Science and Technology Briefs. (1997, 3 February). *Pagers on Indian Tongues Launched*. Available at: ttp://www.indiaserver.com/thehindu/1997/ 03/ test/03/thb10.htm [9 August 1998].

Thirumalai, M. S. (1977). *Language, Thought, and Disorder*. Mysore: Central Institute of Indian Languages.

Thompson, T., & Gaddes, M. (2005). The Importance of Teaching Pronunciation to Adult Learners. *Asian EFL Journal*, 1.

Thornbury, Scott. (2009). *On Interactive Whiteboards (again!)* Retrieved January 18, 2010 from http://www.teachingenglish.org.uk/blogs/scott-thornbury/interactive-whiteboards -again.

Tickoo, M. L. 2003. *Teaching and Learning English*. New Delhi, Orient Longman Pvt. Limited.

Tarone, E. & Yule, G. (1989). *Focus on the Language Learner*. Oxford: Oxford University Press.

Troudi, S. (1994). *The Nature of Speaking Opportunities in English as a Second Language Class*. The Florida State University

Trudgil, P. (1974). *Socio-linguistics: An Introduction*. Harmondsworth: Penguin Books.

Tseng, D.S.D. (1980). Error Analysis, Contrastive Analysis, and the Acquisition of English Communicative Competence. *Journal of the Taiwan Provincial College of Education, 4*, 69-105.

Tully, Mark. (1997). "English: and Advantage to India?" In *ELT Journal* vol. 51 No. 2:157 164.

Twaddell, W. Freeman. (1973). Vocabulary Expansion in the ESOL Classroom. *TESOL Quarterly*. 7:1, 61-78.

Tyrwhitt-Drake, H. (1999). Responding to Grammar Questions on the Internet. *ELT Journal, 53* (4), 281-88.

Underhill, N. (1987). *Testing Spoken Language: A Handbook of Oral Testing Techniques*. Cambridge: Cambridge University Press.

Ur, P. (1996). *A Course in Language Teaching: Practice and Theory*. Cambridge: Cambridge University Press.

Vale, David, & Anne Fountain. (1995). *Teaching Children English*. Cambridge, England: Cambridge University Press.

Verma, M.K. (1998). (Ed.) *Socio-linguistics, Language and Society*. New Delhi: Sage Publications.

Victori, M. & Lockhart, W. (1995). Enhancing Meta-cognition in Self-directed Language Learning. *System, 23* (2), 223-234.

Viswanathan, Gouri. (1989). *Masks of Conquest: Literary Study and British Rule in India*. New York: Columbia University Press.

Vygotsky, L. S. (1962). *Thought and Language*. Cambridge, MA: The M.I.T. Press.

Wallace, J.M. (1991). *Training Language Teachers*. Cambridge University Press: Cambridge.

Wallace, M. (1991). *Training Foreign Language Teachers: A Reflective Approach*. Cambridge: Cambridge University Press.

Walsh, S. (2006). *Investigating Classroom Discourse*. London and New York: Routledge.

Wan, S.E.L. (2004). Second Language Socialization in a Bilingual Chat room: Global and Local Considerations. *Language Learning & Technology, 8* (3), 44-65.

Wang, Y.P. (2004). Distance Language Learning: Interactivity and Fourth Generation Internet-Based Video-conferencing. *CALICO Journal, 21*(2), 373-395.

Warschauer, M., & Healey, D. (1998). Computers and Language Learning: An Overview. *Language Teaching, 31,* 57-71.

______________; *M., & Meskill, C. (2000). Technology and Second Language Learning. In J. Rosenthal (Ed.),* Handbook of Undergraduate Second Language Education *(pp. 303-318). Mahwah, New Jersey: Lawrence Erlbaum*

______________; *(2001). Online Communication. In R. Carter & D. Nunan, (Eds.),* The Cambridge Guide to Teaching English to Speakers of other Languages *(pp.207-212). Cambridge: Cambridge University Press.*

Wei, C.L. (2002). DFLL Learners' Perceptions of Internet Assisted English Writing Instruction: A Case Study. *Journal of Humanities, College of Liberal Arts*, NCHU, 32, 483-503.

Wells, G. (1999a). *Dialogic Inquiry: Toward Socio-cultural Practice and Theory of Education*. Cambridge, UK: Cambridge University Press.

______________; *(1999b). Language and Education: Re-conceptualizing Education as Dialogue.* Annual Review of Applied Linguistics, 19, *135-155.*

Wenden, A. (1987). Incorporating Learner Training in the Classroom. In A. Wenden and J. Rubin (Eds.), *Learner Strategies in Language Learning* (pp. 159-168). New York: Prentice Hall International.

______________; *(1998a). Learner Training in Foreign/Second Language Learning: A Curricular Perspective for the 21st Century.* ED 416 67.

______________; *(1998b). Meta-cognitive Knowledge and Language Learning.* Applied Linguistics, 19 *(4), 515-537.Z*

Whalen, L. (1974). Wordless Picture Books: Every Picture Tells a Story, doesn't it? *Emerging Librarian, 21* (5), 14-17.

Williams, M. & Burden, R.L. (1997). *Psychology for Language Teachers*. Cambridge: Cambridge University Press.

Widdowson, H.G. (1968). "The Teaching of English Through Science". J. Dakin et al., OUP, London

______________; *(1978).* Teaching Language as Communication. *Oxford: Oxford University Press.*

______________; *(1979).* Explorations in Applied Linguistics. *OUP, London.*

______________; *(1983).* Learning Purpose and Language Use. *Oxford: Oxford University Press.*

______________; *(1984).* Stylistics and the Teaching of Literature. *Essex: Longman.*

_____________ : *(1984). Teaching Language as and For Communication. In H. Widdowson (Ed.),* Explorations in Applied Linguistics 2 *(pp. 229-246). Oxford: Oxford University Press.*

Willis, J. (1981). *Teaching English through English*. London: Longman.

_____________ ; *(1996)* A Framework for Task-Based Learning. *Harlow, Essex: Longman.*

Wong, R. (1987). *Teaching Pronunciation: Focus on English Rhythm and Intonation*. Englewood Cliffs, NJ: Prentice Hall Regents.

Woodward, T. (1991.) *Models and Metaphors in Language Teacher Training: Loop Input and Other Strategies*. Cambridge: Cambridge University Press.

Woodward W. Suzanne, (1997), *Fun with Grammar: Communicative Activities for the Azar Grammar series*. Prentice Hall: Regents.

Wright, C. (ed). (2000). *Issues in Education and Technology: Policy Guidelines and Strategies,* London: Commonwealth Secretariat.

Wright, T. & Bolitho, R. (1993). Language Awareness: A Missing Link in Language Teacher Education. *ELT Journal, 47* (4), 292-304.

Yadav, S. (2007). *Language, Literature and Education*. New Delhi: Academic Excellence.

Yang, N. (1998). Exploring a New Role for Teachers: Promoting Learner Autonomy. *System, 26,* 127-135.

Yang, P. J. (1998). Networked Multimedia and Foreign Language Education. *CALICO Journal, 15* (1-3), 75-88.

Yan, X., Zhou, Z., & Dai, P. (2007). Principled Eclecticism in College English Teaching in China. *Professional Teaching Articles of Asian EFL Journal. 17* (Article 1).

Yeh, A. (2003). Telling True Stories: Blending Multimedia in a Task-based Activity. *The Internet TESL Journal, 9* (8).

Yuksel, D., & Yu. (2008). Inside the Classroom: Student and Teacher Questions in a Foreign Language Literature Class. *TESL Reporter, 41* (1), 12-32.

Zhenhui, R. (2001). Matching Teaching Styles with Learning Styles in East Asian Contexts. *The Internet TESL Journal, 3* (7). Retrieved from http://iteslj.org/Techniques/ Zhenhui-Teaching Styles.html